Praise for *The Consultant's Legal Guide: A Business of Consulting Resource*

"I beg you, do not start your own consulting business without first reading *The Consultant's Legal Guide*. And if you already have, read it *now!* I assure you that when you put into practice the sound advice of Elaine Biech and Linda Byars Swindling you will save yourself the heartache and headache of needless legal hassles. Intellectual property is the consultant's present and future value, and attorneys are your essential partners in creating greater value for your business and your clients. Sound legal practices have become as important to the success of small consulting practices as sound financial practices, and *The Consultant's Legal Guide* will help you every day of your business life."

> —James M. Kouzes, coauthor, *The Leadership Challenge*
> and *Encouraging the Heart*

"A great flight plan to avoid turbulence. . . . Whether you are a consultant or the CEO of a Fortune 500 company, this book should be on your desk for a reference in so many areas."

> —Howard Putnam, former CEO, Southwest Airlines and
> Braniff International, and author, *The Winds of Turbulence*

"A well thought out, practical approach to dealing effectively with lawyers and other consultants. If followed, it should help all parties be better prepared and do a better job."

> —Rita Reuss, attorney, and former vice president, Land O' Lakes

"What a gift! Everything you need to know about the legal aspects of setting up a consulting business and then operating it. Better yet, it is written from the client's, not a lawyer's perspective. Best yet, it comes from seasoned pros, who have done it all."

> —Jack Zenger, president, PROVANT, and cofounder, Zenger Miller

"*The Consultant's Legal Guide* is better than an MBA in business relationships. Clear, concise, thoughtful, and thorough. After reading this book, consultants will sleep better at night!"

> —Pamela J. Schmidt, vice president,
> American Society for Training and Development (ASTD)

"This is a terrific resource for any consultant who wants to succeed in today's dynamic marketplace. Read it. Study it. Keep it for valuable reference."

> —Nido R. Qubein, CSP, CPAE, president, Creative Services Inc.,
> and former president, National Speakers Association

"Ah-ha—the missing piece to the puzzle. Biech and Swindling have filled the hole (and an important one I might add) in all the reference books on consulting. Don't start your business without it."

> —Dianna Booher, CSP, CEO, Booher Consultants, Inc., and author
> of thirty-seven books, including *Communicate with Confidence!*

"*The Consultant's Legal Guide* is a must read for every new and seasoned consultant. It provides consultants with a wealth of practical tools and tips to create, improve, and sustain an effective consulting business."

> —Richard Y. Chang, CEO, Richard Chang Associates, Inc., and 1999 chair of
> the board for the American Society for Training and Development (ASTD)

"If the intent was to create a book that provided an instant 'return on investment,' then this exceeds that intent. Almost every page and certainly every chapter present an idea or a caution that could save thousands of dollars. Where was this book when I started my company?"

—Ron Galbraith, CEO, Management 21, Inc., and 1999 president,
Instructional Systems Association (ISA)

"List the top five legal issues in your business, and *The Consultant's Legal Guide* is bound to address them all. Biech and Swindling have written a truly practical handbook that should be on the desktops of all consultants who are trying to make their lives easier and their businesses more successful."

—Diane Hessan, business guru, and author, *Customer-Centered Growth*

"Today consultants not only need to prove their credibility and market themselves, they have to protect themselves as well. They have to protect themselves from misunderstandings with clients and misuse of intellectual property (both theirs and others). These two examples are just the tip of the iceberg. The *Consultant's Legal Guide* should be readily available on every consultant's bookshelf."

—Bob Pike, CSP, chairman and founder, Creative Training Techniques
International, Inc., and editor, the *Creative Training Techniques* newsletter

"Whether you are a start-up consulting business or a veteran in the industry, this is a must read. Elaine Biech and coauthor Linda Byars Swindling delineate the fundamentals for success. Their practical tips and concrete suggestions related to legal issues will save you time, help you steer clear of potential pitfalls, and ensure your ability to build a prosperous business."

—Toni Lucia, managing partner, MANUS—A Right Company,
and coauthor, *The Art and Science of 360° Feedback*

"If you are a consultant, do not pass go. Do not collect $200 until you read this book! Clear, accessible, and practical, *The Consultant's Legal Guide* is an easy-to-use reference that every consultant should have on his or her shelf for answers to any legal question that concerns your business or practice."

—Ann Herrmann-Nehdi, CEO, Herrmann International

"As a management consultant for more than twenty-five years, I wish I had this book a long time ago. It would have saved me a lot of pain and money. Written in plain English rather than legalese, it should be a must for the experienced as well as the budding consultant. Buy it, use it, and don't lend it out."

—George Morrisey, CSP, CPAE, author, *Morrisey on Planning*

"Where was this book when I was starting out? Or last year for that matter? Elaine and Linda provide an awesome compendium for the consultant. It contains everything I learned in twenty-five years of consulting through the school of hard knocks! Here they give it away! If only Elaine and Linda could turn this book into a pill. Every consultant I know would be standing in line!"

—Beverly Kaye, president, Career Systems International, author, *Up Is Not the Only Way,* and coauthor, *Love 'Em or Lose 'Em: Getting Good People to Stay*

"Add *The Consultant's Legal Guide* to the dictionary and thesaurus as office necessities for any existing or aspiring consulting business."
—Steve Cohen, CEO, The Learning Design Group,
and past president, Instructional Systems Association (ISA)

"Elaine's earlier book, *The Business of Consulting,* is an incredible resource and handbook that I've used extensively. This companion piece on the legal aspects of consulting continues the tradition—a practical handbook that hits the mark from an experienced practitioner who has learned these lessons in the trenches!"
—Linda Growney, assistant vice president,
CUNA Mutual Insurance Group

"Finally, a book that is comprehensive on legal questions that most consultants don't ask until it's too late. This is full of practical information that helps training professionals work confidently with their clients."
—Shirley Krsinich, corporate training director,
American Family Insurance

"As the legal and operational pitfalls in successfully running an independent consulting firm multiply, this concise, practical guide expertly fills a critical need. With this book as a companion, consultants can learn from the authors' extensive experience and knowledge and spare themselves the often painful, expensive, and time-consuming costs involved in going it on their own—unprepared. It is a must for every consultant's library—I wish it had been in mine ten years ago!"
—Herbert Cohen, CEO, MOHR Retail Learning Systems, Inc.

"The countess of consultants. Once again Elaine makes you think and guides you effortlessly to understanding. After thirteen years in business, I was shocked to learn how much I didn't know. This book is truly a gift."
—Peggy Joyce, real estate consultant, Re/Max Preferred

"With one book, Elaine and Linda deftly and painlessly eliminate the decades of diverse legal experience, documents and (for many of us) uninspiring-but-needed knowledge you need to acquire to successfully operate not only a consulting business, but any professional organization. Checklists, guidelines, sample legal documents, informative scenarios, you name it—they're all here to help the professional successfully navigate through the numerous legal waters involved in profitably providing their services."
—Raymond T. Halagera, vice president,
the Strategic Management Group, Inc.

"Preventing problems is a lot less expensive in time, money, and aggravation than fixing them. I only wish this book had been available when I was starting my business—even after all these years (and attorneys' fees), I still found some practical suggestions that will help protect my company and keep employee, alliance, and customer relationships healthy and mutually beneficial."
—B. Kim Barnes, CEO, Barnes & Conti Associates, Inc.

"Every consultant and consulting firm needs a copy of this book for their library. . . . and they should refer to it often. It certainly will save time and money and make for more productive meetings with legal counsel. Just the sections on 'protecting work product' and 'avoiding legal problems' alone make it worth the price of the book."

 —Jack Snader, CEO, Systema Corporation

"Linda and Elaine have given consultants an excellent tool for avoiding legal issues. This book is a must have for consultants, trainers, and speakers! It is also a great resource for those of us who interface with outside consultants. Thank you Linda and Elaine."

 —Cindy Hammond, director of training and development, Comdata Corporation

"A masterpiece . . . an absolute masterpiece for any consultant. This cutting-edge information will be one of the most valuable investments consultants can make for their careers. This is a gold mine."

 —Joe Charbonneau, CSP, CPAE, president, Presentations, Inc.

"*The Business of Consulting* was exciting to read and made me feel like I could go right out and start my own business. This new book takes you to the next level *before* you hit the iceberg. Where were you when the Titanic took sail?"

 —Judye Talbot, client

"When you are an expert in a specific subject matter, work process, or content area, making 'the big money' via consulting and sharing your expertise can look so easy and very appealing as a job. However, to be a successful consultant means that you cannot treat your work like you would a hobby. Consulting is a professional business venture with wide-ranging legal ramifications and concerns. In becoming a successful consultant you can choose to stumble along, facing the legal and business challenges as they occur, or you can seek the counsel of these wisdom-makers and avoid a lot of pain. In *The Consultant's Legal Guide,* Elaine and Linda share their wisdom and personally demonstrate the best spirit of business consulting for all of us to model. Thank you Elaine and Linda for your 'wise-full' contribution to our profession."

 —Richard V. Michaels, managing partner, Michaels McVinney, Inc.

Endorsements from the Legal Field:

"*The Consultant's Legal Guide* offers a hands-on approach to avoiding litigation. I heartily recommend it."

 —Robert L. Greening, Esq., Penick & Greening, P.C.

"Elaine & Linda offer a great primer on the legal issues facing consultants. This book should save its readers significant money in legal fees and make them informed consumers when they do seek legal counsel."

 —Joseph B. Conboy, Esq., associate dean of Texas Tech School of Law

"Congratulations on a job well done! This book provides very meaningful information for those in the consulting industry."

 —David B. Moseley, Jr., Esq., Moseley & Standerfer, P.C.

The Consultant's Legal Guide

A BUSINESS OF CONSULTING RESOURCE GUIDE

elaine biech and linda byars swindling, esq.

San Francisco

Copyright © 2000 by Jossey-Bass/Pfeiffer
ISBN: 0-7879-4763-6

Library of Congress Cataloging-in-Publication Data

Biech, Elaine.
    The consultant's legal guide : a business of consulting
resource / Elaine Biech, Linda Byars Swindling. — 1st ed.
        p.   cm.
    Includes index.
    ISBN 0-7879-4763-6 (acid-free paper)
    1. Business law—United States.   2. Consultants—United
States—Handbooks, manuals, etc.   I. Swindling, Linda Byars, date.
II. Title.
    KF390.C65 B54 1999
    346.7307—dc21   99-6480

Printed in the United States of America.

Published by

JOSSEY-BASS/PFEIFFER
A Wiley Company
350 Sansome St.
San Francisco, CA 94104-1342
415.433.1740; Fax 415.433.0499
800.274.4434; Fax 800.569.0443

www.pfeiffer.com

Acquiring Editor: Matthew Holt
Director of Development: Kathleen Dolan Davies
Developmental Editor: Susan Rachmeler
Copyeditor: Hilary Powers
Senior Production Editor: Pam Berkman
Manufacturing Supervisor: Becky Carreño
Interior Design: Claudia Smelser
Cover Design: Laurie Anderson

Printing 10   9   8   7   6   5   4   3   2

 This book is printed on acid-free, recycled stock that meets or exceeds the minimum GPO and EPA requirements for recycled paper.

For Shane and Thad,

the best in any case

For Mom, Dad, Gregg, and Parker,

the verdict is in . . . you are the best.

Thanks for your love, guidance,

patience, and constant support.

CONTENTS

LIST OF EXHIBITS*

---

*▣ Indicates exhibits on disk

ACKNOWLEDGMENTS

The Consultant's Legal Guide is the product of many: the consultants, trainers, and speakers who shared their stories with us, the attorneys who corrected our course, the colleagues who provided advice, and the Jossey-Bass team who always deliver a quality product. There are too many to mention, but we would like to single out a few who went way beyond the call of duty:

- Kathleen Dolan Davies, our editor, who trusted us to do a good job and gave us the flexibility to prove how good we could be.
- Matt Holt, publisher, editor, and friend, for having a vision and introducing two like souls to the vision and each other.
- Susan Rachmeler, our developmental editor, for removing redundancy and creating clarity.
- Josh Blatter and Jamie Corcoran, who took care of hundreds of details at Jossey-Bass.
- Beth Drake, ebb associates assistant, for prodding both of us and ensuring that we met all the impossible deadlines.
- Members of the National Speakers Association—Dick Grote, Bette Price, the late Peter Chantilis (who was both mediator and gentleman), and especially those who believe in our book: Howard Putnam, Joe Charbonneau, George Morrisey, Bob Pike, and Nido Qubein.

- Members of the Instructional Systems Association—Mary Carolan-Doyle, Richard Chang, Howard Cohen, Sally Ewald, Ron Galbraith, Linda Hughes, Beverly Kaye, Dennis McCarthy, Scott Parry, Darryl Sink, Jack Snader, Kathryn Wilson, Jack Zenger.
- Women Speak Business—Lorri Allen, Susan Abar, Sherry Buffington, Peggy Collins, Harriet Meyerson, Vicki Turner, Mellanie Hills—and Tim and Cindy Cocklin and Kathy Reed.
- Mentors Cindy Hammond, Elaine Weeman, Angela Miller, Virginia Clark, Cindy Hamilton, Colleen Rickenbacher, Sue Fry, Suzie Oliver, Mitchell Cathey, Vickie Henry, Sid Stahl, Bud Silverberg, Gail LeMaire, Leslie Penning, Jerry Johnson, and Gene and Betty Garrett for your guidance in a career committed to peacemaking.
- Colleagues and mentors for listening to us, giving us ideas, and bolstering our spirits—L. A. Burke, Vicki Chvala, Ron Galbraith, Linda Growney, Shirley Krsinich, Jean Lamkin, Pam Schmidt, Edie West.
- Karra Guess for her support and her input on real estate issues, Jean Lee for research help, and attorneys Kristin Jordan Harkins, Chris Bloom, Charles Fiscus, and John Monogogna for their insights and down-to-earth explanations of what can be confusing legal topics.
- Texas Tech School of Law's Dean Joseph Conboy for his comments regarding this book and for his constant support for the last eleven years, professor John Krahmer who made even contracts understandable, Dean Kay Fletcher for the practical tips about law practice, and Texas Tech's President of Ex-Students Bill Dean who is always a source of encouragement.
- All the members of the law offices of Withrow, Fiscus and Swindling, your encouragement and help during this time is especially appreciated, and thanks to Lucy Withrow for those much needed chocolate energy boosters.
- Wendel Withrow and David B. Moseley, Jr., whose contributions to this book and the legal profession are countless and who have provided such valued advice over the years.
- Robert Greening, Esq., the best co-counsel one can have when facing the worst litigation attorneys can dish out, and to the Honorable Sally Montgomery and Honorable Bob Jenevein, thank you for entrusting your cases to my care.

- Byron Byars Jr. for his research help and editorial help, and paralegal and mom Pat Byars, for her organization, support, and holding down the fort at work to provide time to write.
- Gregg and Parker for your support, finding ways to occupy yourselves, and allowing mommy to do that book thing.
- Clients for giving us some breathing room when we faced difficult deadlines.
- And Thad—your pride in me helps me move mountains.

INTRODUCTION

In the past, few malpractice suits have been filed against consultants, but that appears to be changing—especially as it relates to intellectual property. So why this book? Why now? Downsizing, disenchantment with the workplace, and the growing tendency for organizations to seek ways to temporarily use professional talent are causing a fast rise in the number of consultants. This growth in the number of consultants brings with it a growing need for more information about legal issues for consultants.

WHY IS LITIGATION AGAINST CONSULTANTS INCREASING?

Although consultants have not been the primary target of litigation to date, that trend seems to be changing. Why is litigation against consultants on the rise? There seems to be a pattern occurring.

First, companies are demanding more of everyone. In the highly competitive marketplace, companies don't have resources to spare. Everything is moving more rapidly. The work is changing. The customer base is changing. And people are changing positions more rapidly. Directors and CEOs change often. Stockholders want immediate return on investments. Individuals as well as corporations are expected to produce more, faster, and with less. This trend means companies change consultants more often as well. It's rare for a consultant to provide the same services to the same client over a number of years. Therefore, consultants do not build up the kind of relationship they may have had with clients in the past. When this lack of relationship is paired with this demanding, results-oriented environment, consultants who don't provide promised results—or, worse yet, have a detrimental effect on company profits—may be held accountable.

An increasing demand for consulting due to downsizing, outsourcing, and other corporate initiatives has increased the workload for consulting organizations. Consultants trying to keep up are facing the same dilemmas faced by their clients. They are pulled in many directions at the same time. Clients push hard to achieve consulting results faster.

Quality may fall as consultants skip steps to achieve a quicker outcome, usually at the insistence of their clients. Some consultants, unwilling to turn down work or bring in appropriate outside help, struggle with finding the time to build quality into their solutions. They lack the time to gather data, analyze the situation, and pilot test the solution. The result is that more and more legal situations are occurring.

Sometimes consultants are so busy taking care of their clients' needs, they forget their own. They get sloppy, skip steps, and soon something slips. When consultants pay more attention to the business services they provide than to their own business, mistakes occur that can lead to litigation.

In addition to an increasing demand on results and time, successful consulting firms may be viewed as having "deep pockets." Times are good in the consulting business. Consulting firms are growing rapidly and making money. Therefore, consultants might be seen as sources of money for companies to target in litigation.

WHAT THIS BOOK COVERS

What kinds of legal issues do consultants encounter? What legal information does a consultant need to know? The following topics are examined throughout the book.

Understanding Legal Terms

As in any business, the legal field has its own language or *jargon*. It helps to remember that many legal concepts date back to Roman times and the original Latin terminology may still be used. In addition, the laws of the United States originate from the influence of many countries. The legal terminology reflects those countries' influence. Also, laws come from legislation, the government, and from the way courts interpreted what was the law, who had the proper rights, or even what is *equitable* or reasonable for the situation.

Legal terms may come from the publication in which the law is located, the name of the person who sponsored the law, or the name of the parties who were in litigation. Just understanding some of the basic legal terms and using the proper terminology help to ensure that you and others are speaking the same language.

You will find a basic glossary of common legal terms in the back of this book. This list is in no way comprehensive. Entire dictionaries are devoted to legal definitions. However, defining these basic terms should aid in understanding some of the legal jargon contained in consulting agreements and various legal situations you encounter as a consultant.

Starting and Running Your Business

Your first encounter with legal issues occurs as soon as you open your business. You will need to determine the legal entity under which you will do business. Should you form a partnership or a corporation? Should you remain a sole proprietor? What about those new business structures—L.L.P.'s or L.L.C.'s? What are the advantages and disadvantages of each?

Incorporating a consulting practice may be an incredible tax savings or may create a huge reporting mess. Knowing how to structure your business to suit your needs is important for every business owner. Did you know that consultants working together may unknowingly form a partnership? Understanding and choosing how to organize your consulting practice prevent those choices from being made for you.

Contracts and Negotiation

Contracts are involved in almost any business relationship. Whether dealing with your clients, other consultants, service providers, or even your landlord, negotiations and contracts are a constant. Therefore, the basics of legal agreements and techniques for negotiating better arrangements are important aspects of being a good consultant.

Working with Others

Regardless of the industry's image, consultants aren't isolated. Working with others usually creates its own legal issues. The legal determination regarding employees and independent contractors is a critical issue and one in which consultants must understand the advantages and disadvantages of each. Legal issues also derive from working with your clients. After reading this guide, you will have an idea of how to proceed when a client has not paid. You will also explore what to do if the relationship begins to sour.

Protecting What Is Yours

Many consultants report that their biggest problem is protecting what is legally theirs from other consultants and from their clients. As an ethical consultant you will also want to know how to avoid infringing upon others' protected work. Protecting work product and intellectual property when working with others is discussed in a number of places in this book.

Avoiding Risk

Finally, this guide will address how to avoid expensive, time-consuming litigation whenever possible. And if you should find yourself facing litigation it shows you how to control legal costs.

A BASIC UNDERSTANDING OF THE LAW IS IMPORTANT TO A CONSULTANT

People who monitor air defense radar expend most of their energy when the radar unit reveals an object that is classified as a threat or can't be readily identified. Legal issues you don't understand can be similar. Understanding basic legal issues, as well as potential pitfalls and solutions, helps you identify the time and energy to spend when those items come up on your legal radar screen.

But what if you always work on a handshake and have never had any problems? You may be blessed with clients and professional relationships that will never sour. Why spend time fixing legal problems that don't exist?

You're right. Most problems are avoided by understanding positions up front and communicating throughout the consulting process. Nothing is as effective in preventing problems as ongoing communication and fostering professional and ethical relationships.

Unfortunately, not everyone works at ensuring good communication or at fostering professional and ethical relationships. Successful consultants are paid a lot of money to point out commonsense problems. Consultants are hired for their ability to troubleshoot and come up with effective and creative solutions. Doesn't it make sense that the same clients who do not see commonsense solutions in their business may not be able to identify commonsense resolutions when dealing with you? Knowing where the potential legal pitfalls or miscommunications could take place will aid you in avoiding them.

WHAT THIS BOOK WILL AND WON'T DO

The guide attempts to communicate real-life situations in easy-to-understand language. It is not intended to frighten you or to invent problems where none exists. Instead, the intent is to provide examples of legal situations faced by other consultants. Many of these situations could have been avoided if the participants had more knowledge up front or had sought legal advice in a timely manner.

At no time should you rely solely on this guide to provide advice or resolve a legal matter. *This book is not legal advice and does not take the place of seeking competent legal help.*

However, this guide should significantly increase your knowledge of legal issues by introducing you to many of the topics of which you should be aware. It also identifies questions you may need to address with an attorney. You will be a better informed client and your time spent in the lawyer's office will be much more productive if you read this book and review the checklists and documents. We have provided some exhibits, examples, and lists of questions on a disk that you may print and take with you.

This comprehensive planning guide has been written in "plain English" to address the legal issues consultants face. It also discusses practical ways to resolve disputes when they occur and to avoid litigation. Chapters deal with real-world examples and situations and then give you the solutions and results!

After reading the book, you should be able to

- Understand the basic legal terms and the need for legal agreements.
- Weigh the legal pros and cons of your choice of business entity.
- Determine whether to hire employees or independent subcontractors and understand the advantages and disadvantages of each.
- Know how to proceed when a client has not paid.

- Negotiate better agreements with your landlords, service providers, other contractors, and clients.
- Protect work product and intellectual property.
- Understand how to avoid infringing upon others' protected work.
- Control legal costs and avoid expensive, time-consuming litigation.

The Consultant's Legal Guide

Selecting an Attorney

This book discusses a variety of legal pitfalls and provides tips for avoiding those legal situations entirely. One of the suggestions you will see repeatedly is to get legal advice from competent counsel. The attorney who handled your friend's divorce or drafted your will may not be familiar with the legal aspects of running a service business and especially the intricacies of a consulting practice.

- *So why do you get legal advice?* Just like a good accountant, a lawyer should be considered a technician whose training and experience can help you stay out of legal trouble in the first place or solve an existing problem at a reasonable cost.
- *When do you need a lawyer?* You should see an attorney before you start a new business. Make an appointment with a lawyer when you are buying or selling an existing business. Legal advice is also necessary when you receive a demand letter from an attorney, a government agency, or any other person. In addition, seek advice if an employee or customer has any serious business complaint or has suffered a personal injury. Never sign a contract with clauses you don't understand.

• *How do you select your lawyer?* The most important consideration is to find a lawyer who handles your specific type of situation on a regular basis. The cost for a specialist may be a little higher, but the matter will be completed quicker and done right the first time. This will probably save you time and money in the long run. You may wish to ask your friends and business associates who have had a similar problem and were satisfied with the legal services they received. Call the attorney's office and ask the legal assistant or secretary if the attorney represents clients in that general type of work on a regular basis.

WHAT QUESTIONS SHOULD YOU ASK BEFORE WORKING WITH AN ATTORNEY?

You should interview a prospective attorney just as you might interview a prospective employee. After all, you will be paying the attorney just as you pay an employee. And you will work just as closely with the attorney as you would with an employee. In addition, you and your attorney will focus on issues and concerns that may be difficult, explosive, and/or uncomfortable.

• *Does the attorney regularly handle this type of legal issue?* Just as the medical profession is highly specialized, law is becoming highly specialized. You don't want to be the guinea pig as your attorney's first or second attempt at a particular issue.

You want an attorney who understands the nature of your business, consulting. It is also important that the attorney has worked with businesses your size. Attorneys are consultants in their own right. They consult with clients regarding legal issues. However, attorneys who have *represented* other consultants will be better able to spot potential problems as well as cost-effective solutions.

• *How much time is required for this project?* Good attorneys are busy attorneys who try to prioritize their work according to the most pressing matter. The level of activity involved in a lawsuit is different from the level of activity required for drafting business documents. If you are involved in litigation, there are definite deadlines and filing requirements that must be met. The time revolves around the court's schedule and there may be long periods when no activity occurs and then a flurry of action happens prior to or after court dates. Drafting agreements, researching intellectual property issues, and negotiating leases may run on their own time line.

Be sure to discover at the outset what time frame you can expect for your particular legal matter. An attorney should be able to give you the best case and worst case scenario for time required to handle your legal matter. There are plenty of good attorneys who are service minded. If an attorney cannot meet your legal needs, go to one who can.

• *Is there a set fee or a flat fee for doing the work?* Many times, attorneys know in advance what they charge for certain legal services. They may have provided specific services often enough to have developed a fee schedule. This is good. It means the attorney not only has a great deal of expertise but also may have the standard documents on a computer. This will save you time and money.

• *Is there a contingency fee option?* Some matters may be accepted on a *contingency fee* arrangement. Used in litigation and collection cases, this type of arrangement means that some or all of the attorney's fees are postponed until the client recovers money. Some attorneys want a reduced hourly rate in addition to the recovery at the end. Some attorneys expect a client to help foot the expenses.

In a sense, the attorney is sharing the risk that you will recover something from another party. A benefit of a contingency fee is that your up-front costs are smaller and that the attorney's interest is much more focused on resolving the case, removing any interest in prolonging the matter to receive more attorney's fees. The sooner the matter is resolved in a contingency fee arrangement, the sooner the attorney receives payment. In the end, attorney's fees can range anywhere from 20 percent to 50 percent of the amount due to the client. Clients may pay many times over the fees they would have incurred on a straight hourly basis. Most business matters and corporate matters will not lend themselves to contingency fee arrangements, but a litigation matter with a high potential for recovery might.

• *If there is no flat fee or contingency fee, how does the attorney bill?* If a set or contingency fee is not used, attorneys bill by portions of an hour, a billable hour. Most attorneys bill either by quarters of an hour or by tenths of an hour. Some might assume that an attorney who is billing by the tenth-of-the-hour method (or in six-minute increments) will be more accurate with the time actually spent on your legal issues. Others argue that many things are grouped together when an attorney bills in fifteen-minute increments instead of recording a six-minute time for each action taken. The truth is that each matter takes a certain time. One method may result to your advantage on one matter and then you may be charged more the next time. Picking your attorney for experience and reputation is more important than picking an attorney based on billing methods. Ethical attorneys will not pad your bill.

- *Does the attorney value bill?* Some attorneys bill for the value of the service received. A contract developed over fifteen years is worth more than the thirty minutes it takes the attorney to revise it. However, a client should not have to pay for hours of research an attorney needs if the contract is only worth a few hours of time.

You may have heard the term *double billing.* This practice occurs in a few law firms. An example is when one project is performed for more than one client. For example, research is needed by three clients. Instead of splitting the research time equally among the three clients, each will be billed the full amount of time. Another example involves one lawyer billing the same amount of time as a junior attorney when only spending a fraction of the time reviewing the junior attorney's work. Also called "padding the bill," this practice results in the senior attorney's higher billing rate being billed or that both the junior and senior attorneys bill the time worked by only one.

The best way to avoid this practice is to review your statements carefully. If you were originally quoted five hours for a project and you see that ten hours were billed or that five hours were billed at the highest billing rate instead of a lower rate, ask why. If you see that a partner of the firm is billing for hours of research or staff-level tasks instead of a beginning attorney or office support, make sure you ask questions about the statement.

- *How do this attorney's fees and billing rates compare to others?* It is a good practice to call at least two lawyers and compare fees as well as estimates of expenses and time. You should not choose your attorney on billing rates alone. While calling other attorneys, it is more important to compare your impression of professional competence. Just as an experienced consultant may save a client time and money, more experienced attorneys know the shortcuts and where potential pitfalls may exist. More experience can also mean that they may not need to charge you for researching the matter.

- *Is a retainer required?* Find out what you will need to pay as a *retainer* or down payment on your legal matter. Attorneys put this retainer amount in a trust fund and use it to reimburse themselves for costs as well as time spent. Many firms require you to maintain a certain minimum amount in the retainer to make sure that the fees and immediate expenses will be covered.

- *Which attorney or assistants will be working on your matter, and will they bill at different rates?* Knowing who will be working on your matter is important for two reasons. First, you usually have hired a certain attorney to perform services for you.

You have a right to expect that the attorney you hired will continue to be involved in your legal matter. However, if the attorney you hired is more experienced, he or she probably bills at a higher hourly rate. If the task at hand requires phone calls, organizing documents, or research that can be performed by a paralegal or a less experienced attorney, it is usually more cost-efficient to have the lower-billing person perform the task.

Learn if others will be involved and what their billing rates are. Some firms may have a *blended rate.* This means that the higher level attorney's rate is reduced and the lower-level associate's rate is raised to find a rate in between. Whatever the practice, it is important to know how fees are determined to ensure your comfort when you see the first bill.

- *What is an estimate of the total fee and costs?* If a lawyer cannot give you a general estimate of what legal services will cost, keep looking! Most attorneys should be able to give a best and worst case scenario. Also, be clear on what that estimate will cover. For example, ask if any research time will be required and, if so, how much.

- *What are the other costs involved?* The extras can cost a lot, especially in litigation. You may have filing fees, deposition costs, service fees, and expert fees in addition to what the law firm is charging for its attorney's time. Also, find out about the office costs up front. Will there be expensive long distance calls, overnight mailings, or courier fees? Are you expected to reimburse the firm at its cost for copies, phone calls, and faxes or will those be charged at a significantly higher rate? For example, one firm may charge $1 per page for incoming faxes, another may charge 25 cents per page for copies made on its in house copier.

Law firms have become amazingly thorough in tracking business charges by using codes on copiers, phones, and fax machines. Those costs add up. If an attorney is in court representing you, you may be charged parking costs, mileage, and meal expenses for everyone working on your lawsuit.

- *Does the attorney charge travel time when traveling to another city on your behalf?* Most attorneys will charge travel time, but might charge at a reduced rate. Others may be billing you at their normal rate because they are also preparing for your hearing or meeting during the travel. For example, the time on the airplane may be spent reviewing your documents and drafting questions. Attorney billing practices are as different as the attorneys themselves. Be clear how services are charged before you receive your first statement.

• *Can this attorney refer you to someone else if necessary?* In hospitals, doctors can refer you to specialists if your medical situation exceeds their training or expertise. The same is true in the legal profession. In a law firm, attorneys may have colleagues with different areas of expertise to whom they can refer you. Even if an attorney does not practice with the referral attorney, attorneys are ethically required to bring in other lawyers or refer the case when the matter is beyond their experience. Beware of attorneys who think they can do it all. Exhibit 1.1 provides a list of questions to guide your discussion with an attorney you are considering hiring. In addition to these questions you should compare the attorney's fees and billing rates with those of others.

🖫 Exhibit 1.1. Questions to Ask a Prospective Lawyer.

• Does the attorney *regularly* handle this type of matter for this type of client?

• How much time is required for this project?

• What time frame can I expect for this legal matter? (Best case and worst case scenario.)

• Is there a set fee or a flat fee for doing the work?

• Is there a contingent fee option?

• If there is not a flat fee or contingency fee, what is the hourly rate?

• What is the minimum amount of time that will be billed? (Usually fifteen minutes if billing by quarter of an hour or six minutes if billing in tenths of an hour.)

• Does the law firm practice value billing?

• What, if any, retainer is required?

• Do I have to maintain a certain minimum amount in the retainer?

• Which attorneys or assistants will be working on my matter?

• Will they be billed at different rates?

💾 **Exhibit 1.1. Questions to Ask a Prospective Lawyer, Cont'd.**

- What is an estimate of the total fee and costs? (Best and worst case scenario.)

- How much research time do you anticipate will be needed?

- What are the other costs involved?

- Are long distance calls anticipated?

- Will overnight mailings or courier fees be necessary?

- Am I expected to reimburse the firm at its cost for copies, phone calls, and faxes or will those be charged at a higher rate? What is that higher rate?

- If an attorney is in court representing me, will I be charged for parking costs, mileage, and meal expenses for everyone working on the lawsuit?

- Am I charged travel time if an attorney is traveling to another city on my behalf?

- What is the billing rate for travel time?

- Does the attorney refer to other attorneys if a matter is beyond his or her expertise?

- Does the attorney return phone calls promptly?

- Can you reach the attorney in times of emergency, either through office staff or a mobile or home phone number?

OTHER CONSIDERATIONS

As in any business situation, you will want to ensure good communication. Clear, complete, and candid discussions will help you build a positive working relationship with your attorney.

 • *How can you ensure good communication and a positive working relationship with your attorney?* Make sure you understand what the lawyer is telling you. Does the lawyer use words you understand or define those words you don't? Do the answers to your questions create even more questions in your mind? Do these answers make sense? Do you feel your questions were answered completely? Do you feel as though your attorney has your best interest in mind? Once you leave the conference, do you feel comfortable calling with a question you forgot?

If you are uncomfortable with any of your answers to these questions, watch out. Some clients are actually too intimidated to ask questions. Don't forget that you are the boss in your legal matter. You deserve to have questions answered in words you understand and explained in a way that makes sense to you. Also, if you don't ask questions, some important fact may not be revealed to your attorney. Legal matters many times are influenced by one change in the factual situation. Failure to ask or contribute a piece of information may result in advice that does not resolve your legal situation. Exhibit 1.2 identifies questions you should ask yourself before hiring an attorney. If you answer any of the questions with a no, it may be a red flag for how the two of you will communicate in the future.

Exhibit 1.2. Questions to Ask Yourself When Choosing a Lawyer.

- Do you understand what the lawyer is telling you?
- Does the lawyer use words you understand and define those words you don't?
- Do the attorney's answers to your questions clarify your concerns?
- Do those answers make sense?
- Do you feel your questions were answered completely?
- Do you feel as though your attorney has your best interest in mind?
- Would you feel comfortable calling the attorney with questions?

• *Look around the attorney's office and meet the staff.* As much as possible, an attorney's office should make you feel comfortable. While the surroundings are not as important as the actual service provided, they do speak volumes about the lawyers' priorities. A law firm decorated in marble and furnished with expensive artwork may mean that clients pay more for the services or it may mean the lawyers are especially effective at what they practice. Files left lying about may mean a busy practice or a disorganized lawyer. An attorney who does not introduce the legal secretary, or worse yet treats the office staff with disrespect, may not be courteous when representing you to others. Your abilities of observation and perception are just as important when choosing a law firm as they are when you are consulting.

• *Remember, your attorney may change firms.* Attorneys change law firms. Law firms merge, downsize, and break up. Names change, people move, and new lawyers join the staff. Change is a fact of life in the practice of law. It is your decision if you want to follow your attorney or remain where you are. While some lawyers agree to not contact you or try to take your business, this is ethically prohibited in most jurisdictions. It is the clients' choice who will represent them. You have the right to follow your lawyer to a new place of business or stay with the existing firm. You are the boss. You make the decision to do business with whomever you wish.

• *Attorneys are bound to ethical standards.* Just like consultants, attorneys have rules of conduct and professional standards. Unlike those of consultants and many other professions, lawyers' standards and professional rules are not just guidelines. An attorney who does not follow the professional rules can face punishment by the state bar association. A copy of the professional rules to which an attorney must adhere may be found at a law library or obtained through your state or local bar association. It is interesting reading and can give you some idea of behavior to guard against. Believe it or not, many jurisdictions even require that attorneys post information or give their clients information about how to file grievances against lawyers.

GETTING THE MOST FROM ATTORNEY SERVICES

Use the checklist in Exhibit 1.3 to prepare yourself for your first meeting with an attorney.

• *Prepare for your meeting.* Have a list of questions or a brief summary of a transaction that has occurred, identifying all the parties involved and any unusual concerns or facts. Just as in the doctor's office, you may forget to tell your lawyer all the "symptoms" or details. In this case, follow up with the documents or information after the meeting.

• *Bring all necessary materials.* If you have a sample contract or a draft of a document, bring it with your comments about what you like or dislike. Bring your notes of conversations and copies of correspondence. If you have been sent a demand letter, bring not only the letter but your draft of a brief written response to the letter as well as any contract, correspondence, purchase order, etc., to which the demand relates.

🖫 Exhibit 1.3. Checklist for Maximizing the Benefit of Attorney Services.

❑ Prepare for your meeting.
- Have you developed a list of questions?
- Have you written a brief summary of the transaction that has occurred?
- Do you have a list of all the parties involved?
- Are there any unusual concerns or facts?

❑ Bring all necessary materials.
- Do you have a contract or a draft of a document? Have you written your comments about what you like or dislike?
- Have you brought your notes regarding conversations?
- Do you have copies of letters?
- Do you have copies of your responses?
- Have you prepared a draft of response to a letter?
- Did you bring a pad of paper with you to take notes?

❑ Find out what you can do to keep the legal costs down.
- Are there records you could obtain? What documents are needed that you could gather?
- Ask how you can make the job easier.

❑ Clarify what your attorney is to do.
- Make sure the attorney will get your approval if actions will exceed your initial agreement.
- Ask what is expected of you.

❑ Obtain a written fee agreement that includes a brief description of work to be performed.
- Ask for a fee agreement that clearly explains what you can expect as well as what the lawyer expects of you. Read it carefully before signing. If you desire, take the agreement with you to review before signing.
- Make sure you have a copy when you leave.

❑ Determine if a specific staff member can be a point of contact if the attorney is often unavailable.

- *Find out what you can do to keep the legal costs down.* Can you can obtain records or certain documents needed? Determine what information you could provide that will make the job easier.

- *Clarify what your attorney is to do.* Make sure the two of you are on the same page and that actions beyond your initial agreement will be cleared by you before they are started.

- *Obtain a written fee agreement that includes a brief description of work to be performed.* Your fee agreement should clearly explain what you can expect as well as what the lawyer expects of you. Ask for a copy of the agreement and read it carefully before signing. You may want to take the agreement home and review it carefully before signing.

- *Remember that time is what the attorney sells.* As discussed, unless it is a flat or a contingency fee, attorneys bill by the hour. Any time spent handling your legal matter including phone calls and visits to the office usually will be billed. Regardless of what the media would have you believe about people hating attorneys, many clients like their lawyers and enjoy talking with them. One thing some clients may experience is being billed for the time spent in conversations regarding kids and sports. You want a good relationship with your lawyer. However, it is appropriate to cut those conversations short or jokingly ask if this small talk is "on the clock" or if "the meter is running." If so, it is appropriate to tell the attorney that you want to stick to business and catch up later.

How to Be Dissatisfied with Your Legal Experience

- Ignore your potential problems. Avoiding the issue usually results in more complication and expense. You can pay the lawyer now or later. Later is invariably more expensive.

- Fail to ask questions and seek explanations.

- Avoid finding the right fit or personality in your attorney.

- Rely on the *TV Guide* or other ads to find your lawyer or just pick someone out of yellow pages.

- Be content to never meet or speak to your attorney. Speak only with a secretary or assistant from the initial consultation forward.

- Don't question fees or the scope of agreed work.

HOW TO LIMIT THE USE OF LAWYERS

Much of an attorney's work on your behalf is getting organized and looking for documentation to support your position. The more organized you are and the more written support you have, the more you can limit the attorney's time. In addition, several legal situations can be prevented or at least decreased through your careful attention to correspondence, documents, and your relations with others.

As a good consultant, you should not think about how to get yourself out of legal trouble, but rather how to prevent it from occurring in the first place! The suggestions in Exhibit 1.4 can be used to limit—or even prevent—your need for legal services.

Exhibit 1.4. Tips for Limiting Your Need for Lawyers.

- Read everything you sign.
- Read the fine print.
- Respond to customer or employee complaints in a timely manner.
- Show professional courtesy and concern for persons with complaints.
- Keep a written log of phone conversations and other business activities.
- Confirm business agreements or resolutions by letter.
- Consult with an attorney before a small problem becomes a big problem.
- Have good insurance.
- Have a good bookkeeping system.
- Save receipts—make a paper trail.

- *Read everything you sign.* In the hurry of running a business, people don't always take time to really read and understand documents. Don't be intimidated by impatient looks or comments stating, "This is just standard language," or "Nobody reads this. They just sign." Take the time to read everything and ask questions about language you disagree with or don't understand.
- *Read the fine print.* People are often surprised about the power of this tiny text. Spend some time carefully reading the small stuff. Conversely, pay great

attention to the large bold print. It is generally conspicuous because the law requires it of certain important matters.

- *Respond to customer or employee complaints in a timely manner.* People want to be heard and acknowledged. If you don't respond to others, you are basically telling them that they don't matter and if they want their complaint solved they need to go elsewhere.

- *Show professional courtesy and concern for people with complaints.* Becoming defensive will keep you from listening to the real issues and resolving a problem. Make sure you understand the other side before responding. People who don't receive respect or a response from you may seek it with a competitor or in court.

- *Keep a written log of phone conversations and other business activities.* Writings kept in the course of regular business may later be used as reference if a disagreement arises. Also, those same documents may be introduced as evidence in a trial.

- *Confirm business agreements or resolutions by letter.* This practice ensures that both parties understand the agreement or resolution. If the agreement is not accurately reflected to the other party's satisfaction, the inconsistency can be ironed out right then.

- *Consult an attorney before a small problem becomes a big problem.* Get advice while the problem or relationship can be repaired, not after a problem has reached a point of no return.

- *Have good insurance.* Proper insurance can protect your business assets. Make sure you use quality providers, not the company submitting the lowest bid.

- *Have a good bookkeeping system.* Records that are organized in a timely and orderly fashion exude professionalism and confidence. Creditors, clients, and others may simply take your word for any discrepancies if your bookkeeping is organized and current. Also, as a consultant, you don't have the luxury of being disorganized or appearing less than professional.

- *Save receipts and create a paper trail.* Reimbursements require proof. Business deductions require receipts. Be able to show what you spent and what that money was spent on. This documentation may also be used as proof that you really did do work in certain locations or did buy those supplies. Good expense tracking also helps reassure people that you are not letting other matters slip through the cracks.

Your goal should be to avoid litigation wherever possible. You know you need an attorney for business dealings, contract review, complaints, and a host of other issues. Meet with that same attorney and discuss what you can do daily to limit your legal exposure.

The Relationship of Ethics and the Law

Just like many other professionals, consultants have ethical standards that they are expected to follow. Strictly adhering to ethical practices sets you apart in many ways as a consultant. Professionalism distinguishes you from consultants who are not as professional and ethical. Clients notice ethical behavior and you are identified in their minds as someone who is trustworthy and dependable. In addition, your peers will characterize you as someone with whom to conduct joint projects or to whom they would recommend their own clients in comfort.

The ethical approach will be discussed throughout this book. Nothing works better in preventing lawsuits than being professional and above reproach. Nothing sounds better to a jury than someone who did the right thing and is ethical. A list of important ethical practices is discussed in this chapter. Keep a list of your ethics in your desk to remind you of your commitment to professional standards.

CODE OF ETHICS

Most professional associations that represent consultants, such as the Institute of Management Consultants, have codes of ethics. If you don't know your association's code of ethics, call the member services line and ask that it be sent to you.

As an independent consultant you will establish your own code of ethics. You will develop a set of ethical standards that you choose to abide by as you do business. Having your own ethics is both a privilege and a responsibility. As an independent consultant you are privileged that you can choose your ethical standards instead of being forced to live by others' ethics. As a consultant, ethical behavior is also a responsibility. As a consultant, you have the ability to influence and to increase the public's respect and trust for the consulting profession.

If you have the courage to face the truth and do what's right, even when it means turning down work or upsetting a client, you will always feel good about the services you provide.

ETHICS OF CONSULTING

Many of the legal problems consultants face can be avoided through adherence to ethical standards.*

Consultant to Client

When delivering services to a client, good ethical practices also serve to help protect you from lawsuits. Exhibit 2.1 identifies a long list of ethical standards that will help keep you out of court. The following discussion of the items expands on what they mean in practice.

- *Deliver only the highest quality products and services.* A client should have no defense for nonpayment and no valid claim against you if your services are as promised, of the highest quality, and delivered without problems.

- *Accept only projects for which you are qualified.* If you turn down jobs that are beyond your competence, you have not misrepresented your abilities or held yourself to a standard the client expects but that you cannot deliver.

---

*Note: The material in this section is adapted from the discussion of ethics in Elaine Biech, *The Business of Consulting,* San Francisco: Jossey-Bass/Pfeiffer, 1999, pp. 188–192.

Exhibit 2.1. The Ethics of Consulting.

As a consultant, I am committed to the highest ethical standards of delivery of services and business operations. I am committed to:

- Delivering only professional-quality products and services.
- Delivering projects at a reasonable price and on time, wherever and whenever possible.
- Accepting only projects for which I am qualified.
- Turning down jobs beyond my competency.
- Learning on my own time.
- Turning down projects that are inappropriate for me.
- Placing my client's interest ahead of my own.
- Being willing to say I don't know.
- Always being honest with the client even if my words are not what the client wants to hear.
- Accepting only work that I can manage with high quality.
- Accepting only work from organizations that I respect.
- Choosing work that supports my values and my reputation.
- Keeping proprietary and confidential information confidential.
- Avoiding all conflict of interest situations.
- Working myself out of a job to create my clients' independence.
- Repaying any loss caused to my client by my actions.
- Taking responsibility for my actions.
- Informing the client immediately when problems arise or errors occur.
- Completing all work myself or advising the client before I use additional people.

Exhibit 2.1. The Ethics of Consulting, Cont'd.

- Avoiding working with competing clients at the same time.

- Conducting regular self-examination of my practice.

- Assessing my progress and results and learning from the experience.

- Continuing to provide excellent services that the client may never comprehend.

- Watching business expenses as if the money were coming out of my own pocket.

- Adhering to a consistent pricing structure and clearly spelling out any differences with clients or work.

- Charging only for the work that needs to be done.

- Charging only what I earn.

- Charging only for reasonable expenses actually incurred and verified with receipts.

- Splitting the travel costs between two clients when only one trip was made.

- Discussing what my client expects from me.

Source: Adapted from Biech, E. *The Business of Consulting.* San Francisco: Jossey-Bass/Pfeiffer, 1999.

- *Learn on your own time.* Once again, if you do not have the expertise, do not charge the client to obtain it. While something new is always learned with each project, charging your client to get up to speed on a consulting technique is not usually ethical.

- *Turn down projects that are inappropriate.* If you are asked to do anything that is inappropriate from any standpoint, say no.

- *Place the client's interest ahead of your own.* This basic principle will protect you more than most lawyers' advice. Do not take advantage of your client even if your actions may never be uncovered. Not taking advantage of your client in even small ways will greatly decrease the force of an allegation that you have acted improperly or unethically. A client who knows you take a taxi, not a limo, or who receives a refund for a project that has been overbid, will be less likely to question your truthfulness on contract performance.

- *Be willing to say I don't know.* Being honest with a client will gain more respect and fewer lawsuits than "faking it 'til you make it."

- *Accept only work that you can manage with high quality.* Don't overextend and miss deadlines or cut corners to meet everyone's needs.

- *Accept only work from organizations that you respect.* Organizations that you do not respect, or whose business purpose may undermine your own values, will hurt your reputation. Also, those are usually the same clients who later refuse to pay or find fault in your consulting.

- *Hold all confidential information close.* Never divulge any proprietary information or information about your contract. While it may not appear so, it could give some other company a competitive advantage.

- *Avoid even an appearance of a conflict of interest.* If you have the potential to benefit personally from any information you gain, you should not accept the project. For example, if you know that you will be in competition with the client in the future, you should not accept the project.

- *Create your clients' independence.* The goal of every consultant should be to go into organizations, complete the work, and leave the clients better able to take care of themselves.

- *Repay any loss caused by you to the client.* Inform the client immediately when problems arise or errors occur. No matter what the error, if you are responsible, own up to it and take care of it. This is not only an ethical issue; you may be held legally liable if anyone is hurt or the business is damaged in any way as a result of your error.

- *Keep the client apprised if work is not on schedule.* If you find yourself in a bind and unable to complete an assignment, go to the client before you turn the project over to someone else. There could be another solution. Perhaps the client can take on more responsibility for the project, or perhaps the client was hoping to delay the project but didn't want to change the agreement. You'll never know unless you ask.

- *Avoid working with competing clients at the same time.* Due to the sensitivity of information to which you may be exposed, it is likely that it could have negative consequences if shared with the competition. Some consultants take this one step further. Due to the size and nature of many of their contracts, they will not work with a client's competition for a full two years after their last contact.

- *Conduct regular self-examinations of your practice.* During and after consulting engagements, assess your progress and results. Learn from the experience.

- *Continue to provide excellent services that the client may never comprehend.* Someone will notice. And even if they don't, you know you did what was right.

- *Adhere to a consistent pricing structure.* Establish a fee structure and stick with it. Identify a clear and consistent pricing structure for all of your clients. Your structure should clearly spell out any differences, e.g., special rates for dealing with specific clients such as non-profits or government, fees for different kinds of work, or fees that vary depending on where the work is completed. Be consistent.

- *Charge for the work that needs to be done.* It may be tempting to charge more when you know the client has more in the budget. Don't do it. You won't feel good about it. In addition, don't add on services that the client really doesn't need.

- *Charge only for reasonable expenses actually incurred.* Expenses are petty little things that can begin a distrustful relationship. One way to avoid a problem is to build things such as telephone calls and express mail into your daily fee. The advantage is that you don't need to track them or present them to your client for payment.

Travel expenses should always be charged at cost and verified with receipts. Don't exaggerate mileage and don't exceed reasonable expenses. The question you should ask yourself is, "Would I spend this if I were at home?" For example, "Would I eat this lobster dinner if I were at home tonight?" If the answer is no, it is probably not a reasonable expense.

Double dipping—charging two clients for the same trip—is one of the worst ways a consultant violates the trust between consultant and client. There is nothing worse than having your statement reviewed and having to explain unethical discrepancies under oath.

Your fee structure, your expense report and how you deliver your product are all important aspects of building an ethically strong relationship with your client. The bottom line, however, is that the ethical overtone will be dependent upon the personal and professional relationship between individuals.

How can you determine if you are doing what you must to build this relationship? Ask your client. Discuss it. Your client may not be aware of your standards or what you do to maintain them. This kind of discussion builds respect for you.

Client to Consultant

The problems some clients are facing could be avoided through implementing and adhering to their own ethics systems.

Unfortunately, sometimes companies are first exposed to ethics through your professional behavior. Many times you may be setting the standard of professionalism. While you have no control over your client's behavior, you should be aware of some of the things clients may do that undermine your relationship with them.

Some clients simply do not know better and need educating from you. In other cases, the client may have an agenda that does not meet your standards. Typically you learn about this during the early stages of the relationship. Turn the project down and find something else. These same clients and their agendas inevitably turn their attention on you later. This attention may involve attacks on your work, questions regarding results, or refusal to pay.

Sometimes the client's agenda isn't apparent until later in the project. You may see warning signs along the way. The client may have unrealistic expectations of you or may begin to withdraw commitment from parts of the project. What do you do? You should be honest and candid with the client to resolve your concerns. Put your concern in writing to the client. If the client will not get back on track you can either work within the boundaries you've been given or terminate the relationship in accordance with your contract and ethical rules.

What unethical actions or danger signs might you encounter? Prior to your accepting the project, the client might exhibit some of the items identified in Exhibit 2.2.

Exhibit 2.2. Early Warning Signs.

The potential client:

- Wants to "pick your brain."
- Offers you lower pay than you quoted.
- Asks for a proposal in order to get the minimum number of quotes, without any intention of giving you the job.
- Requests samples of product from several consultants, then puts them together and develops its own program based on information belonging to the consultants.
- Already knows the solution to the problem.

You may also find that during the project, the client exhibits some of the behaviors identified in Exhibit 2.3.

Exhibit 2.3. Warning Signs on the Job.

Beware of a client who:

- Reveals an agenda that does not meet your standards.
- Seems to have a hidden agenda.
- Has unrealistic expectations of you.
- Withdraws commitment from parts of the project.
- Fails to provide data and information as promised.
- Is slow to approve work.
- Is slow to approve invoices.
- Shifts gears in the middle of the project.
- Refuses to remove barriers for you, such as difficult staff.
- Ignores your recommendations.
- Presents your ideas to management without sharing the credit with you.
- Requests that you change or omit information from a report.
- Brags about controlling or taking advantage of others.

The best way to address any of these issues is to hit them head on and candidly discuss them with your client.

When your name is on the project, your reputation is on the line. Remember that your reputation is your most valuable asset. Protect your ethical reputation as carefully as you would a priceless treasure.

Place a high value on your talents and your high-quality service. Think highly of yourself. Don't sell out on your integrity; don't negotiate your reputation away. As a consultant your principles are always in jeopardy. Ethical decisions can make your job harder in the short term, but will serve both you and the profession well in the long term.

Setting Up a Consulting Practice

Shirley had been a sales rep for an office furniture company for six years. One aspect of her job was to provide time management and assertiveness seminars at expositions and conferences, and for customers. Her seminars drew large crowds and rave reviews from people who told her she should conduct seminars full time. When her application for the sales manager's position was rejected, she decided it was time to strike out on her own. She gave a two-week notice and opened a small consulting practice called Personal Development. She knew what she wanted to do, so she didn't waste any time on a business plan. She would offer training and consulting to small companies and individuals in topics such as assertiveness, stress management, time management, and conflict resolution.

Four months have passed. Shirley has entered into agreements with service providers that she has recently found out are bad deals and not needed for her practice. She wants out of those agreements. She spent $2,500 for a license to teach materials that not one client has requested. Shirley wants to ask for her money back. Although Shirley has worked hard at selling her seminars, she has conducted four "brown bag lunches" and only one full-day session, billing a total of $1,900 during the four months. She has lots of leads, but no signed contracts. She has used up most of her cash reserves setting up her practice and marketing it. Shirley now wonders if she should begin to look for a job or take out a loan. She is on her way to a networking lunch with one of the most successful consultants in town to ask his advice.

Commentary

Shirley had no business plan, no written marketing plan, and no more idea of marketing tactics than what she'd used for furniture sales. She did not do any market research. Except for her presentation experience, she knew little about the consulting business. Therefore, her mental marketing plan (going after small businesses and individuals) was flawed. Shirley found that individuals rarely pay for their own learning experiences and small businesses have little discretionary funds for training and consulting. Small businesses also take longer to make decisions to buy things like Shirley's training programs. Entering into expensive agreements without checking prices was a mistake, as was purchasing a license to sell a service no one had requested. A visit to an attorney might have helped Shirley understand her rights under those contracts. Also, after the fact is the wrong time to network with the pros. Shirley should have asked lots of questions and put a plan together first. Plan the work, then work the plan.

PLANNING FIRST

Most people who embark on a trip to a new destination do some preparation. They look at a map to see where the place is located. They ask others who have visited the locale. They may ask directions along the way. They find milestones to mark their progress.

As a consultant, you need to take some basic legal steps in running your business. The importance of good professional advice has been stressed in the first chapter. However, the most caring, knowledgeable professional cannot effectively help you unless you have some type of plan or map of your business. That map is most commonly known as a business plan.

Usually, the consultants who fail are those who start without thoughtful and proper planning. They are the consultants who have unreasonable expectations and unrealistic time lines and who do not seek appropriate professional advice.

BUSINESS PLANS

Even if your plan is very basic, organizing your thoughts and goals on paper allows you to clearly communicate them to others, especially your attorney.

Before determining how to set up your consulting practice, you need to determine what type of business you are creating. The best way to do this is to prepare a written business plan. A business plan is a written strategy for achieving goals and meeting the associated costs. Business plans are working documents that you should refer to regularly and revise as needed.

A plan should describe the nature of your business. The description should include the types of services you offer and how you distribute those services. The plan should discuss the management of the business and introduce the key players in the business, and their duties, compensation, and benefits. The worksheet in Exhibit 3.1 will assist you with the planning.

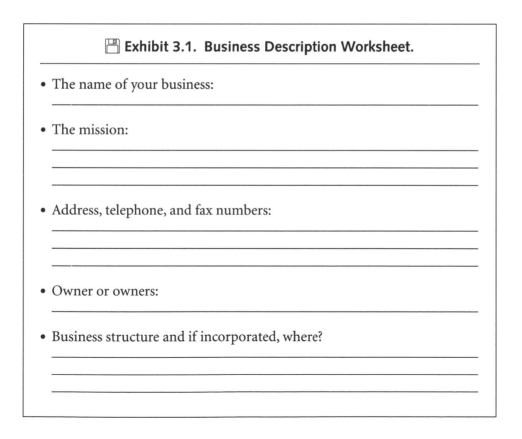

🖫 Exhibit 3.1. Business Description Worksheet.

• The name of your business:

_____

• The mission:

_____

_____

_____

• Address, telephone, and fax numbers:

_____

_____

_____

• Owner or owners:

_____

• Business structure and if incorporated, where?

_____

_____

_____

💾 Exhibit 3.1. Business Description Worksheet, Cont'd.

- Brief history of the business (e.g., is it a new business or an expansion of an existing business?):

  _____

  _____

  _____

- Start-up date:

  _____

- Specific activities to raise revenue:

  _____

  _____

  _____

- Services or products provided:

  _____

  _____

  _____

- Reasons why the business will succeed:

  _____

  _____

  _____

- Key players in the business:

  _____

  _____

  _____

- Relevant experience each contributes:

  _____

  _____

  _____

- Duties, compensation, and benefits of key players:

  _____

  _____

  _____

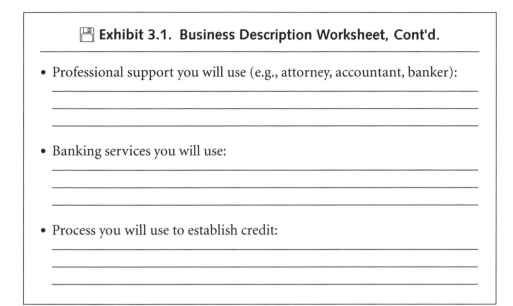

Exhibit 3.1. Business Description Worksheet, Cont'd.

- Professional support you will use (e.g., attorney, accountant, banker):
  _____
  _____
  _____

- Banking services you will use:
  _____
  _____
  _____

- Process you will use to establish credit:
  _____
  _____
  _____

Business planning includes financial planning. A good financial plan will cover your profit and sales objectives over a determined future period. It will also allow you to anticipate costs and help you plan actions to take when you are not meeting your goals. Exhibit 3.2 is a worksheet that will assist with your financial plan.

Exhibit 3.2. Financial Plan Worksheet.

- What assumptions are you making as a basis of the plan (e.g., market health, start-up date, gross profit margin, required overhead, payroll, and other expenses)?
  _____
  _____
  _____

- What expenditures will you require for start-up?
  _____
  _____
  _____

💾 Exhibit 3.2. Financial Plan Worksheet, Cont'd.

- What are your cash flow projections (revenue less expenses) for each month of your first year?

  Jan.: _____   Apr.: _____   July: _____   Oct.: _____
  Feb.: _____   May: _____   Aug.: _____   Nov.: _____
  Mar.: _____   June: _____   Sept.: _____   Dec.: _____

- What are your three-year cash-flow projections?

  Year 1: _____
  Year 2: _____
  Year 3: _____

- Where do you expect to get financing and under what terms?

  _____
  _____
  _____

- How will the money be used (e.g., overhead, supplies, marketing)?

  _____
  _____
  _____

- What is your personal net worth?

  _____
  _____
  _____

Your business plan should incorporate a marketing plan that addresses your advertising strategies and identifies your competition. The worksheet in Exhibit 3.3 asks the questions you'll need to answer to develop your marketing plan.

💾 Exhibit 3.3. Marketing Plan Worksheet.

- What are the demographics of your expected client base?

  _____
  _____
  _____

- What is the size of your potential market?

  _____
  _____
  _____

- What percentage of the market do you expect to penetrate?

  _____
  _____
  _____

- Who are your competitors?

  _____
  _____
  _____

- How does your product or service differ from theirs?

  _____
  _____
  _____

- What experience do they have?

  _____
  _____
  _____

- What is your pricing strategy and structure?

  _____
  _____
  _____

- How does your pricing strategy and structure differ from that of your competitors?

  _____
  _____
  _____

Creating your business plan may seem like a lot of work, but the results are worth it. Keep your business plan handy when making decisions. Show it to your attorney so that your legal decisions are based on the nature of your business and support your future plans. Legal advice that takes into account your business description, financial plan, and marketing plan is more effective for your particular needs. At the very least, you should check your business progress against your original plan quarterly. Your business plan will keep you focused and provide reminders of your legal requirements and ethical expectations.

SCENARIO

When the urban renewal consulting firm where Rory worked filed Chapter 11 bankruptcy, he decided to open his own company. He knew that he needed to appear larger than a one-man show to get appointments with city managers in his state. He knew that being incorporated was critical to this appearance. At a family gathering Rory's uncle Jake told him about a friend who had saved thousands of dollars by incorporating by mail in a state on the East Coast. Rory incorporated by mail and began a series of other cost-saving measures. To save the cost of a business checking account, Rory used his personal checking account to pay for the few business expenses he incurred the first year. Two months ago he started paying himself a salary. He has recently received several pieces of correspondence that he does not understand: a letter from the state in which he resides stating that he never filed the proper forms to do business as a foreign or alien corporation, a letter asking for unpaid franchise fees, and a demand letter asking for payment from some attorney claiming that a former client is about to sue Rory personally. Rory is wondering if he should see an attorney and what is the cheapest way to pay for it.

Commentary

Some attorneys look forward to meeting a client like Rory. His savings schemes have actually created more expensive legal problems. First, incorporating right off the bat might not have been in his best interest. Rory might not have had assets to protect or have understood the corporation requirements. Another entity might have better suited his needs while creating the professional appearance desired.

Second, incorporating outside his state was probably a mistake. When you conduct a *significant* amount of business in a state other than the one in which you have incorporated, you have filing requirements and must usually pay a fee for the privilege. Rory conducts all his business in his resident state so he probably should have incorporated there.

Third, Rory may have lost any limited liability protection a corporation gives him against the former client. He has broken the most fundamental rule of maintaining a corporation, that of following the formalities. He has not kept current with his franchise fees and he has failed to keep business funds separate from personal ones.

BUSINESS ENTITY OR STRUCTURE

One of the most confusing things any business owner faces is how to structure a business. The decision is important for a number of reasons. The entity you choose affects your taxes and your potential for liability if something goes wrong. Your business structure affects your ability to raise money as well as the perception of your business by your clients and other consultants. You should explore the different types of business entity and the characteristics of each. Then you, your accountant, and your attorney can determine which entity best serves the needs of your business.

Don't skimp on using professionals here! Go to an attorney familiar with your business requirements and an accountant familiar with your financial requirements. You need advice to properly draft the documents to create your business as well as to protect it. Choosing the right business entity has become more difficult but also more exciting since the number of business structure choices has exploded in the last few years. The typical general partnership, with its threat of personal liability for all partners, and the standard corporation, with its strict reporting requirements, have given way to entities that are much more flexible. Invest time in understanding all your options as well as your potential for risk.

In the United States, there are basically five types of business structures:

- Sole proprietorships
- Partnerships (general and limited)
- Corporations (C and S)
- Limited liability companies
- Limited liability partnerships

Naturally, if you are forming a business entity outside the United States, you will seek additional experienced professional advice. However, it is also important to note that laws vary from state to state. Therefore, if you are planning to do business outside your state, you need to learn about those distinctions as well.

As you compare the different business entities, consider these basic issues:

- The cost of forming
- Filing or the process of formation
- The cost of maintaining and operating the entity
- The formalities of operating the entity
- Liability risks
- The ability to transfer ownership interest
- The length of time you expect your business to exist
- The amount of privacy you require in business operations
- Any other legal restrictions

As you can see, some of the same information contained in your business plan will be used to make the legal decision of how to structure your business.

SCENARIO

Sam and Bill sketched their partnership agreement on a napkin over dinner. Two months later they both gave notice to their respective employers and opened the doors to The Action Planning Group. They were swamped with business right from the start and never got around to completing the legal work for incorporating the business or even a partnership buy-out agreement. Their services were in high demand and within two months they hired their first employee. Three years later, with ten employees, they developed a philosophical rift and decided to go their separate ways. Now they are in court battling over ownership of seminar materials and of the company name. The napkin and all its good intentions have been long forgotten.

Commentary

Partners Sam and Bill have quite a few issues that will be decided for them in court. The judge or a jury—with no prior knowledge of Sam and Bill—has to determine name ownership, asset distribution, client ownership, property rights of seminar materials, location of the business, and maybe even which employees continue to work with each partner. If Sam and Bill continue fighting, they could use up any resources they have accumulated in the partnership as well as their personal resources arguing about who owns what and what the napkin actually said. The need for early planning is extremely apparent in this sort of situation. A few dollars spent planning up front could have saved thousands of dollars later.

Just like marriages, business relationships have a honeymoon stage where everything is rosy and any little fault is forgiven. Like newlyweds, new business owners don't think anything will go wrong. Now Sam and Bill are in the divorce stage of their business marriage. A well-written partnership agreement would have served as a prenuptial agreement spelling out what each partner contributed and how those assets would be distributed upon separation.

What will happen to Sam and Bill? Perhaps the judge or their attorneys will get them to mediation. Mediation is an alternative way to resolve disputes that allows the parties to help in the settlement process. Perhaps, they will arrive at a settlement as quickly as possible—before all of their assets are depleted and their credibility with clients and other consultants is gone.

CHOOSING THE PROPER BUSINESS ENTITY

Do you have others who will own the business with you? How are you going to distribute profits? What are the tax consequences? Are you thinking about incorporating or forming a limited liability company to avoid or limit your loss exposure? Since limiting liability is such an important part of choosing the proper entity, you need to know where your potential liability lies. Your exposure to liability risks is discussed in Chapter Thirteen. The worksheet in Exhibit 3.4 will assist you with questions to ask while you decide which business entity will best meet your needs. Many answers should come directly from the business plan worksheets (Exhibits 3.1 through 3.3).

🖫 Exhibit 3.4. Business Entity Selection Worksheet.

Questions to ask yourself as you decide on the best business entity for you.
Review the answers with your attorney and accountant.

- What type of business are you creating?

  _____
  _____
  _____

- What services are you offering?

  _____
  _____
  _____

- How will you distribute those services?

  _____
  _____
  _____

- Where will the business operations be located?

  _____
  _____
  _____

- Who will own this business?

  _____
  _____
  _____

- How much of the business will each own?

  _____
  _____
  _____

- Who will manage the business and what role will each play?

  _____
  _____
  _____

🖫 Exhibit 3.4. Business Entity Selection Worksheet, Cont'd.

- What is your financial plan?

  _____

  _____

  _____

- How much capital will you require? When? In what form?

  _____

  _____

  _____

- What are your start-up costs?

  _____

  _____

  _____

- What are your income projections?

  _____

  _____

  _____

- How will profits and losses be allocated?

  _____

  _____

  _____

- What are the financial resources of the owners?

  _____

  _____

  _____

- What are the assets of the business?

  _____

  _____

  _____

- What action will you take if you are not meeting your financial goals?

  _____

  _____

  _____

📁 **Exhibit 3.4. Business Entity Selection Worksheet, Cont'd.**

- Who is your competition?

  _____
  _____
  _____

- What is your marketing strategy?

  _____
  _____
  _____

- Where is your customer base located?

  _____
  _____
  _____

- How long do you plan on being in business?

  _____
  _____
  _____

- Do you plan on selling the business one day?

  _____
  _____
  _____

- Will you want to sell a part of the business to raise money? (Stock or membership interest?)

  _____
  _____
  _____

- Do you plan on transferring the business to a family member?

  _____
  _____
  _____

💾 Exhibit 3.4. Business Entity Selection Worksheet, Cont'd.

- Do you have any estate planning issues regarding the business?

  _____
  _____
  _____

- Are there any special tax issues regarding your type of business?

  _____
  _____
  _____

- Are there any special laws or regulatory constraints on your type of business or on the owners?

  _____
  _____
  _____

- What is your potential exposure to risks and liabilities?

  _____
  _____
  _____

- What is your potential risk in addition to the equity invested in the business?

  _____
  _____
  _____

- How will you keep track of the legal requirements or formalities of your business entity?

  _____
  _____
  _____

- What happens upon death, disability, retirement, or departure of a principal?

  _____
  _____
  _____

Sole Proprietorships

A *sole proprietorship* is the simplest form of business structure. Sole proprietorships are not considered separate legal entities. Since the company is not considered separate from the owner, it dies when the owner does or when the owner decides to pursue other interests. Owners manage their businesses as they see fit without justifying their actions to partners or stockholders. Unlike a corporation requesting permission from a state government, there is no registration requirement other than an assumed name if a sole proprietor wants to do business in another state.

Usually your Social Security number serves as your company's federal taxpayer-identification number. Federal tax reporting for sole proprietorships is the easiest of the five structures, just requiring the addition of a Schedule C to list business income and take deductions for expenses.

Sole proprietors pay income tax on net profits. As a sole proprietor, you incur no additional or separate tax liabilities beyond your profits. However, self-employment taxes, without the contribution from an employer, may come as a shock to many new sole proprietors. As a sole proprietor, there are no filing fees or recording requirements. The only filing most sole proprietors do is filing an assumed name certificate.

The fact that no separate legal entity is created is usually considered an advantage. However, it also poses some concerns. First, your business dies with you because there is no continuing interest or separate entity to survive. Second, you face unlimited liability as a sole proprietor. While owners of other business structures may be limited to what they have invested in the company, the entire amount of your legal or tax liability becomes your personal liability. For example, if your client sues you for business reasons, you are personally liable for the full amount of the debt. Your personal assets may be used to satisfy that debt. While insurance may provide coverage for this type of situation, it is important to know the expensive pitfall if no protection is in place.

Partnerships

A *partnership* is a familiar business structure to most. A partnership is an effort of two or more persons engaging in business with the goal of making a profit. The traditional partnership is known as a *general partnership,* but other, more limited arrangements are possible.

General Partnerships. Unless otherwise agreed upon, each *general partner* has a direct and equal voice in managing the business. Instead of identification by the owner's Social Security number, a partnership has a separate federal employer-identification number, known as its FEIN.

Although a partnership files a tax return, it pays no separate federal tax. Each partner pays a pro rata share of income tax on net profits, whether or not those profits are distributed. The business losses and income are reported on each partner's personal tax returns.

As with a sole proprietorship, there are some liability concerns. Partners in a general partnership share unlimited personal liability for the acts of the partnership or any of the partners. Therefore, if you are in a partnership with a consultant who makes a big error, you will most likely share in the responsibility and liability. And you may have to pay for the error.

General partnerships can be created by an agreement of parties or even a perception of the public. If you want to form a general partnership, the best way to do so is by written agreement spelling out who will be involved, what each has contributed, the distribution of profits, the sharing of loss, and the nature of the partnership. The division of profits can be shared equally or on a percentage basis, resulting from the contributions of cash, experience, property, labor, and perhaps even reputation or earning power of each partner.

As in any situation, an oral agreement will be only as clear as the memories of the partners involved. A written agreement, on the other hand, can be shown to outside parties both to acquire additional partners and to reflect the terms of the actual agreement. In the absence of a partnership agreement, most jurisdictions have adopted the Uniform Partnership Act or similar legislation to provide the terms of the partnership agreement for you. You can eliminate having those terms imposed on your partnership by documenting your own agreements.

It is possible to inadvertently form a legal partnership by simply acting as one or being perceived as one. Attorneys are a good example of how a partnership can form unintentionally but exist for liability's sake. Even if two attorneys are sole practitioners in the eyes of the IRS, they may be considered partners by the general public. If the attorneys share office space and work jointly with clients, they must make their separate status known or they will be considered a partnership for liability purposes. The same principle applies to consultants. If you are performing joint projects for a client with other consultants and sharing expenses, it is important to maintain your separate status. Use separate stationery. Hand out business cards that reflect your individual business instead of a shared name. Have separate signs on the door. Explain to your client that you are bringing in another consultant with a separate business to help on a project. If you don't take these steps, you may be facing liability for another consultant's errors because you were perceived as partners.

Unless provided in a written agreement, a general partnership may be terminated by the agreement of the partners, by the death of one or more of the partners, or by the bankruptcy of one of the partners. A partnership interest can be assigned, but the assignee does not have full partnership rights. That means that if you wish to give your interest in the partnership to your spouse or a child, or sell it to an outsider for profit, the recipient's rights extend only to sharing the profits. The recipient will not have a say in the management or how the profits will be disbursed.

Limited Partnership. A *limited partnership* is created by a written agreement of the parties. What distinguishes this partnership from a general partnership is that it provides a way to limit the liability faced by some of the partners. L.P.'s are used as passive investment vehicles in which the investors will not be active in the business, will accept no risk beyond their investment, and want the tax advantage of flow through profits and losses. In a limited partnership, there are two types of partners, general and limited.

General partners face the same type of unlimited personal liability for the acts of the partnership or other partners. However, limited partners are only limited to the amount of their partnership investment. For this privilege of avoiding liability, the limited partner has limited rights in managing the business. Unless you have some very rich friends who want to invest their money in your consulting business and you are willing to be personally liable for it, you probably will not be looking at a limited partnership.

Limited Liability Partnership. A *limited liability partnership* or L.L.P. is different from a limited partnership. An L.L.P. is a general partnership where the partners are given limited liability status in certain areas. While L.L.P. partners can manage the company just as in a general partnership, partners are provided some limits on their personal liability. Therefore, the limited liability pocket exists to protect your other assets.

Corporations

A corporation is probably the most recognizable business structure. Corporations can be formed as *C corporations* or as *Subchapter-S corporations*. Many of the rules for both types of corporations are the same.

Combined Rules for C Corporations and Subchapter-S Corporations.

All corporations are treated as separate and distinct legal entities. The liability for the owners or shareholders is limited to the amount of assets of the corporation. If all the rules have been followed to maintain the corporation's separate status, the most shareholders can lose is the amount invested in the company. However, incorporating is not a way for you to avoid your own wrong actions. The shield protects against liability from contractual business obligations as well as acts of other employees or owners. No business entity will protect an owner from his own acts, especially intentional ones.

Ownership interests or shares in a corporation can be transferred. Therefore, the corporation has perpetual existence and does not die when an owner dies or no longer wants to be a part of the company. The business is managed by directors who set policy and appoint officers. Shareholders elect the directors.

To form a corporation you must file articles of incorporation, receive a charter issued by a state, create corporate bylaws, and fulfill other state requirements.

There are some drawbacks to incorporating. For example, it is possible that you may lose some control over the management of your business, especially if you have other shareholders who vote against you.

Check with your accountant regarding the tax implications. You may experience double taxation on the profits because the corporation pays income tax on net profits, with no deduction for dividends paid to its owner, you. Corporations incur other expenses including fees required for organization.

You will probably have to pay a state franchise and/or income tax, prepare annual reports, and keep up with corporate formalities such as minutes of meetings and corporate resolutions. Remember, to prove the corporation is a separate entity it is important to keep all these documents current.

The limited liability protection is one of the most important functions of a corporation. If the corporate formalities are not followed, owners risk losing the corporation's limited liability status and can be held personally liable. This reaching into personal assets is called "piercing the corporate veil." For example, if you treat the corporate bank account as your personal account, a court may rule that your creditors can pierce the corporate veil and reach into your personal assets.

All of this discussion is aimed to show that incorporating is made for reasons other than the ability to have the initials "Inc." or "Corp." after a business name.

Special Provisions for Subchapter-S Corporations. S corporations or S-Corps are standard corporations but enjoy the advantage of avoiding federal income tax at the corporate level. Both the number and types of owners are limited in an S-Corp. The structure allows only U.S. citizens and organizations to serve as shareholders. Also, the maximum number of shareholders in an S-Corp is seventy-five.

An advantage of the S-Corp is that you will avoid double taxation on income to the corporation and dividends to you. The income is passed through to the shareholder to report on your personal return. Creating an S-Corp, however, requires a special filing and has some restrictions some owners don't like. Your accountant is probably very familiar with S-Corps and can tell you whether this structure meets your needs.

Limited Liability Companies

Although the protection from double taxation is a definite advantage for S-Corps, many people are beginning to use limited liability companies. A *limited liability company* or L.L.C. has a corporate look but qualifies for other partnership or corporate tax status under federal law at the owner's election. Under most state laws the L.L.C. is very flexible and may, unlike partnerships, even allow only one member or owner. For example, an L.L.C. can be run like a traditional corporation with many levels of management or managed at just one level. Some of the terminology also changes. The term *shareholder* used in corporations is replaced by *member* and the term *director* is replaced by *manager*. Articles of *organization* are filed instead of *incorporation* and the L.L.C. is governed by its *regulations* instead of *bylaws*.

Both the L.L.P. and the L.L.C. are more relaxed entities and combine limited liability protections without all of the corporate formalities. Some jurisdictions impose different taxes on L.L.C.'s and partnerships. Make sure to consult your tax advisor on this issue.

The greatest problems you may encounter with either of these entities is that both are relatively new. That means that many attorneys or accountants are just becoming comfortable with them. In addition, you still face the potential that they may not be recognized in other states or by the IRS as planned. However, these entities are rapidly becoming accepted.

The chart in Exhibit 3.5 provides you with a comparison of characteristics of some business entities. Some of the names and filing requirements may differ depending on your state. Consider these different aspects before selecting a business entity.

ENTITIES FOR CERTAIN PROFESSIONS

Some professions must file slightly different types of entities. For example, licensed professionals such as attorneys, architects, certified public accountants, doctors, and dentists cannot form a limited liability company, but can form a *professional* limited liability company or P.L.L.C. In other circumstances, professionals can form Professional Corporations (P.C.) and Professional Associations (P.A.) but not standard corporations. The reason for this different treatment is to limit the owners of a business or practice only to the licensed professionals and to impose more restrictions on liability. Your attorney will tell you if you need to have this different filing due to a licensing requirement.

FILING ASSUMED NAME CERTIFICATES

When people or businesses use names other than their legal name, they file assumed name certificates. For example, sole proprietor Maria Smith may want to name her consulting business Smith and Associates or The Smith Group. (Note: Depending on her state's laws Maria may not be able to use the words *Company, Co., Incorporated, Inc., Corporation,* or *Corp.* in her title because she has not incorporated.) Maria will need to first check the assumed name filings to make sure no one is using her name. Then Maria will pay a filing fee and file an assumed name certificate in the states and individual counties in which she will be doing business.

You may be familiar with the term *doing business as* or *d/b/a.* This term can also refer to incorporated businesses or partnerships using assumed names. Using a d/b/a also lets you to attempt a business and later sell the name or start again if the business does not succeed. One other note, if you or your business changes name, you will want to publish the name change. This gives creditors fair warning and lets individuals know that the business will now be known by another name. Generally, newspapers have forms to fill out to publicize these name changes.

Exhibit 3.5. Comparison of Basic Business Entities.

Entity	Owner Liability	Participation in Management	Ownership	Formation Requirements	Name
Sole Proprietor	No limits.	No restrictions.	One.	None. File assumed name if doing business under different name.	No special requirements.
General Partnership	No limits.	No restrictions.	At least two partners.	Partnership agreement (may be oral) and file assumed name certificate.	No special requirements.
Limited Partnership	No limits for general partners. Limited for limited partners.	Restrictions for limited partners.	At least one general partner and one limited partner.	Partnership agreement (may be oral) and file certificate with Secretary of State.	Must have "Limited Partnership," "Ltd.," "Limited," or "L.P." in title.

Exhibit 3.5. Comparison of Basic Business Entities, Cont'd.

Limited Liability Company	All members have limited liability for company debts.	No restrictions. ("Managing" members make decisions.)	One or more members. (Some states may require at least two members.)	File Articles of Organization and adopt regulations.	Must have "Limited Liability Company," "LLC," or "LC" in title. ("Limited" and "Company" may be abbreviated.)
S Corporation	Limited liability for all shareholders.	No restrictions. (Shareholders elect directors to make decisions. Directors appoint officers for daily decisions.)	One to seventy-five shareholders.	File Articles of Incorporation, adopt bylaws, and file "S" election tax form with IRS.	Must have "Corporation," "Incorporated," "Company," or abbreviation of these in title.
C Corporation	Limited liability for all shareholders.	No restrictions. (Shareholders elect directors to make decisions. Directors appoint officers for daily decisions.)	One or more shareholders.	File Articles of Incorporation and adopt bylaws.	Must have some form of "Corporation," "Incorporated," "Company," or abbreviation of these in title.

ORGANIZE TO GET STARTED

Setting up your consulting practice is a manageable task. Use the worksheets in this chapter to develop your plan. Then make a list of everything you need to do to ensure you complete all the details. The checklist in Exhibit 3.6 will get you started. Most important, get legal and financial advice from professionals before you get too far down the road.

💾 Exhibit 3.6 Start-Up Checklist

❑ Describe the business, its services and products.
❑ Identify your market.
❑ Analyze your competition.
❑ Assess your skills.
❑ Name your business.
❑ Determine your financial requirements (budget) and your pricing structure.
❑ Identify start-up costs.
❑ Select an accountant.
❑ Determine your business structure.
❑ Check on zoning laws, licenses, taxes.
❑ Select a location.
❑ Develop a business plan that includes:
  ❑ business description
  ❑ marketing plan
  ❑ management plan
  ❑ financial plan
❑ Select a banker, attorney, and insurance agent.
❑ Arrange for financing (or set aside capital for a worst case scenario).
❑ File documentation to legally register your business.

Source: Biech, E. *The Business of Consulting.* San Francisco: Jossey-Bass/Pfeiffer, 1999, p. 74.

Starting Your Office

Juan and Al saw that their two consulting firms complemented each other nicely. Three months ago they formed a partnership and signed a two-year lease on a space that included a conference room and two offices with lovely views of the lake. They are paying a premium for the location. The building was sold one week after they moved in. Since that time, the hall areas have not been cleaned, the public bathrooms are often out of supplies, and the outside walkways and entrances have often been left buried in snow. To make matters worse, the tenant next to them has erected a sign that interrupts their lake view.

Commentary

Juan and Al do have a right to expect that the public areas in the building are kept to certain standards. Hopefully, they have a clause that states those standards are of a similar type of building. The failure to shovel snow also presents a safety hazard to them and their clients. If they have not complained to date, it could be argued that they accept the building's condition by their silence over the last three months. A review of their lease will tell them what their options are regarding complaining and what the landlord is required to do to remedy their complaints. If it was a standard form lease, the original landlord probably had the right to transfer or *assign* the terms of Juan and Al's lease to the new owner.

Juan and Al probably won't be able to get out of the lease. The conditions discussed are not so terrible as to make the space uninhabitable. As far as the sign goes, the tenant next to them may have violated his lease regarding signage. If so, Juan and Al can ask that their neighbor's lease be enforced. Another option might be to approach the neighbor about moving the sign and offering to pay for the cost of moving it. If the problems are not corrected to Juan and Al's satisfaction, they need to seek legal advice on their options under the lease and their state's law.

LEASING YOUR OWN SPACE

Having an office in a nice office building adds to your appearance as a professional. You feel more professional since you actually leave your home every morning for the workplace. This is important to many consultants who are just starting out in the business. In addition, in the right building, you may receive referrals.

As you might expect, there are some drawbacks with leasing your own space. Leases are typically drafted first by the landlord, and are originally very one-sided in favor of the landlord. If office space is in high demand, a landlord has a choice of tenants and can charge what the market will bear. If space is not at a premium, you may have some additional flexibility.

Depending on the size of space you need, the amount you are willing to pay, and the length of time you are willing to stay, a landlord may be more accommodating. That is not to say that a smaller tenant does not have negotiating room. Remember, a landlord does not make money on unleased space. Be prepared with the benefits of having you as a tenant when you negotiate the amount of your rent.

A landlord may negotiate your rental rate around several issues. Will you bring in other lessees? Are you willing to take the smaller space that the landlord has had trouble filling? Is there some space already "finished out" with existing construction that is compatible with your needs or do walls need to be built and carpet laid? And here's the major benefit to a landlord, will you always pay on time? Just as a good credit history is important for acquiring a loan, a history of paying rent in a current manner is extremely important to a landlord. Also, you may be asked to provide letters of credit in addition to a security deposit to ensure your rental payments.

Regardless of your firm's size, there are some areas of flexibility. If possible, have someone who understands real estate help you negotiate the lease. The questions in Exhibit 4.1 should be useful to consider before negotiating a lease.

Exhibit 4.1. Questions to Consider Before Negotiating a Lease.

- How much space do you need?

- How much can you afford to pay for space?

- Is location important to your business?

- How long can you commit to stay? (Many typical leases require a three- to five-year commitment.)

- Will you be able to attract other lessees for the landlord?

- How often are you in your office?

- Are you willing to take that smaller space that the landlord has had trouble filling?

- Do you care how the space is finished out?

- Would you be willing to take space as is instead of requiring the landlord to make additional finishes or remodeling?

- Will you always pay on time?

In addition to negotiating your rental rate, consider the following items when negotiating your lease:

- The expense acceleration portion of the rate. The expenses are the operating costs built into the rent to cover maintenance, security, and services.

- The amount of build-out costs, remodeling costs, or tenant improvement allowance. Find out what's typical from other tenants.

- The amount of parking, number of covered spaces, and whether there are reserve parking spaces for you, your employees, or your visitors.

- The cost of additional parking if you need it—or the possibility of exchanging unneeded parking space allocations for other things you want.

- A way to abate rent if services such as electricity are not available. *Abate* means the contractual ability to suspend rental payments in whole or part until the problem is corrected. It's better to get this in writing before the need occurs.

- A way to terminate the lease if the space becomes uninhabitable. *Uninhabitable* could refer to extreme violations of the safety code. However, don't assume that a lease will be automatically terminated unless the problem is severe—a complete loss of electricity or malfunction of the heating, ventilation, or air conditioner system (HVAC), for example.

- The amount of the security deposit as well the possibility of interest on the deposit. In some cases the security deposit can be returned after a period of time.

- Your ability to fix problems or "self-help" clauses and the effect of those repairs as a credit on your rent.

- The possibility of avoiding personal guarantees or letters of credit to guarantee payment of the lease. You have selected a business entity to ensure limited liability to you. This is one case when you should attempt to exercise that right. However, in some cities, personal liability is very difficult to avoid. Also, can the landlord put a lien on your property if you don't pay?

- The management construction fee to supervise the construction of your space should be kept as low as possible.

- The need for relocation agreements. These should be made prior to relocation, and should include both relocation within the building and to other locations owned by the landlord. Relocation space should be absolutely compatible in size or building location.

- Sublease rights and assignment rights. Remember that you want to keep your options open regarding finding another tenant if necessary. You may leave the consulting business because you change your mind, become ill, or get a job offer you can't refuse. And don't rule out the possibility that your business may be so wildly successful that you outgrow the space before the lease is up.

- The signage. Consider not only your own signage, but how others' signage might affect your space.

These points of negotiation are found in Exhibit 4.2.

Exhibit 4.2. Questions to Consider in Lease Negotiations.

- What is included? What is extra? (Electricity, signage, parking, and so on)

- What is the common area maintenance fee portion of the regular rental rate?

- Can you set expenses after you determine what they actually are during the first year?

- Is there negotiating room on the amount of build-out costs, remodeling costs, or tenant improvement allowance?

- Can you have more parking spaces or covered spaces?

- Can you have reserved spaces for you, your employees, or your visitors?

- If parking spaces are not of major importance, can your rent be reduced or can you have something else in lieu of those parking spaces?

- What are the costs of additional parking?

- Is there a way to abate rent if services such as electricity are not available or the heating, ventilation, or air condition system malfunctions?

- Is there a way to terminate the lease if the space becomes uninhabitable?

- What is your ability to remedy the problems yourself (self-help) and deduct the amount from your rent?

- Can you reduce the amount of the security deposit?

- Can you receive interest on the deposit when it is returned?

- Can you avoid personal guarantees, letters of credit, and landlord liens on your lease?

- What actions cause the rent payments to accelerate or become due on a faster payment schedule?

- How low can you make the management construction fee if finish-out is required?

- Can you agree not to be forced to relocate?

Exhibit 4.2. Questions to Consider in Lease Negotiations, Cont'd.

- Can you have an agreement that allows you the choice of terminating the lease instead of relocating?
- Do you have sublease rights and assignment rights, and what restrictions or approvals are required?
- Can the landlord add signage to advertise your presence?
- Who controls the heating, ventilation, and air conditioning for your space?
- What can be done to enforce the rules of the building against other tenants?
- What are your remedies if the building changes ownership?
- What can be done if the landlord/leasing entity does not comply with its own rules?
- Can all building construction be conducted after hours?
- If your quiet enjoyment of the lease premises is disturbed, what concessions or remedies do you have?
- What type of security is offered?
- What happens if other tenants are disturbing you?
- How much will your rent increase if you renew your lease?
- What are the terms of your renewal options? (For example, if you have a five-year lease, do you have the option to renew the lease for two additional five-year terms?)
- When do you have to inform the landlord you are renewing your lease?
- How much time do you have to cure a problem or default once you are notified by the landlord? (For example, a ten-day opportunity to cure a financial default once notified and thirty days if the default is nonfinancial.)

Duties of the Landlord

In a well-negotiated lease, a landlord has the duty to maintain the building in the manner of a building of similar quality. The landlord must provide quiet enjoyment of the leased property. For example, the building should be quiet during office hours and tenants who disturb others should be handled by the landlord.

Duties of Tenants

Tenants have to pay their rent in a timely manner. They must keep their space clean and contact the landlord before major remodeling. Tenants usually have a duty to notify a landlord if there is a change in the tenants' business status, such as when the business is sold or enters bankruptcy. Tenants generally must use space as required under the restriction of the lease.

SUBLEASING FROM OTHERS

Do you actually need your own lease? Perhaps you can arrange to sublease extra space from another business. For example, maybe your accountant knows of a business that has some spare office space or your banker knows a company that would welcome someone to subsidize a portion of the rent. When you sublease from another company, you may have the benefit of office systems such as phones and equipment already in place.

However, in subleasing it is important to maintain your own separate identity for legal and professional reasons. Does the space have a separate entrance for your clients? Can you add an additional sign that distinguishes your office from that of the lessor?

Also, review both your agreement for the space and the lessor's lease agreement with the landlord. As a sub-tenant, you will be expected to abide by the lease agreement. Also, if subletting space is against the business owner's lease, both you and the business owner could find yourselves evicted by the landlord. Usually tenants must get permission from the landlord before subletting or assigning their space to someone else. If permission is needed before subleasing, make sure that permission is given in writing to the business owner with a copy to you. Reprinting stationery and notifying people of an address change due to a lease disagreement detracts from your business, both in terms of the time it takes to deal with the problem and in the message of impermanence and poor planning it sends your clients.

SHARING OFFICE SPACE

If you decide to share office space with someone else, make sure you make it known to the public that each is a separate business. You will want to avoid the appearance of a partnership if one doesn't exist. You will need your own letterhead and must ensure that the phones are answered in a way that does not imply a partnership. Make certain that each party using the space has his or her own business sign.

If you are sharing an office, make sure that those items you need to keep confidential are protected in a locked filing cabinet and that phone calls are made behind closed doors. Your chief concern is not simply exposing private matters to other consultants but also exposing information to their visitors and clients. Confidentiality issues will be discussed in Chapter Seven.

Ensure that all the individuals sharing the space are liable under the lease. You may remember stories of college roommates who moved out of apartments leaving one roommate responsible for the rent. . . . If you and your fellow office space sharers have a disagreement, it is tempting to leave if your name is not on the lease. You may want to try a space-sharing relationship on a trial basis. It's wise for all involved parties to agree to meet after a probationary period to discuss how the arrangement is working.

EXECUTIVE SUITES

An effective solution for many businesses is establishing an office in an executive suite. Executive suites are typically managed by a company that leases a large amount of space and then divides the space into many different offices. Their popularity has grown due to the cost-saving features of sharing conference space, office support, copiers, and phone systems. Business owners can choose from a menu of options and pay as they go.

Just like any tenant, executive suite owners are subject to their own lease arrangements and to their own landlords. Executive suite owners that lose their space may have no place to move the businesses. When renting from them it is always a smart idea to ask how long the executive suite has had its lease with the building and the duration of the current lease. Another drawback may occur when contracted services change with a new management company or owner. Unless a new management company agrees to abide by the terms of your original agreement, the executive suite services may change, sometimes drastically.

Shop around. Executive suites run the gamut for amenities, service, and quality. Remember, if you are unhappy with an executive suite's office staff, you don't have the ability to discipline or terminate them. You are a recipient of services when you are in an office suite. Ask about the executive service's reputation before you lease. Are current tenants happy with the services they are receiving? To help you when considering leasing options, answer the questions found in Exhibit 4.3.

🖫 Exhibit 4.3. Questions to Ask Yourself Regarding Lease Options.

- Do you actually need your own lease?
- Can you arrange to sublease extra space from another business?
- Does your accountant or banker know a business that has some extra office space?
- If you sublease, what office systems could you use?
- Is there a receptionist available?
- Could you use the existing phone systems?
- Would you have access to office equipment such as copiers and fax machines?
- Is the office already furnished?
- How could you keep your identity separate?
- Does the space still allow for privacy?
- Does the space look professional?
- Does the space have a separate entrance for your clients?
- Can you add an additional sign that distinguishes your office from that of the lessor?
- Is a sublease allowed under the lease?
- Can you abide by the current lease agreement?
- Is the current lease holder in good financial condition?
- Why does the current lease holder want to lease the space?
- What happens if you and the current lease holder have a dispute?
- Does the current lease holder have permission to add you as a sub-tenant?
- Could you find someone to share office space with you?
- Do you have a way to protect confidential information?
- Could you find an executive suite situation?
- What is included in the executive suite arrangement?
- Are other tenants happy?

It started innocently enough. Cassandra started providing a résumé-writing service to make some extra spending money. Word spread fast that her résumés and advice got results. She decided to resign from her job and pursue her résumé consulting practice full time. Her business plan included working out of a spare bedroom in her condo to eliminate the cost of renting office space. Three months into her new endeavor, when she was just beginning to build her clientele, her condo association sent her a notice. The letter stated that the homeowners agreement she had signed prevented her from "conducting business in her residence in which any monetary transactions occur." She needed to cease operating her business venture immediately.

Commentary

What's a hard-working consultant to do? It appears Cassandra has chosen a neighborhood that genuinely cares about the appearance of its property. One thing Cassandra could do is figure out if there have been any other violations of the policy. Does she remember a neighbor holding regular kitchen parties in her condo or someone who regularly conducts singing lessons? Have certain condo owners been allowed to conduct business without notification or are the rules universally applied?

Next, she should visit an attorney who knows about residential real estate law and homeowners associations. She should take the agreement and the letter to her lawyer for a review and a quick response. There may even be a state law protecting her home office. Cassandra needs to think through her options. Maybe she could meet clients at a separate conference room if the traffic flow is the real issue to the association. Perhaps she could show other violations and ask for the same type of exception. Maybe she will get herself elected to the condo association and change the rules. In the worst case, Cassandra could find another condo where owners are more concerned with property upkeep and not the business conducted by the residents.

HOME OFFICES

A few years ago, a home office might have implied you were less than professional. In the present era of telecommuting and flexi-place arrangements, a home office is more often seen as a smart business decision. To work successfully at a home office, maintain your office for conducting business only. In addition develop a plan so that you will minimize sounds like dogs barking and children playing. Don't allow household chores to distract you.

Be careful about deducting a proportionate amount of your home's utility costs, taxes, or rent for your home office.

While it is certainly a financial advantage to do so, deductions for home offices are potential red flags to the IRS and may make you more prone to audits for tax implications. Review the decision to deduct home expenses that support your home office very carefully with your accountant before proceeding. Also, see if any other rules apply, such as depreciation.

In addition, keep in mind that the IRS may require proof that your home office is used exclusively for business. If your family or you use your phone, fax, or computer for anything other than business purposes, you may not be able to deduct those equipment items as business expenses.

If few clients will visit you at your office, working out of your home is a wonderful option. If you must meet clients at your home office, it is better to have a separate entrance. However, avoid meeting clients at your home if at all possible. You might be subject to various government requirements for bathrooms, wheelchair ramps, fire exits, business permits, etc. You may also require special insurance if your general homeowners policy excludes commercial uses of your home. In addition, some neighborhoods have homeowner restrictions that are violated by having clients come to your home.

A better alternative is to meet clients at their offices or use conference rooms of other public meeting spaces or businesses. Some executive suites allow you to rent conference rooms just when you need them. They also can serve as a mailing address and even provide a professional receptionist while you maintain your office at home.

While most federal employment laws regarding discrimination will not apply to your business until you have fifteen employees, you are still responsible for the safety of your workers. Therefore, be careful about hiring employees to work in your home office unless you can comply with OSHA and other federal and state laws covering workplaces. Some consultants use independent contractors or allow their employees to work at home as well.

START YOUR OFFICE ON THE RIGHT FOOT

Whether you decide to lease space or start your consulting practice from a home office, don't cut corners. The Start-Up Checklist (Exhibit 3.6) in the preceding chapter will help you with planning all that needs to be completed. The Start-Up Cost Worksheet (Exhibit 4.4) will help you determine how much money you will need to start your practice.

💾 Exhibit 4.4. Start-Up Cost Worksheet.

	Estimated Cost
Professional Advice	
Attorney	$_____
Accountant	$_____
Furniture	
Desk and chair	$_____
Filing cabinet	$_____
Book cases	$_____
Table	$_____
_____	$_____
Equipment	
Computer	$_____
Computer software	$_____
Printer	$_____
Copier	$_____
Typewriter	$_____
Fax machine	$_____
Adding machine	$_____
Calculator	$_____
Telephone system	$_____
Answering machine	$_____
Postage scale	$_____
Postage meter	$_____
_____	$_____

📁 Exhibit 4.4. Start-Up Cost Worksheet, Cont'd.

	Estimated Cost
Office Supplies	
Stationery	$_____
Paper:	
Fax	$_____
Printer	$_____
Special	$_____
Three-hole punch	$_____
Pens, pencils	$_____
Tape, glue, other adhesives	$_____
Scissors, rulers, misc.	$_____
Seminar Supplies	
Pocket folders	$_____
Three-ring binders	$_____
_____	$_____
Marketing Supplies	
Business cards	$_____
Brochures	$_____
Pocket folders	$_____
_____	$_____

Source: Biech, F. *The Business of Consulting.* San Francisco: Jossey-Bass/Pfeiffer, 1999, p. 61.

Notice that the first item on the list is professional advice. Be certain to plan for whatever advice you will need to start out right.

Contracts and the Law

SCENARIO

Thad left his internal consulting job to open his own practice a year ago. At that time he signed a three-year contract with his local print shop to type and duplicate all of his materials. He has recently spoken with a number of colleagues who use various desktop publishers and work out of their homes. The cost of goods is less than half what Thad is paying. He is wondering how he can get out of his contract and prevent this situation from happening again.

Commentary

Thad is facing what many know as buyer's remorse. He has negotiated an agreement that he now believes is not as good as what everyone else has. It should be noted that Thad's agreement with the print shop is an unusual one. Most print shops work per job unless there is a negotiated rate. Thad needs to review his contract as well as his reasons for wanting to change the arrangement.

Thad has to explore some options and, of course, run them past his attorney. Thad may be able to renegotiate with the print shop to print materials the desktop publisher creates. The desktop publisher may be able to send the materials electronically to the printer thus saving Thad the design and set-up fee.

Thad has to determine whether he will spend more billable time bringing the new desktop publisher up to speed and reviewing work product. It may cost less to turn his documents over to his already proven quality printer. Many people forget how much time supervising others or bringing people up to speed can actually take.

Thad also needs to consider if the print shop even cares about the change. Thad is probably a small client compared with others. Perhaps the print shop would be willing to cancel the agreement. Also, Thad may be able to refer the print shop to other organizations who need printing on a larger scale.

Thad has options that he needs to explore before worrying about breaching his agreement. To prevent his hands from being tied in the future, Thad should consider making shorter contracts or adding clauses that give him the benefit of competition. For example, if Thad can find competitors willing to perform the same services at less expense, the provider will match it or allow him to get out of the agreement.

CONTRACTS

Throughout this book you will encounter discussions regarding contracts. There has been a push both by business people and many attorneys to create plain language agreements. However, most contracts are still filled with Latin words and many do have certain clauses with a particular legal significance known as *terms of art*. For instance, a jurisdictional clause regarding where a legal dispute would be determined in court does not seem important when signing most agreements. However, if disputes will be decided by New York law and heard by New York judges and you reside in Los Angeles, the clause becomes significant. International contracts and relationships must be closely examined both for jurisdiction and laws that apply.

Contract Basics

A brief review of what constitutes a contract is helpful. Contracts can be oral or written. They can be simple or complex or somewhere in between. All contracts need contracting parties, the people who will be bound by the agreement. The parties need a description of the subject matter of the contract or what it is the parties are agreeing to do. For instance, a consultant may agree to provide consulting service for a client within a specific area of the company or a specific geographical location. The description of what each party has offered to do must be clear.

An *offer* is basically a promise to do something or to avoid doing something in the future. An example of avoiding some act in the future would be if your landlord promised not to put another consulting firm in the same office space as you. In order to form a contract, there must be an offer and there must be acceptance of that offer. Another offer back or a *counteroffer* does not mean the offer has been accepted. In fact, it is a rejection of the original offer. Also, an inquiry cannot form a contract.

A contract should spell out the terms and conditions of the agreement. It should describe what is required from both parties for the contracted work to be a success. It also provides what conditions are not acceptable to the parties and how to resolve disputes if they occur. Contracts should also have a *recital of consideration.*

What is consideration? Does that mean that the parties treat each other with respect? Not quite. Consideration in the legal sense means the value that will be exchanged. The client's consideration is the money to be paid the consultant. The consultant's consideration to the client is the service to be provided.

A contract should be signed. It should also spell out who is signing or for whom. For example, the signature block of an officer of a company should include the company name, the person's name, and how the person represents the company (i.e., Big Bucks, Inc., by Fran Smith, its President). The date the contract is effective should be listed as well as the date the agreement was signed by each party.

Ability of Parties to Form Contracts

There are also some legal requirements before parties can form a contract. All parties involved must have the capacity to form an agreement. Each must be old enough, generally at least eighteen, and have the mental ability to enter into an agreement. Also, for a contract to be upheld by a court, it needs to be shown that the parties understood they were entering an agreement, that the contract is for legal acts, and that the parties entered into the contract freely and not as a result of fraud, undue influence, or duress. It is not likely that your next advertising agreement will be made under duress because someone has held a gun to your head. However, consultants face allegations of fraud if their clients claim deception or fraudulent misrepresentation of consulting abilities.

Six months ago Mario met the VP of human resources for a large manufacturing company at a neighborhood party. The VP was impressed with Mario's knowledge of employee benefits. Mario bragged about his expertise in employee benefits. In reality, his only benefits experience is that he received health insurance from his former employer and he has read through that policy in great detail. Since he was sure the VP wouldn't check on certification, Mario also mentioned that he held the high-level human resource designation Senior Professional in Human Resource (SPHR) and that he was Employee Benefits Certified.

To Mario's surprise, the VP called him the following Monday and asked him to assist with a special project. Mario said yes, figuring he could get some good advice from his brother-in-law who runs an insurance company. It's the least his brother-in-law can do. Besides, Mario intends to refer the client to his brother-in-law for a small finder's fee for himself.

Three months after Mario's consulting project, the client is complaining. Employees are reporting that conditions formerly covered under the old health insurance policy are no longer covered under the new and more expensive policy recommended by Mario. Also, transferred 401(K) accounts are now showing fees for the transfer that weren't supposed to occur. The manufacturing company is seeking a refund of all monies paid to Mario. The company also wants a reimbursement for the cost of the transfer and is demanding to be returned to its former health policy. The company has threatened to bring a lawsuit against Mario for misrepresenting his experience and for fraud. The company is also looking into charges with the state insurance commission.

Commentary

Here Mario had a definite plan to deceive his client. He not only held himself out as an expert but invented credentials to go along with the scam. He isn't an SPHR and has no type of benefits certification. The company probably does have a good claim for fraud and misrepresentation. The fact that Mario received a kickback from the insurance company run by his brother-in-law also shows that the advice will certainly not be regarded as unbiased or to have the best interest of the client in mind. Mario has problems on many fronts.

Avoiding Claims for Fraud

Consultants may hold themselves out as having qualifications they don't possess by padding their education or puffing up their credentials or experience. Don't be tempted to do this. Your mom was right. Honesty is the best policy. If you don't have experience in an area, admit it. Either refer the work, bring in another consultant, or let the client know what is necessary for you to get up to speed. Don't fake it or you may be looking at a claim of misrepresentation or fraud.

Statute of Frauds

Fraud in making a contract was just discussed. There is another legal concept that has the word *fraud* in it, the Statute of Frauds. Usually, a contract can be oral or written. However, certain types of contracts must be written to be upheld by courts. A quick review of these types of contracts will help you know when you *must* have it in writing.

Under the legal concept of the Statute of Frauds, contracts for the sale of land, sales of goods over a certain amount of money, contracts that cannot be performed within a year's time, and promises to pay for the debt of another must be written. Also, written agreements are needed for promises by a personal representative to use personal funds to pay the debts of one who has died, or agreements made in consideration of marriage. There are also some specific requirements under the uniform commercial code when you are in the business of selling goods.

Get It in Writing

People most often have problems with agreements or contracts when they are not written because everyone remembers the agreement differently. Sometimes parties' versions change over time. Even if people use written agreements, they may use forms that don't suit the situation or that include language they do not understand.

SERVICE PROVIDERS

When you consider all the areas in which you must make decisions, nothing can be as time-consuming or as important as determining your service providers. If your phone system does not work correctly or your office equipment does not perform as promised, you risk losing business as well as looking unprofessional. The list of service providers alone is daunting. You will probably need to form a relationship with providers for most of the services listed in Exhibit 5.1.

Exhibit 5.1. Services and Goods Most Consultants Need.

- Advertising
- Telephone service
- Long distance carrier service
- Copier maintenance
- Printer maintenance
- Courier
- Security
- Office space and equipment
- Office equipment repair
- Furniture

- Electrical service
- Computer maintenance or repair
- Yellow Pages advertising
- Postage meter
- Cleaning
- Landscaping
- Building maintenance
- Internet access
- Utilities
- Credit cards

Negotiating with Service Providers

As clients push to receive more services for less cost, you should reexamine the costs associated with vendors and service providers. Surprise changes by vendors or noncompetitive service rates will prevent you from staying competitive. One way consultants can hold their vendors to their agreements is through more formalized purchase order processes. This type of process forces vendors to be more careful in calculating services and the final bill. You should also shop around or accept bids, especially for large-ticket items such as computers or office equipment. Unfortunately, you are at the mercy of some of your service providers. You may be forced to accept what is offered, on the terms it is offered. For instance, if the temperature reaches 104° and you do not have air conditioning, you will be willing to pay what it takes to get the problem fixed as soon as possible. If the power goes out in your building, you are forced to deal with the power company's schedule for repair. See Exhibit 5.2 for additional questions to consider when negotiating with service providers.

▨ Exhibit 5.2. Questions to Ask When Negotiating with Service Providers.

- Will your vendors agree to submit purchase orders?
- Have you shopped around or acquired bids for large-ticket items such as computers or office equipment?
- What services can you reclaim that you once outsourced? Should you?
- Have you delegated your administrative work to a lower-paid person?
- Have you brought in an expert for services you only need occasionally?
- What options are available for this particular service?
- Have you compared companies and services?
- Do you know the competitors' prices and services?
- What do you actually need?
- Have you asked for all discounts, concessions, and add-ons?
- Are there materials suitable for your needs that the provider wants to unload at a reduced cost?
- When do the services start? Stop?
- Is your approval required or does the service renew automatically?
- Do you have the ability to approve assignments to other service providers?
- What happens if the service is unsatisfactory or delayed?
- Is training offered by the service company?
- Is there a help line for understanding a product or service?
- What happens if you or the service provider go out of business or sell the business?
- What is the cancellation policy?
- Will you need upgrades?
- Should you own or lease pieces of equipment?
- Are payment plans available?

Know Your Options

To negotiate effectively, you must understand all the options available. Always compare companies and services. Be armed with knowledge about competitors' prices and services as well as your actual needs.

For example, the quality of your printed material is important to your appearance as a consultant. Do your homework. Different paper grades and finishes cost different amounts. A two-color process may be as much as 25 percent less than four-color work. Your printer may have leftover materials for folders or brochures. There may be a way to lay out your materials at the same time and print all of your pieces—brochures, note cards, and business cards—together, saving you additional set-up fees.

You may need to negotiate with service providers regarding the dates a service will begin or stop. You may want to limit automatic renewal provisions or the continuation of your service without your approval. You will probably want to approve any assignments to another service provider. Discuss the servicing of a product and provisions if a service is unsatisfactory or delayed.

It is helpful if a service provider offers training or a help line to understand its product or service. Why have something if you don't know how to use it? Negotiate a provision to cover what happens to the deal if you or the service provider go out of business or either of you decides to sell the business. Learn about the policies regarding cancellation and for the provision of upgrades, if any. You may want to explore the benefits of ownership of hardware or equipment compared to the benefits of leasing. Also, be sure to discuss your options for payment plans.

Ongoing Service Relationships

Just as consultants have ongoing relationships with clients, you may have ongoing relationships requiring a lot of interaction with certain service providers. You may deal daily with a courier service. You may have a cleaning service or be in constant contact with a receptionist service. After these ongoing relationships are established, altering the terms or changing services can be difficult. Therefore, it is imperative to understand the relationship before it begins and to have means for correcting problems when they arise. Exhibit 5.3 is a service agreement with a computer consulting firm. Notice the provisions regarding increasing fees and that services cost more during certain times of the day.

CopyCenter Equipment Maintenance Service Contract

Copier _____   Customer _____

Serial # _____   Location _____

Starting Date _____   _____

Initial Meter _____   Sales Rep. _____

In consideration of the promises and agreements herein, CopyCenter "Dealer" hereby agrees with the above Customer to maintain the listed copier upon the following terms and conditions.

1. Dealer will supply all labor and materials; including all replacement parts at no additional charge (except as stated in point "4" below) required to maintain copier in its present condition throughout the agreed term. All maintenance work will be performed during regular business hours.

2. For the purposes of such maintenance, Dealer agrees to inspect copier as frequently as may be reasonably requested by the Customer and, in any case, at least once during each Preventive Maintenance period or after _____ number of letter-size copies.

3. As part of this agreement, and at no additional charge, Dealer will provide the following copier expendables: photodrums, upper and lower rollers, cleaning rollers, cleaning blades, calls, and all parts required through normal use. In addition, at no extra charge, Dealer will perform emergency service calls during regular business hours.

4. Following the monthly reading of the copy meter for letter-size copies, the Customer shall pay the Dealer in accordance with the following schedule:

_____

Exhibit 5.3. Sample Service Contract, Cont'd.

5. Supplies used in said copier shall be purchased from or approved by CopyCenter.

6. Either party reserves the right to cancel this agreement upon 30-day notice.

7. Dealer is not responsible for damage through acts of God.

8. A power protection device is provided at No Charge as long as Customer maintains a CopyCenter Maintenance Service Contract. CopyCenter Maintenance Contract does NOT cover damage due to power surges unless approved protection above is in use. Should Customer elect NOT to purchase protection above or acquire a CopyCenter Maintenance Contract, Customer must initial following box to indicate above protection was recommended and waived. [   ].

9. Any special terms or conditions shall be stated here:

_____

Customer Acceptance:

By:_____

Title:_____

Date:_____

Another ongoing relationship occurs when you lease pieces of equipment. It is important to know what happens when the copier breaks down or you exceed the copies you agreed to in your contract. The time needed to repair a broken LCD projector is as important as the cost of repairing it, if you use the projector weekly for presentations. The equipment lease shown in Exhibit 5.4 is a sample of those you may encounter. It should not be used as a legal document without additional legal advice.

Exhibit 5.4. Sample Equipment Lease.

COMPUTERS HELP SERVICES, INC.

Helping you achieve your business goals with computers that work.

6231 121st Street #254

New York, NY 10012

February 10, 2000

Ms. Creative Consultant

Consulting Plus

143 Inventive Ave

Madison, WI 12543

RE: SERVICE CONTRACT

Dear Ms. Consultant:

Please read this letter carefully. It describes the terms and conditions under which we provide technical services to the client on a service contract basis. Our policy requires that each client sign a copy of this letter agreeing to the terms and conditions described below before we can engage in representation.

PER CALL SERVICE. Computers Help agrees to provide technical services to you on a service contract basis. You agree that you will be charged and obligated to pay for services for each service call in accordance with the fee schedule and payment terms stated in this agreement. You understand that this service contract is based on availability of service personnel.

REQUESTING SERVICE. You agree to request service by contacting Computers Help by telephone or fax and will provide the following information: your name, your contact, and your phone number, and a complete description of the problems and/or the types of services required.

Exhibit 5.4. Sample Equipment Lease, Cont'd.

FEE SCHEDULE. All support will be billed at Peak and Off-Peak rates. The Peak rate hours are Monday through Friday, excluding national holidays, between the hours of 8 A.M. and 6 P.M. Off-Peak rate hours are weekends, national holidays, and Monday through Friday after 6 P.M. and before 8 A.M. **Please see the attached fee schedule for our current rates and our agreed Reduced Rate for the next six months.**

It is our policy to bill clients periodically for fees and out-of-pocket expenses. Each support assistant records the time required to perform services, and these time records are the basis for the bills. These bills will generally describe services performed and the expenses incurred. For large expenses, we may request the supplier to bill you direct.

Because of the detailed nature of our statements, our clients usually do not have any questions about them. However, if any questions should arise, please call us promptly so we can discuss the matter.

Computers Help will be entitled to receive compensation from you for all equipment provided and for all services rendered, pursuant to the provisions of this agreement, up to the time of termination.

PAYMENT TERMS. You will receive a discount of 5 percent for any amounts paid within fifteen (15) days of the service. You will be obligated to pay the full amount when payment is made within thirty (30) days of the service. Any balances outstanding after thirty (30) days of the service will be subject to a monthly service charge of 1.5 percent. This service charge will be added to the balance due.

By your execution of this engagement letter, you agree that we are relieved from the responsibility of performing any further work should you fail to pay any statement for fees and expenses (including bills for expenses received from third parties).

Exhibit 5.4. Sample Equipment Lease, Cont'd.

LIMITATION OF LIABILITY. You agree that any damages incurred as a result of actions, omissions, representations, or reliances associated to Computers Help shall be limited to the amount of payment received by Computers Help from you during the preceding 12 months.

In addition, you shall save, hold, and keep harmless and indemnify Computers Help from and for any and all payments, expenses, costs, attorneys' fees, and from and for any and all claims and liability for losses or damages of any nature occasioned wholly or in part or resulting from any acts or omissions by you or your agents, employees, guests, licensees, invitees, sub-tenants, assignees, or successors, for any cause or reason whatsoever arising out of or by reason of the occurrence of your performance of services as contemplated herein.

TERM OF THE AGREEMENT. You and Computers Help agree that this agreement shall be effective for a period of 12 months and shall terminate unless otherwise agreed to in writing. Either party has the right to terminate this agreement upon 30 days of written notice to the other party.

NO WAIVER. You agree that if your performance or nonperformance under this Agreement provides Computers Help with a reason to terminate this Agreement, and Computers Help decides to continue the relationship, such decision of continuation shall not constitute a waiver by Computers Help of the same nonperformance or default by you if the action continues or is repeated.

MISCELLANEOUS. This Agreement represents the entire understanding between you and Computers Help with respect to the matters contained in this Agreement and it may be amended only by an instrument in writing signed by both you and an authorized representative of Computers Help. If any provision of this Agreement is held or declared by a court of competent

Exhibit 5.4. Sample Equipment Lease, Cont'd.

jurisdiction to be void, invalid, or illegal for any reason, such provision shall be deemed to be altered to the extent necessary to conform it with applicable law, and such actions shall not in any way invalidate or affect any other provision of this Agreement. You and Computers Help agree that: (i) this Agreement and all matters pertaining thereto shall be governed by and construed in accordance with the laws of the State of New York; (ii) this Agreement has been entered into in New York, New York, and it shall be deemed for venue and all other purposes to be performable in New York.

Please sign a copy of this letter in the space below, indicating your agreement to the terms and conditions set forth above. After we receive your signed copy of this letter and the required deposit of $1,500.00, we will commence our service of your organization.

Sincerely yours,

COMPUTERS HELP SERVICES, INC.

I have read this letter and agree to the terms stated therein.

COMPANY: _____

By: _____   **Date:** _____

Printed name: _____

Its: _____
[position]

Reclaiming Outsourced Tasks

Some consultants want to limit the service providers with whom they have a contractual relationship. They do not want to spend time negotiating or reviewing others' work product. While consultants now have the option of using technology for many tasks that were outsourced in the past, thinking through the legal issues before entering into an agreement can eliminate many concerns. In addition, before you decide to acquire new technology or take on another administrative task, decide if it's the best use of your time. Be careful that your time isn't spent learning complex computer programs or doing work that you could give to a lower-paid person or an expert already up to speed.

Negotiating with Professional Service Providers

Think through what you need from a relationship with a service provider before you enter into an agreement. If you are clear on your expectations up front, you can avoid disputes as well as concentrate your energies and time on higher-level tasks where you earn a higher rate.

Attorneys. Negotiations with attorneys are discussed in detail in Chapter One. The most important area of negotiation regarding legal services is to understand what is covered and what is not. Also, find out what steps you can do yourself.

Accountants. You can save money in several ways by negotiating with your accountant. See if you can keep your books yourself on a computerized program and then submit the information at the end of each tax period. Determine the easiest way for information to be maintained. For instance, sorted receipts and well-kept mileage logs may decrease the cost of an accountant's services. Identify the slower times of the tax year. Maybe you could deliver your materials to the accounting firm in off-peak times for a slight reduction in costs. The last-minute client may be charged a premium.

Banks. It's true that many banks no longer have personal relationships with their clients. Instead, some banking relationships are built with computers. If possible, find a banking institution where human contact remains important. This relationship helps when obtaining a line of credit, transferring funds, or resolving a disputed bank charge. Independent or community banks offer the best opportunity for satisfactory relationships with start-up and small businesses. You need a banker, not just a bank.

What happens when your clients have not paid, but all the office expenses are due? An operating line of credit from a bank may be the answer. Operating lines of credit are much easier to get before you need the money. You might structure a loan so you are able to draw on a line of credit as needed to supplement cash flow and then pay it back as soon as cash is available.

Legal Remedies Against Service Providers

SCENARIO

When Lorraine opened her career management consulting firm she decided to work out of her home. Rather than get a business telephone line, she simply got a second personal line. Her telephone has been out of order for a day or more every month for the past three months. She has called and complained but all the telephone company tells her is that it is a problem at "central" with overloaded lines due to new construction. Each time they say their only obligation is to have the telephone repaired within twenty-four hours. Lorraine's telephone is her link to her clients. Today, in a fit of anger, Lorraine told them how important this service was to her survival. The telephone company's response was, "If you are operating a business out of your home, you must change your service to a business line." Business lines cost much more in Lorraine's city.

Commentary

Lorraine is facing a problem many face. Instead of paying for the service she needed, she tried to make do with a less expensive option. Unfortunately, Lorraine now does not have as much negotiation power as she might have had with a business line. She also risks having her phone line canceled or being assigned a different number and paying more money. Sometimes those bargains end up costing more than what one bargains. As in any business relationship, there are legal options when service providers do not perform as agreed. Your remedies may range from an apology, a partial refund, or even damages for the business lost due to failure to perform. If you are disappointed with one instance of service but respect the company, use it to your advantage in negotiation. Ask for more services at the same price to make up for your inconvenience or its error.

If you are interested in pursuing your legal options against a service provider, make sure that your agreement is spelled out. Also, document what service was agreed on and exactly how that service failed in delivery, including the costs you incurred to correct the problem and/or the amount of lost business resulting from that failure.

Employment Issues

chapter SIX

SCENARIO

Jenkins and Schmidt have been providing advice to the MacDougal Corporation for several years. MacDougal is an engineering firm that designs and manufactures hydraulic systems for the aerospace industry. Several months ago a Jenkins and Schmidt consultant facilitated a meeting that involved a potential new supplier for MacDougal. The purpose of the meeting was to discuss ideas for resolving a recurring problem with a particular part produced by MacDougal. During the meeting the consultant stated that perhaps the small supplier should try its hand at making the part. The meeting ended on a pleasant note. Two months later the potential supplier returned to MacDougal with the part manufactured to specifications and the problem resolved. In the meantime, MacDougal solved the problem itself and doesn't need the supplier's services. The supplier is now suing MacDougal for reimbursement of investment and potential lost sales. In turn, MacDougal is suing Jenkins and Schmidt for breach of the consulting contract and acting outside the contracted responsibilities.

Commentary

This confusion regarding roles is a common problem for consultants and their clients, especially after they have worked together for several years. The Jenkins and Schmidt consultant led a facilitation and suggested a solution that might resolve the recurring problem with a part. However, it appears that the potential supplier did not understand that the consultant was independent from the company and did not have the authority to bind the company for future purchases. If it appears that the consultant has authority to act for MacDougal or serve as its agent, the supplier can say that it relied on the consultant's "apparent authority."

How will Jenkins and Schmidt defend itself? Well, if representatives from Mac-Dougal were also present at the facilitation, they should have spoken up and stated that they did not want the potential supplier to work on the part until they had a stab at it. Also, the supplier could have asked for a commitment from MacDougal to buy parts if the supplier fixed the problem. In this case, MacDougal and the consultants could argue that the potential supplier did not have a contract.

How do Jenkins and Schmidt and MacDougal prevent a consultant from having apparent authority to act for the company in the future? Both parties have an obligation up front to explain the consultant's role as an independent participant who is neither the agent nor the employee of MacDougal Corporation.

WORKING WITH OTHERS

One of the issues with having people work for you is that they can be considered your *agents*. Unless people outside your organization are informed differently, your agents are considered to have the same power as you, the owner, possess. Your bank doesn't know that you really don't want that large withdrawal from your bank account and the manufacturer doesn't know that you haven't authorized the order of expensive computer equipment if you have permitted or authorized employees to perform similar acts in the past.

As long as you have honest employees who do not act outside the scope of their job, their agency status does not create a problem. However, watch those trusted employees with access to key information or financial matters. For example, have safeguards to monitor the bookkeeper who has access to your checkbook or accounts. Make sure you have written policies regarding what staff members can say to clients, who can order equipment, and who can contract on behalf of your business.

To limit your employees' authority, the agency relationship should be clear. Spell out what, if any, authority employees have in making commitments on your behalf. Explain that employees should not make any representations that they possess any greater authority. Your first step, however, should be to decide whether you actually have an employee or if you have an independent contractor.

Employee or Independent Contractor?

What's the big deal about employees and independent contractors? Having employees creates additional expenses, including taxes you pay to the government. Many employers try to avoid employment taxes and unemployment insurance by designating true employees as independent contractors. With the increased cost of office space, the popularity of home offices, and more flexible work schedules, the lines of employer/employee relationships are blurring. Many businesses find it hard to compete and play by the rules when others in the same industry are reclassifying true employees as independent contractors. Firms that misclassify make it difficult for firms that follow the rules to stay competitive financially.

The government pays special attention to independent contractor relationships. Over the years many organizations have tried to avoid employment taxes and benefits by characterizing their workers as contractors instead of employees. Governmental entities want to be paid their money and will make a determination based on a worker's real function and not what terms the parties use to refer to each other. Failure to properly classify workers as employees will result in IRS penalties, state commission audits, attention from the Department of Labor, and even lawsuits from your employees. So how do you determine the correct status for your workers? The IRS has twenty factors to determine if an individual is an employee or an independent contractor.

To prove that you are legitimately using independent contractors you must have as many factors as possible point to independent control of a contractor's business.

- Does the employer control when, where, and how the work is done?

  If so, the relationship will probably be viewed as that of employer/employee. Independent contractors are more likely to set their own timetables, provide their own place to work, and determine what method will be used to complete the work.

- Is the individual provided with training on how to do the job?

  Independent contractors are usually already trained. If you're providing training, your worker may be viewed as an employee. However, some companies provide specialized training in company policies or training techniques to ensure compatibility with the organization's culture or to enhance a consultant's already acquired skill. This training may not be viewed as an employee trait.

- Are the services performed integrated into the business's operations?

  This question looks at whether the services are a regular part of business operations such as those an employee might provide, or a separate service provided by a contractor. For instance, a window washer would not be considered an integral part of the services offered by a manufacturing company.

- Must the services be rendered personally?

  If the services can be performed by an independent contractor's employees or agents instead of personally like an employment relationship, the contract relationship is supported.

- Does the business hire, supervise, or pay assistants to help the contractor?

  Contractors usually prefer their own people to support them and usually don't rely on business to offer the additional support they offer employees.

- Is it a continuing relationship?

  This question looks at the nature of the relationship. Is this a one-time project for a contractor or a continuing relationship with an employee?

- Who sets hours of work?

  The answer to this question determines if you have a contractor who can control the hours he or she works on the project. An independent contractor might work until midnight two days straight to complete the project but an employee may have hours set by the employer, for instance working only between the hours of 8 A.M. and 6 P.M.

- Does the individual work full-time solely for the business?

  Independent contractors may have many projects and clients at a time. An employee usually has just one master.

- Does the individual perform work on the business premises?

  Employees usually perform work in the same areas or have a home base. Independent contractors work in different locations, have different clients, and may even perform work in different premises of the same business.

- Who directs the order or sequence of the work done?

  Once again, the response determines if the employer or the contractor controls the assignment.

- Are regular oral or written reports required?

  In consulting, reports will be required to show project results. In employment, reports are required to show use of time.

- Is the worker paid weekly, hourly, on commission, or by the job?

  Workers paid weekly or hourly wages appear to be on an employer's payroll and are likely to be considered employees. Workers paid by the job appear to be more independent and are thus more likely to be considered independent contractors. Further, a contractor isn't paid unless the job is completed.

- Are business or travel expenses reimbursed?

  Employees are usually reimbursed for travel. With independent contractors, any reimbursement must be negotiated as part of the contract.

- Who furnishes tools and materials necessary for the job?

  Employers usually supply tools and materials for their employees. Contractors have those items as tools of their trade.

- Does the individual have a significant investment in facilities used to perform the services?

  Contractors may own or lease their place of business. Employees don't usually have that expense, unless working from home.

- Does the individual realize a profit or loss?

  Typically, employees don't lose money if a project does not go as planned.

- Can the individual work for a number of firms at one time?

  If so, the individual may be considered an independent contractor.

- Are the individual's services available to the general public?

   This question seeks information similar to that of the preceding question. Independent contractors are able to offer their services outside of the particular company or companies with whom they are currently working. Employees provide services to their employer or to those whom their employer designates.

- Can the individual be subject to dismissal for reasons other than nonperformance of agreed-on tasks?

   Employees are subject to rules and company policies, which means factors other than performance could make an employee subject to dismissal. Contractors are subject to the terms of their contract.

- Can the individual terminate the relationship without incurring liability for failure to complete a job?

   Employees can quit employment. Contractors that quit a project may be responsible for damages, finding a replacement, and other duties under their contracts.

The Internal Revenue Service can provide you with additional information distinguishing independent contractors and employees. Some of the key characteristics are compared in Exhibit 6.1. See which characteristics more clearly fit your situation.

SCENARIO

Kristin downsized her small consulting practice two years ago so that she could ease into retirement. Mike had worked for her for three years prior to that. As a result of the downsizing, Kristin asked Mike to continue to work as an independent contractor. She would guarantee him enough work to cover his salary and benefits for two years. In exchange he would work from his home office and would not report to work every day. He could pick up additional consulting jobs as long as they did not interfere with Kristin's client work. She and Mike put their agreement in writing.

After two years of this independent contractor arrangement with Mike, Kristin terminated the relationship at the start of her retirement. Today, she received a notice that Mike was requesting unemployment benefits. Mike listed

Exhibit 6.1. Characteristics of Employees vs. Contractors.

Employee	Independent Contractor
Employer controls place of work.	Contractor controls place of work.
Employer sets hours of work.	Contractor sets hours of work.
Employer pays by the hour or through salary.	Contractor may charge by the job, although more and more contractors charge by the hour.
Employer furnishes tools and materials for job.	Contractor has all tools of trade.
Employer owns place of business.	Contractor owns or leases place of business.
Employee is paid regardless of job completion.	Contractor doesn't get paid if job isn't done.
Employer is the only recipient of services.	Contractor offers services to public.
Employer controls how work is done.	Contractor controls methods of work.
Employee is subject to company policies and rules.	Contractor is subject to terms of contract.
Employer provides all training to do the job.	Contractor is trained expert.
Employee works full time for company.	Contractor has many jobs; time for different companies.
Employee can quit employer relationship without incurring liability.	Contractor that quits is responsible for damages, finding replacement, other contract duties.

Kristin as his last employer and stated the reason for his termination from employment as loss of business. In addition, the notice mentions that Kristin owes past unemployment taxes and penalties and that she may owe the federal government past employment taxes.

Commentary

Kristin finds herself in a common situation. Increasingly, companies forced to downsize have entered into continuing contractual relationships with former employees. At the outset, it appears that Kristin covered her bases through her written agreement. However, Kristin's defense lies in proving that she treated Mike as an independent service provider rather than as an employee she could control.

So what happens to Kristin? The downside for Kristin is that she may need to pay federal and state employment taxes as well as penalties spanning two years. In addition, Kristin could be held accountable for the unemployment payments Mike is seeking.

From the scenario, it appears that Mike was outside Kristin's immediate control. The more distinctions Kristin can show between the time Mike worked as her employee and the time Mike did contracting work for her the better. Kristin can show she paid Mike by the job or only on the work completed, not a salary. However, Kristin's guarantee to ensure Mike's income level for two years might be interpreted as payment of a salary. In her defense, Kristin should show that the duties Mike performed required specialized skill and that she did not supervise Mike during this time. For example, Mike happens to be ISO-certified and worked with the client at its work site without Kristin's presence. Proof that Mike set his own hours, furnished his own materials, and had other clients during this time will also support her position.

How to Avoid This Confusion

A written contractor agreement that clearly spells out your relationship and states that the independent contractor is not an employee of your company will help insulate you. Be very careful to define projects and roles when contracting with your former employee or when you have employment relationships as well as independent contractors. Treat the independent contractor as a separate entity, just as you would a service provider such as a printer or computer expert. Payment needs to be per job and upon your approval of the work product. This means that rather than establishing a salary or an hourly rate, you should determine the scope of the work and the outcomes and then determine a fee for the completed project or portions of the project.

On the other side, how do you keep your client company from being seen as your employer? Look over the twenty IRS factors and make sure that the separation between control over your work and work environment is obvious. Also, make sure you have a clear agreement showing your status as a consultant. Remember that government agencies disfavor independent contractor status and will find in favor of an employee relationship if at all possible.

HIRING ISSUES

If you do decide to hire employees, there are a number of hiring issues that you should be aware of. The first contact you will have with an employee is during the application and interview stage. The costs of incorrect hiring procedures are large. When you do not have good hiring policies, poor employment risks are hired and your risk for lawsuits increases.

It is a good policy to have applicants complete your specific application form in addition to providing you with their résumé. Many people have résumés prepared by professional résumé writers. If the job requires at least basic reading and writing abilities, you can eliminate many candidates just by reviewing the completed applications. It also gives you the opportunity to obtain their signature that everything provided on the résumé is true and correct. Later, if you find an employee has lied to you regarding a degree or certificate or experience, the application can be used as evidence of what you were told. A word of caution about applications—make sure your attorney reviews yours before you use it. The laws have changed regarding what constitutes an appropriate question. Years ago you could ask about marital status, workers' compensation injuries, and other issues that are no longer permitted. Also, be careful before using a form you buy from an office supply store, generate on your computer, or copy from another business. Many of these forms do not reflect the changes in the federal law or the laws of your state.

The interview process is used to see if the applicant has the skills, talent, education, experience, and drive to fill the position your firm has open. Always be honest about the job. Do not make false promises or create unrealistic expectations with the applicant.

Your goal is to make an applicant feel as comfortable as possible. Good interviewers only speak about 30 percent of the time and allow the applicant to speak the majority of the time. *You* already know about the job and your firm. Wait until you make sure that the applicant's education, experience, and responses to your interview questions are a fit for the position before you spend time discussing all the benefits of working in your company.

Ask an applicant open-ended questions. Question gaps in employment history. If an answer on the application is that a person left the last job for personal reasons, ask what those personal reasons were. Check if licenses and certifications are valid. Make sure you avoid answering for the applicant. Do not ask a question and then answer it for the applicant. For example, "At our firm we need hard workers. Are you a hard worker?" What else is an applicant going to answer but "yes"?

SCENARIO

Bob, the administrative officer of a medium-sized consulting company, interviewed candidates for the receptionist position. Last month he interviewed Cleo, who he thought had a great track record and a pleasant personality. He thought he would offer her the position, but later interviewed Franklin, a terrific candidate with years of receptionist experience. Bob called Cleo to tell her that Franklin was a better fit at this time and that her résumé would remain on file. Today he received a letter from the state Equal Employment Office stating that he was being investigated for possible gender discrimination against Cleo. He thought back to the interview and remembered that he had the utmost respect and genuine concern for Cleo. He knew that his intentions were good. Out of respect he asked her if she wanted to be addressed as Ms. or Mrs. or Miss. He was concerned about how she would find child care on the far side of the city. And he was concerned about how she might juggle a hectic schedule, long work days, and caring for three children. She was a steady runner-up for the job, but this letter has him puzzled.

Commentary

Be aware that you run the risk of a lawsuit if the questions you ask in an interview are inappropriate. Unless your interview questions relate to the objective criteria of the job, avoid them. Questions that relate to children and marital status have nothing to do with how someone performs a job. Ask applicants if they think they can meet the job requirements. Review your applications carefully for inquiries regarding age, race, religion, absences from a job, or prior illnesses or injuries. Delete references to all of these items in your application and during your inverview.

Exhibit 6.2 provides a list of appropriate interview questions. Although this is a start, you should seek legal advice to address your specific requirements before interviewing others.

💾 Exhibit 6.2. Acceptable Interview Questions.

These questions are considered acceptable or safe questions to use during an interview. They are also open-ended questions that require more than a yes or no answer.

- Sometimes we have to work overtime. How do you feel about that?

- All employees are required to undergo a drug screening as a condition of employment. Do you have any objections?

- We need people interested in their career goals. Can you tell me what yours are?

- Do you know of any reason you could not perform the job as I have described it to you?

- What did you like the most about your last job?

- What did you like least?

- What would you have changed about your job if you could?

- What characteristics do you dislike among coworkers?

- What was your most difficult problem? How did you solve it?

- What sort of people would you prefer not to work for?

After the Interview

After you complete an interview, list your objective impressions. Compare the person's résumé to their application and the responses they gave you. Many times the application will not match either the verbal responses that someone gives you or a résumé.

Check an applicant's references. Ask an applicant's former supervisor if he or she would hire the applicant back again. Ask about the applicant's strengths and weaknesses. Make sure you document any phone calls and any responses even if the applicant's past employers will not discuss the applicant with you.

SCENARIO

Brian was hired by the consulting arm of one of the big accounting firms. When he applied for the position, Tracey, Brian's future supervisor, thought he was a dream come true. On the day of his interview, two of Tracey's team members called in ill. She had a major project that needed to be facilitated that afternoon. Following his interview, she shared her dilemma with Brian, who volunteered to help her out. She filled him in about the project on the drive to the client's location. Once they began working with the client, Brian did a terrific job, fielding questions as if he'd been on the project from the start, cajoling the doubters in the group into believing in the design, and resolving the conflict between the two factions in the group. Tracey hired Brian on the spot. Now, six months later, she cannot believe the turn of events. It seems that Brian lost his temper in a team meeting with a team member who was harassing him about his motives for the implementation plan. Brian yelled, pounded his fist on the table, and kicked a chair over. The client has sent Tracey a letter demanding payment for the broken chair and return of its money. When Tracey called several of Brian's former employers, she found reluctance to talk about Brian's performance. When she continued to probe, one former supervisor admitted that Brian had a history of violence and that the supervisor had learned that Brian was discharged from the Navy for repeated fighting.

Commentary

This is one time when a quick fix ended up creating more problems in the end. Brian has a history of violence that former employers were willing to discuss.

This means that there will be witnesses to his bad temper if the case reaches trial. However, Tracey didn't bother to do even a brief reference check after she saw Brian's good initial results. When a violent person is hired and that violence could have been determined, employers like Tracey can be sued for negligent hiring.

Even though Tracey really liked Brian as an applicant, she still needed to follow her hiring practices. She should have paid Brian as an independent consultant for the major project and then told him she would contact him after completing her other interviews and her own hiring process. Skipping steps when dealing with employees is where many potential lawsuits arise.

Avoiding Problem Employees

On occasion, people bring lawsuits against companies for hiring dangerous employees. If an employee has a history of violence in previous jobs and hurts a customer or another employee, you can defend yourself against a lawsuit if you have documented your attempts to research the applicant. Employers are promoting laws that would protect open disclosure of an employee's past performance. Currently, it is difficult to obtain employment information other than dates of employment and position held. However, some managers and human resources personnel will give you additional information if you promise not to reveal the source in order to prevent you from hiring someone they know will cause you problems in the future.

A note: if someone calls you requesting information regarding *your* former employee, give neutral references *only* as company policy, e.g., dates worked, position held. Protect yourself. Sometimes private investigators pose as potential employers and ask about former employees to get evidence of slander.

The Polygraph Protection Act prohibits you from using a lie detector test on applicants unless your firm is involved in security, safeguarding money, or working with controlled substances. Therefore, you must listen for stories that do not ring true.

There are other methods to find out information about applicants. Some organizations use formal background checks. This approach is fine if you make sure that the company running the checks for you is credible and in compliance with the law.

Alternative Staffing

Some organizations use placement companies or a temporary or staffing company to place people. Temporary arrangements allow you to spend some time with that individual before you form an employer/employee relationship.

Alternative staffing services are becoming very popular. They will pay for the employees' taxes and employment benefits and handle screening and any disciplinary problems for you. You usually pay a premium for these services. Because you are a coemployer with the staffing service, you are still responsible for day-to-day supervision and must provide a safe workplace free of discrimination. The greatest benefit of using alternative staffing is that you eliminate most of your worries about the technicalities of employment rules and concentrate instead on being a consultant. If your temporary person does not work out, you just request a replacement.

Employee Agreements

Employers have employees sign a number of agreements as part of their employment. These agreements may spell out terms for tuition reimbursement, relocation expenses, nondisclosure of information, noncompetition, and details of the employee relationship. If you expect your employees to sign any type of agreement, it is much easier, both practically and in enforcement, if it is signed as a part of the initial paperwork before an employee starts. Later in the employment arrangement, employees may question your motives and the reason for the agreement. Also, an issue arises of whether you have to pay something extra to receive their signature.

Non-compete agreements that prohibit work after termination in similar fields or locations are difficult at best to enforce against employees. Some jurisdictions prohibit them entirely. Be sure to have an attorney who knows this type of agreement draft it narrowly with respect to the type of conduct, the location, and the time duration. Most consulting firms are more concerned with disclosure of client names or trade secrets than competition from a former employee. Nondisclosure agreements are more readily accepted by the courts.

If you are currently employed and want to begin a consulting practice, make sure consulting is allowed under your current employment agreement or company policies. Some professors have this ability. You may have a right to moonlight as long as your consulting does not interfere with your regular duties and you are not consulting with businesses similar to your employer. Also, some consultants leave a full-time consulting practice to return to the corporate environment. If you plan on drawing a salary and continuing your consulting on the side, make sure your new employer is aware of this arrangement.

SCENARIO

Geoff, the owner of a small but growing consulting firm, has been working with the manufacturing VP of a large paint manufacturer for almost two years. The paint manufacturer is Geoff's bread-and-butter client, consistently providing enough work to pay all the overhead for his thirteen employees and six independent contractors. The VP drops in on Geoff regularly. While there, he enjoys flirting with Geoff's staff—especially the receptionist, Dorie. He brings her candy, asks her out, gives her back rubs, and teases her mercilessly. Dorie told Geoff how uncomfortable she was with the VP's behavior. Not wanting to upset the client, Geoff responded that it was harmless. He explained that the VP was married, had always been a flirt, and didn't mean anything. Geoff asked Dorie to put up with it and told her he would remember her efforts at bonus time next year. Dorie finally left Geoff's company, citing personal reasons. Almost a year later Geoff received a letter from Dorie's attorney requesting damages for the sexual harassment and hostile work environment experienced by Dorie.

Commentary

If the letter was sent more than three hundred days after the employee quit and the employee has not filed a complaint with the Equal Employment Opportunity Commission (EEOC), then the employee has lost the right to bring a sexual harassment claim under the federal law, Title VII of the Civil Rights Act of 1964—usually referred to simply as Title VII.

Most defense attorneys would take some comfort in the size of Geoff's business, thirteen employees. The federal law protecting against sexual harassment, Title VII, does not apply to employers with fewer than fifteen employees. However, some of the consultant's six independent contractors may actually be considered employees. As discussed earlier, businesses don't always properly classify independent contractors.

States have their own employment laws and their own courts have interpreted those laws. If a state chooses, it can decide to offer more protection for employees than what is offered under federal law.

If an employee has been subjected to unwelcome touching or comments, a lawyer can find a way to sue the employer. The law decided through the years by the courts—the *common law*—allows people to sue under claims of personal assault and battery as well as intentional infliction of mental anguish.

If this scenario also falls under the federal or state employment laws, the consultant may have to defend against quite a few problems in addition to the personal assault, battery, and mental anguish charges. Not only has the employee experienced a hostile work environment but her employer has told her that her cooperation will be remembered at bonus time. This "go along to get along" comment shows that Geoff, the consultant, did not take steps to investigate or remedy the situation as required by law. The Supreme Court has ruled that employers have a duty to have policies to prevent discrimination and a duty to train employees in those policies, as well as a duty to investigate and remedy a situation if one occurs.

It is clear that employers like Geoff have to pay attention and correct situations where harassment occur, as well as have good training and policies in place. This situation is a traditional *quid pro quo* sexual harassment claim. In Latin, "quid pro quo" means "this for that." Asking the receptionist to tolerate the sexual harassment in exchange for a positive effect on her job is a violation of Title VII. Demoting the receptionist or not giving her the raise because she refused the advances would also be a violation of Title VII. Even more important, the employee was subjected to a hostile workplace and Geoff did nothing about it.

If Geoff does not have the requisite fifteen employees to fall under federal law, he still faces some exposure. Forcing an employee to tolerate unwelcome advances could be considered intentional infliction of mental distress. Also, judges and juries are not going to like Geoff's cavalier attitude or approach to Dorie's complaints.

HOW TO AVOID HARASSMENT

As an employer, one has a duty to immediately investigate and take action where necessary to correct instances of sexual harassment. This duty exists even if the harassment comes from someone outside your immediate control. The consultant should have pulled the client aside and said, "We have a strict policy against sexual harassment at our company. Please don't flirt or make sexual advances toward any of our people." Here comes the big question—if the client doesn't stop the advances, do you drop the client? If you cannot ensure that the receptionist can be insulated from client advances, you drop the client. Clients that don't respect others and don't follow your requests may be the same clients who don't pay their bills or who ignore your advice within their own organizations.

COMPLAINTS AND INVESTIGATIONS

What are your duties as an employer? You must let people know what behavior is not allowed and where to go if they have a complaint. It's best to have a complaint process and also to allow employees to bring complaints to neutral, uninvolved management, someone other than the immediate supervisor. In fact, it is good to have people of different genders available. For example, a female employee may feel more comfortable bringing sexual harassment charges to another female. An organization must ensure that there will be no retaliation against employees who lodge good-faith complaints. The investigation must be *immediate* and *treated seriously* by an impartial party. The investigation must also stick to the incident in question or related behavior—just the facts!

To ensure procedural fairness, obtain all versions of the story including witness interviews. Ask open-ended questions and don't suggest the response. Document all your steps and make sure all employee discipline is tailored to the offense. This also helps to avoid a potential suit by the disciplined employee.

Ensure confidentiality to the extent possible, but make no blanket promises. Keep the investigation results on a need-to-know basis with management and involved parties. Determination must be based on objective findings and both parties must be informed of their rights to internal appeal, if any. Employers who don't follow the rules to correct a situation within their own organization are not popular with the EEOC.

SCENARIO

Hawkins and Hawkins contracted with Joe, a sales consultant, to develop the training for launching a new product. The consultant was known for keeping his audiences laughing. Unfortunately no one checked on what was so funny. A number of jokes were directed at female buyers and others at the female sales employees who were in the audience. Female attendees were heard to say, "This just confirms the company hates women." Later, the training programs were used as evidence of gender discrimination when an EEOC charge and a lawsuit were filed against the company.

Commentary

Here Hawkins and Hawkins have placed Joe the consultant in a training position, a role in which he clearly appears to speak for the company. This apparent authority, coupled with the lack of follow-through on the comments made by female attendees, works as evidence against Hawkins and Hawkins.

SCENARIO

It was black and white. The data proved it. The consultant's study addressed the pockets of greatest inefficiency—those areas where overhead and payroll were highest. As a result, a list of employees who would be terminated was created. Unfortunately, no one checked the list for patterns or potential problems. After pink slips were distributed, someone added another layer of data. It turned out that 90 percent of the employees terminated were over fifty and had been with the company more than fifteen years. The former employees are now suing the company for age discrimination.

Commentary

Once again, acting without reflecting on the overall results of those actions has placed another consulting client on the lawsuit firing range. Unfortunately, the consultant's information was not complete. While most human resources departments would catch the potential for age discrimination claims, many companies still do not have trained individuals in that role. The fact that a personnel or human resources department may be underdeveloped does not mean that all consultants have to acquire a master's degree in human resources. It does require a consultant who works with a company in human resource issues such as interviewing, performance review, disciplinary action, termination, and other areas concerning employment to make sure that the company reviews his or her suggestions with their employment attorney and human resources department before implementing recommendations.

HELPING YOUR CLIENTS AVOID LIABILITY

As discussed in both scenarios, the company was held liable for the actions of an outside vendor. Clients can be held liable for the actions of their consultants. These scenarios show liability with gender and age discrimination. However, the liability with other employment issues such as discrimination on the basis of race, religion, national origin, and disabilities is just as prevalent.

The secret to helping your client avoid employment problems caused by your consulting is quite simple. Be sensitive to possible areas of discrimination. If you have a question, run it past your attorney, the client's human resources department, or the legal counsel for your client. Ask for a copy of the client's employee handbook and make sure you have all the current employment policies.

YOUR EMPLOYEE POLICIES AND HANDBOOK

Even if you have only one employee, the best way to avoid misunderstandings is to have written policies and to communicate them. Make sure policies are written in clear language. Distribute policies and have a signed statement in each employee's file that the policies were received and that the employee had an opportunity to ask questions. At the beginning of any policy or handbook you should have an Equal Employment Opportunity statement. EEO policies prohibit discrimination against employees or applicants on the basis of age, race, color, religion, sex, national origin, and/or disability. EEO policies also outline the ramifications of violating the policy. You probably want a *disclaimer*—a statement that your company policies can change and that policies in place prior to the distribution of this handbook are no longer in effect. Make sure to write down and distribute any changes to your company policies. There are so many employment laws that this is one area not to take shortcuts! Have your attorney review your policies before you implement them.

As an employer, you need to make decisions regarding work hours, breaks, vacation time, rules, discipline, safety, dress code, and other issues. To help you consider some of the employment issues you must decide, answer the questions provided in Exhibit 6.3.

Some issues may be determined for you by outside requirements. If you have workers' compensation or receive federal grants, you may be required to have a drug-free workplace policy. Under a drug-free workplace policy, you must state that drugs are not permitted and have a reporting requirement if an employee is convicted of a drug-related crime. However, there is no mandatory drug testing.

Some clients may require you to have workers' compensation or an employee health plan to cover any employees on the client's premises in order to qualify for the job. Workers' compensation is explored more thoroughly in Chapter Thirteen.

Exhibit 6.3. Employment Policy Issues.

Decisions to consider with respect to your employment policies:

- How many employees do you need?

- What is each employee's job description?

- When are your work hours?

- How long are lunch breaks?

- Do you have coffee breaks?

- What is your policy on vacation?

- How much time do you allow for sick leave?

- What constitutes a violation of your company's rules?

- What is your policy on harassment?

- Where would an employee go with a complaint?

- Are employees allowed to look in their personnel file?
  (Note: In some states, this decision is left to the employer.)

- Will you give your employees health benefits?

- How will you train your employees and distribute your policies?

- How will you make sure policies and procedures are followed?

- How safe is your workplace?

- Do you comply with OSHA standards?

- Do you prohibit guns and other weapons at your workplace?

- How will you check an applicant's references and qualifications?

- How will you determine an applicant's potential for violence?

- How will you discipline employees?

- What actions can get an employee fired?

- How will you investigate potential problems?

Exhibit 6.3. Employment Policy Issues, Cont'd.

- Will you have a written consent to search your employees' desks or lockers?

- Where do employees park?

- What is the dress code?

- What is your policy regarding dealing with clients?

- What constitutes a reasonable business expense?

- Are there safety rules?

- When is the company open?

- Whom do employees contact in emergencies?

At-Will Employment

If your employee is not under a contract for employment, he or she may be employed *at-will*. If your state has at-will employment, it means that either the employee or employer can terminate the employment relationship for any reason without any prior notice to the other. The at-will status is great for employers. It is important that you do not change the ability to fire at will by forming a contract with your employees. For instance, your employee handbook might include the phrase "Nothing in this handbook or policy constitutes a contract or changes an employee's at-will status."

Communicate Your Policies

One of the most common employee complaints is that the rules were not communicated. The communication of policies does not end at an employee's orientation. Continue to communicate policies throughout the employment relationship. Begin with the first offense and don't let one instance go by without commenting or addressing it. Do not hide performance issues in evaluations. If an employee is not meeting expectations in an area, let the employee know what is expected and what needs to change.

Not only should all policies be discussed, certain laws must be posted in a place employees frequent, such as the break room. Usually these posters are available for a nominal charge from each government agency or can be ordered from private vendors that compile the necessary state and federal material into one large poster. The required posters can notify employees about minimum wage, overtime compensation, unemployment benefits, protection against polygraphs, drug-free workplaces, and the availability of workers' compensation.

Disciplinary Procedures

At the very least, develop simple employee policies that show employees what you expect of them and outline disciplinary procedures such as an oral warning, written warning, probation period, and termination. Stay calm, stick to objective facts, and remain in control of the situation during all conversations.

Counseling and disciplinary actions must be reflected *in writing* and *signed* by the employee. Document, document, document. Not only are records important as evidence for trial, keeping good records is extremely important if an employee later files any type of complaint against you with a government agency. If you don't write it down, it usually didn't happen as far as the government is concerned.

All meetings and disciplinary counseling should provide the employee an opportunity to ask questions. If possible, have employees state their positions or responses in writing. These responses are very effective evidence if the employees change their explanations at a later date.

Usually, people want an opportunity to respond to accusations. Instead of having that response become a heated exchange, provide a written appeal form that allows employees to request review of any action you take. This is an opportunity for you to consider the employee's response, as well as your actions. You may have acted hastily or made a decision without adequate information.

Avoiding Litigation

The most frequently occurring legal issues during employment can be avoided by following basic guidelines. Here are some of the "rules" of managing employees:

- *Be perceived as fair.* Even if the actions you take are completely legal, the *perception* of fairness is more important.

- *Follow the policies in place.* Don't reinvent the wheel each time a situation comes up. Refer to the language in the policy or handbook when you are counseling an employee.

- *Do not make quick decisions; speed gains you nothing.* Sleep on your decision, ask other owners how they handle such a situation, and contact your employment adviser, be it your attorney or human resources personnel.

- *Communicate and apply the rules equally.* Don't deviate or show favoritism if you have more than one employee. If other people supervise your employees, make sure they are trained in your rules and policies.

- *Discuss confidential matters on a need-to-know basis only and keep an employee's confidential information private.* Share information with other employees or outsiders only on a need-to-know basis with disciplinary matters. This is a good guideline with personal information of any kind, including medical conditions and/or drug testing. Separate employee files for medical information should be kept confidential under lock and key or password if computerized.

- *Investigate all claims of wrongdoing.* Document findings and actions taken. Quick and effective investigation and remedial action is required under many employment laws.

- *Read all notices and requests for information from government agencies.* Learn about the government agencies: the EEOC, OSHA, Department of Labor, Unemployment Commission for your state, etc. Pay special attention to deadlines. Different agencies have different response times. Most are short.

- *Have a way to resolve conflicts internally.* Provide a mechanism for employees to resolve their problems in the workplace. The alternative is to allow an employee to find someone to listen to their concerns outside your organization. That person is usually a government representative or an attorney.

- *Respect your employees' personal space and do not use intimidation as a management technique.* Employees can bring civil action for violating common rules of decency under the legal cause of action known as *torts*. Torts are generally property or personal claims and can result from touching your employee improperly (assault and battery) or forcing an employee to stay in a locked office (false imprisonment). Torts also cover actions where an employee's good name is ruined (defamation or slander), something private is made public (invasion of privacy), or you have mentally injured the employee by causing mental anguish or inflicting emotional distress.

- *Document, document, document.* Keep a detailed employee file documenting each employee's evaluations and incidents. Use objective observations, not subjective conclusions. Also, make notes to the file when an employee refuses to sign a reprimand or disciplinary action.

Specific Employment Laws

Ask your accountant what employment taxes you must pay. Not paying taxes is one of the big dangers you face. Many employment laws do not affect businesses with less than fifteen employees. Under normal business circumstances, if your consulting firm has less than fifteen employees, you probably will spend less time worrying about employment laws. However, as a consultant, you work directly with other companies' employees and management. Many times your suggestions have a direct impact on a company's employees.

Some of the laws affecting employment are as follows:

- The Employee Polygraph Protection Act of 1988 prohibits the use of lie detectors unless private employers provide certain security services or are involved in the manufacturing, storing or distribution of drugs.

- The Drug Free Workplace Act of 1988 requires businesses with government grants and/or workers' compensation to have policies regarding drug-free workplaces.

- The Occupational Safety and Health Administration (OSHA) Act of 1970 requires employers to provide a safe workplace for employees.

- The Immigration Reform and Control Act of 1986, administered by the Immigration and Naturalization Service (INS), requires proof of citizenship or authorization to work and completion of a form known as the I-9 form. Before you interview an applicant, you will need to make sure that the applicant is a U.S. citizen or authorized to work in the United States.

- The Fair Labor Standards Act of 1938, or FLSA, provides for the minimum wage to be paid by all employers, regardless of the size of their organizations. The FLSA also provides for overtime, which is generally paid at time and a half for hours worked over forty hours a week by non-exempt employees. It also sets the rule that minors must be over fourteen or sixteen years of age to work depending on the place of employment and eighteen years of age to work in hazardous jobs.

- The Equal Pay Act of 1963 states that people should be paid equal wages for equal work regardless of gender.

- Title VII of the Civil Rights Act of 1964 prohibits employers with fifteen or more employees from discriminating in any aspect of employment on the basis of race, color, religion, sex, or national origin.

- The Age Discrimination in Employment Act of 1967 (ADEA), which was amended by The Older Workers Protection Act in 1990, protects employees who are forty or older. The ADEA prohibits employers who have twenty or more employees from discriminating on the basis of age in any employment decisions, including hiring, firing, promotion, compensation, and disciplinary action.

- The Americans with Disabilities Act (ADA) was enacted in 1990. The ADA protects qualified individuals with disabilities in all aspects of employment who work or apply with companies of fifteen employees or more. The ADA also requires that employers provide a reasonable accommodation to those people with disabilities unless that accommodation imposes an unreasonable hardship. The ADA caused quite a stir among businesses concerned that they would be forced to pay for expensive remodeling or equipment. While some changes required constructing accessible bathrooms and ramps, many of the required changes were not costly. Those readjustments consisted of things like restructuring job duties, rearranging furniture, raising or lowering desks, installing cup dispensers, and providing instructions in writing or orally. It appears that many more ADA cases than expected are being found in favor of the employer.

- The Family Medical Leave Act of 1993 (FMLA) offers unpaid job-protected leave to employees whose company employs fifty employees or more within a seventy-five-mile radius of each other. The employee must have been employed at least twelve months and worked at least 1,250 hours (about 60 percent of a normal work year). The employee may take up to twelve weeks of unpaid leave if the employee or a family member is seriously ill or for the birth or adoption of a child.

- The Pregnancy Discrimination Act (PDA) of 1978 adds to the pregnancy coverage in the FMLA. The PDA applies to employers with fifteen or more employees and requires that pregnant women be provided (at the very least) the same type and amount of leave as that given to employees for other temporary medical disabilities. Just as in Title VII, there are protections against treating a female employee differently just because she is pregnant unless she requests reasonable accommodation due to her condition. For instance, it would not be unreasonable for a pregnant employee to ask that she not have to climb stairs if her doctor has told her not to do so.

- Both the Vietnam Era Veterans' Readjustment Assistance Act of 1974 and the Rehabilitation Act of 1973 require separate affirmative action plans for Vietnam veterans and disabled veterans as well as handicapped individuals when the company has federal contracts of $50,000 or more.

- The National Labor Relations Act of 1935 (NLRA) gives employees the right to form, join, and assist labor organizations ("unions") and to bargain collectively with their employer. Employees also have the right not to join the union unless the union has contracted otherwise with a company.

In addition to these federal laws, there are a number of other laws protecting workers, ranging from informing of continuation of benefits, and protection of credit history and bankruptcy, to protections for jury duty and layoff notices. Also, each state's Workers' Compensation Act requires you to notify employees if workers' compensation is available. Each state also has unemployment laws regarding payment of wages upon termination. Usually unemployment benefits can be protested by the employer if the employee was fired for misconduct.

You may have heard of affirmative action. Affirmative action is often misunderstood and feared. An affirmative action plan provides a statistical analysis of your company and shows the "underutilization" of people in the protected groups we have discussed. For instance, if it were shown that people of a certain race or gender were not represented, the plan would indicate the reasons as well as possible corrective measures to take. A plan is supposed to provide for steps to be taken to improve the representation of these protected classes in the workforce. As a consultant, you might see these plans in place at your clients' businesses.

A list of policies and laws you should consider when you have employees can be found in Exhibit 6.4. Review them and prepare your responses before discussing them with your attorney.

⊞ Exhibit 6.4. Policies to Consider When You Have Employees.

All handbooks should have a clear equal-employment statement prohibiting discrimination against employees or applicants on the basis of age, race, color, religion, sex, national origin, and/or disability, and the ramifications of violating policy. There should be a *disclaimer* or statement that policies can change and that past policies are no longer in effect. If employment is "at-will," you must have a statement that clearly spells out that the handbook is not a contract, that explains employment-at-will, and that provides that terms of employment can only be changed to a contract if done in writing by the president or other appropriate officer.

Consider including policies in these areas in your handbook:

- Drugs, alcohol, and violence
- Termination (effect on benefits, pay, references, appeals and severance or wages in lieu of notice, if any)
- Appeal rights
- FMLA leave (if fifty or more employees)
- Absence and tardiness
- Vacation
- Military leave and jury duty
- Grievance and complaint procedure
- Internal investigation policy
- Discipline policy (providing for immediate termination if severe misconduct)
- Harassment of any kind (sexual, racial, age)
- Benefits (e.g., discounts, health insurance, workers' compensation, profit sharing plans, pension funds)

```
┌─────────────────────────────────────────────────────────────────┐
│            💾 Exhibit 6.4.  Policies to Consider                  │
│              When You Have Employees, Cont'd.                     │
│  ───────────────────────────────────────────────────────────     │
│                                                                   │
│  • Probation periods                                              │
│                                                                   │
│  • Definitions, policies, and benefits affecting exempt and non-exempt │
│    employees, as well as full-time, part-time, and seasonal workers │
│                                                                   │
│  • Holidays, personal days, and sick days                         │
│                                                                   │
│  • Compensation (e.g., paydays, overtime, deductions from paycheck, │
│    bonus, comp time, unused leave, and distribution of paycheck)  │
│                                                                   │
│  • Conflicts of interest with employee                            │
│                                                                   │
│  • Trade secrets and confidentiality                              │
│                                                                   │
│  • Employee assistance program, if any                            │
│                                                                   │
│  • Reporting illegal acts or exercising legal rights              │
│                                                                   │
│  • Basic company policy for all employees (e.g., parking, dress code, │
│    seniority, customer relations, business expenses, coworker solicitations, │
│    off-premises conduct, safety rules and emergencies, hours of operation, │
│    treatment of fellow employees, transfers, and promotions)      │
│                                                                   │
└─────────────────────────────────────────────────────────────────┘
```

SCENARIO

Ian caught Sandra, one of his consultants, in a compromising situation with a client. The company policy was very specific and he clearly had the right to fire her but didn't. Unfortunately, Ian never keeps his mouth shut. He told the story several times at parties, embellishing the details just a bit more each time. Ian now faces slander charges brought against him by Sandra.

Commentary

Libel, slander, and defamation of character are legal liability areas of which employers must be aware. Ian should have terminated Sandra and kept his mouth shut. Ian's desire to be the hit of the party has placed him in a precarious legal position. His embellished accounts created false information and may expose him to damages for slander.

Issues When Firing

Chances are you or someone you know has been terminated. Your own separation from employment may be why you are now consulting. Even if it is expected, separation of employment is a stressful event. Regardless of the reason, terminations should be performed in a manner that is respectful of the employee.

If termination is for performance reasons or misconduct, document those objective reasons. Properly performed exit interviews are helpful in documenting an employee's response. You should remain calm and state the documented reasons for termination.

Be prepared to give your terminated employee any transition information as well as a last check at the meeting. Transition information consists of information regarding what severance pay, if any, is available, the time for which health benefits will be extended, and any other business that needs to be resolved or explained to the terminated employee.

If you are terminating an employee because you have to downsize, you might tell your employee of any future chance for rehire or for contract or part-time work. If you will not be contesting the application for unemployment benefits, you can tell the employee so.

Some former employees are concerned about the reference you might give. Especially if you are terminating for misconduct or failure to perform up to standards, confirm that your firm's policy is to give only dates of employment and position held.

If necessary, provide the terminated employee an opportunity to express in writing any dissension or any appeals to you to reconsider your decision. Writing an appeal can be therapeutic as well as nonconfrontational. Some employers provide separation letters that spell out the transition information as well as discuss the written opportunity to appeal and/or respond.

After termination, have all calls regarding the employee forwarded to you. For safety, make sure to change all computer passwords as well as door locks after terminating someone. To help you remember these termination guidelines, a checklist has been prepared (Exhibit 6.5). Review it with your attorney and revise the checklist to agree with your own company policies.

⊞ Exhibit 6.5. Checklist for Terminating an Employee.

- Document objective reasons for termination.
- Perform exit interview in private.
- Be respectful.
- Remain calm.
- Document employee responses.
- State the documented reasons for termination.
- Explain severance pay, if any.
- Explain the time for which health benefits will be extended.
- Give any other transition information and last check.
- If downsizing, explain opportunities for rehire or contract and part-time work.
- If you are not contesting unemployment benefits, tell the employee.
- Explain your reference policy.
- Listen to the employee's side but remain in control of the situation.
- If necessary, provide the terminated employee an opportunity to write an appeal or response.
- After termination, have all calls regarding the employee forwarded to you.
- Change all computer passwords.
- Change door locks and pass codes.

Wrongful Termination

Cases for wrongful termination or firing in retaliation are growing areas of the law. Be very careful about terminating an employee who

- Contacted a state or local agency regarding rule violations by your company
- Made complaints to management about other employees' violating company rules or any law or regulation
- Alleged wrongdoing of any kind by an immediate supervisor
- Refused to commit an illegal act

Provide the opportunity for your employees to communicate, voice their concerns, or report things that they believe are illegal or unethical. Do not take any negative action or retaliate against employees who make a good-faith use of your reporting policy.

chapter SEVEN

Working with Other Consultants

SCENARIO

Lola and Cora own Conference Design, a meeting planning service. They specialize in computer and engineering conferences and are hired by companies and associations to coordinate the transportation, hotels, meals, speakers, suppliers, meeting space, sightseeing, and decorations. Lola started the business seven years ago out of a spare bedroom in her home. When the business grew too large for her to handle alone, she formalized the company name and invited Cora to join her. They only have an agreement regarding profit division. Conference Design has become so successful that additional office space and staff are required to meet clients' needs. One of the new hires is Lola's husband, Hank, a retired military officer. Hank is not the best communicator. In fact, on several occasions, he has offended clients, requiring Lola and Cora to make amends. Hank believes that he is "the man behind the scene" and that Lola's success is primarily due to his advice over the years. Hank's ineptness and ego are driving Cora crazy! Cora has been unable to speak frankly with Lola about the situation. Cora feels the best thing to do is for her to leave. She has bounced this idea off a few of the clients, all of whom have asked her to take them with her when she leaves. When Lola got wind of Cora's plans, she threatened to sue Cora for tortious interference with business relations.

Commentary

So many times, growth brings unanticipated reactions. The combination of personalities and talents that makes one consulting group unique may also result in its dissolution when new personalities are added. Before working with other consultants, it's always a good idea to determine what to do if the dynamic is changed by adding additional personalities. What course of action should you take if you determine that it does not make sense to work together?

Cora and Lola are in deep trouble. Here, personalities clash—in essence, Lola would be asked to choose between her friend and business partner, Cora, and her own husband, Hank. When family members are part of the problem, it is almost impossible to fix the situation. Cora and Lola should try to get some neutral person, a mediator or a mutually respected colleague, to help them reach a resolution that is tolerable to both. Speaking frankly in this method may cost Cora her friendship with Lola, but it will clear the air and may force Lola to make future decisions on the role Hank will play. As for the lawsuit for interference with existing business relations, Lola may have a claim. Cora would have been wiser to have left first and then let clients choose with whom to do business. A better way to handle this is for the preexisting business owner to write a letter informing clients of the change. If done properly, this serves as good public relations for the company losing the partner or employee. Since Cora is leaving, she might suggest that Lola write a letter to their clients informing them of the separation. For instance, the letter could state that Cora is embarking on a new business and that Lola and the company wish her well in her new endeavors. Lola could go on to state that Conference Design will continue to provide clients the high-quality service that they have come to expect. This type of letter accomplishes a couple of things. First, the separation looks like it was done civilly, which makes clients relax. Second, it informs clients that Conference Design will continue in business. As an added benefit, such a letter makes Lola look like a hero. Whether Cora will be able to convince Lola to send such a letter remains to be seen.

TYPES OF RELATIONSHIPS WITH OTHER CONSULTANTS

It's logical for you to consider how consultants might work together for more than one project. You may even wish to create a permanent business structure with other consultants as discussed in Chapter Three. However, what happens if you want to perform occasional joint ventures or need a hand on a large project? Maybe you need a consultant's special expertise on rare occasions. These situations pose different legal concerns. For instance:

- *Does the consultant you use to provide special services to one of your long-term clients have your permission to continue the relationship after your project has ended?* If so, you may risk losing your client to this consultant. You may want to negotiate a finder's fee on future business. Even if you do not have financial concerns regarding future contact, it is important to discuss it with the other consultant.

- *Can the consultant later perform services that you usually perform for the client?* Once again, you need to consider the possibility that you are finding a replacement for yourself and decide what limits need to be set before bringing someone new into the project.

- *Is there a time limit before the consultant can approach the client?* Define those time limits, if any, before your client can be approached by the other consultant.

- *Under whose name are the consulting services performed when you and another consultant are involved in a joint project?* If you are not in partnership with the other consultant, determine what liability risks you face if the consultant does not live up to the contract. Also, if you receive payment and then pay the consultant, do you have additional tax consequences?

- *Can the consultant with special expertise make agreements without your prior approval?* Decide what authority the consultant has regarding agreements for additional work and changes before you find yourself committed to projects you do not wish to do.

- *How do you ensure that the information you provide regarding your consulting techniques remains confidential?* Spell out what you expect from the other consultant regarding confidentiality of your own consulting techniques. Something unique to you and your practice may be easily copied or revealed to competitors if you do not communicate the need for confidentiality. You may want an agreement so that both of you are clear on what is considered secret.

• *How can a client ensure that the confidential information shared with the added consultant remains confidential?* Make sure that the consultant understands that client information is confidential. A written agreement serves not only as notification to the other consultant but also as a tool in your defense if information is leaked.

Exhibit 7.1 provides a list of various questions to explore regarding consulting relationships.

💾 Exhibit 7.1. Questions to Answer Regarding Consulting Relationships.

• Does the consultant have your permission to continue the relationship with your client after your project has ended?
• Can the consultant later perform services that you usually perform for the client?
• Is there a time limit before the consultant can approach the client?
• How will you keep the consultant from competing against you and using your own information?
• Under whose name are the consulting services performed when consultants are involved in a joint project?
• What are the consultant's ethics?
• How are you going to determine if the consultant is meeting your standards?
• Do you have a review period?
• Can the consultant with special expertise make agreements without your prior approval?
• How do you ensure that the information you provide regarding your consulting techniques remains confidential?
• How can a client ensure that the confidential information shared with the added consultant remains confidential?
• How are these rules discussed?
• What happens if you and the consultant have a disagreement?
• How do you dissolve a relationship that's not working?

HOW ARE THE RULES DETERMINED?

Adding more people to the consulting mix always adds additional worries to accompany the additional benefits. While some generally accepted professional guidelines exist regarding the relationship issues faced when working with other consultants, just as many differing opinions exist. It is strongly recommended you have a written understanding regarding your guidelines so nothing is left to interpretation.

There are many legal issues to explore. Even if you decide to do nothing about these issues, you should at least make an informed decision not to act. You should also explore the kind of relationship you wish to form. Exhibit 7.2 outlines some questions to ask before determining what shape a relationship might take.

Exhibit 7.2. Questions to Ask Yourself About Shared Consulting Arrangements.

- Do you want a continuous business relationship?
- Do you want to formalize the relationship by forming a business entity?
- Is this an occasional joint venture?
- Do you need a hand on a large project?
- Do you need a consultant's special expertise?
- What do you want out of this relationship?
- What do the other parties want out of this relationship?
- What potential problems could occur if you set up a formal relationship?
- Are there advantages to setting up a more formal relationship?
- Who benefits if a formalized relationship is created?

SCENARIO

Michele has had her own training practice for ten years. When she lands a contract that is too large for her to handle alone, she subcontracts with other trainers. Although she does not ask the subcontractors to sign a non-compete agreement, she verbally tells them that if the client offers them additional work while working on her contract, that work rightfully belongs to her. All offers must come to her first. Then, if she is unable to meet the client's needs, she may turn it back to the subcontractor for a finder's fee or make some other arrangement to share the additional work. Michele just found out that Frank is working for one of her clients, whom he met on a contract the two of them completed last month.

Commentary

Michele may lose this battle. By her own admission, she tells her subcontractors that if the client offers additional work while working on her contract, that work belongs to her. Michele now has the burden of showing that Frank was approached by her client *while* he was working under Michele. As the contract just concluded last month, Frank probably was contacted during that time. However, *proving* that he was is a different story.

Michele needs to make some tough business decisions. Does she have her former client get involved by telling her when the work started? If she does contact her client, will her questions about using Frank make people defensive because the client chose to use Frank? Will the client admit that Frank first suggested the work during Michele's contract? Will the client avoid both Frank and Michele in the future?

Does Michele hire an attorney to write Frank a demand letter asking for her lost percentage? Does she call Frank and ask him for her percentage on his new contract? Does she remind Frank of their agreement and ask to also work on the project? Does she just put a big black mark against Frank and avoid him for future consulting projects?

Michele's decisions should be based on the amount of money she is losing, the opportunity to be hired by the client at a later date, and the action that will result in a resolution as quickly as possible. Two years spent battling over a small amount of money when Michele does not have all the facts is not a good investment of time. Chapters Fifteen and Sixteen provide a more in-depth look at when and how to bring lawsuits. Perhaps Michele will work out a new arrangement with Frank whereby he provides the service and she receives a percentage of the fee.

What could Michele have done to avoid this situation? Avoiding potential legal situations comes from recognizing them first.

WORKING WITH SUBCONTRACTORS

It is generally believed that subcontracting consultants should not market their own consulting services to the client. Ethically, the client belongs to the primary or general consultant. The primary has invested in marketing and establishing a relationship with a particular client. A subcontractor gives up the right to represent his or her individual firm or even discuss it. That right is relinquished in exchange for the work.

Under this guideline, a subcontracting consultant should not discuss the relationship with you, contact the client directly for more work, or make agreements on your behalf for additional work. If a client approaches a subcontracting consultant, the offer should be reported immediately to the primary consultant. What ethically should happen and what actually does can be two different stories. Subcontracting consultants offer services directly to the clients every day. Proposals for services without the expense of the primary consultant's cut are attractive to clients. Clients may like the subcontractor's credentials or consulting style better than that of the primary.

Preventing a Subcontracting Consultant from Marketing to Your Client

Some consulting firms ask their subcontractors to sign agreements to protect the relationship developed with a client. For instance, some consultants have a no-solicitation agreement that a client is not "fair game" and should not be approached by the subcontractor until at least two years past the final contract date. These no-solicitation agreements spell out what a subcontractor should do if approached, as well as the penalty for accepting or inquiring about work outside the primary consultant's control.

Non-Compete Agreements. Non-compete agreements with strict terms are difficult to enforce because most states and courts want people to have the ability to work. As a general rule of thumb, if money might come out the government's pocket (e.g., unemployment benefits, fewer employment taxes, more jobless people on welfare, or time spent in court arguing about restraint of trade), it is a good bet that the government will be against that arrangement.

Here are some standard terms of non-compete agreements that a consulting company might require you to sign if you want to be one of its independent consultants:

- You agree that you are receiving special training or knowledge or something of value.

- You acknowledge that the information you will receive is confidential, is valuable, and is a legitimate business interest to be protected.

- You cannot contact a current client after your relationship ends with the company for a limited period of six months (or one year or two years). Note: Most courts won't allow time periods they consider too "restrictive," which means too long. Unfortunately, each court determines what is too long based on the facts of each case. Check with your attorney to make sure you have established a reasonable time limit for your state and industry before having anyone sign such an agreement.

- You cannot consult in certain geographical areas for a specified time period. This may be limited to using just the special consulting techniques you learned at the company. Again, check with your attorney to determine if you have defined a reasonable geographic area.

- You cannot help someone else contact clients or try to take away customers or employees of the company.

One of the best reasons to have a non-compete agreement is to clearly spell out what behavior is considered against the rules, or *unfair*, by the parties. Also people also use non-compete agreements in an attempt to keep information confidential.

Non-Disclosure Agreements. A better way to keep information confidential is through a non-disclosure agreement. Non-disclosure agreements identify what information is considered private, or a *trade secret*, and what property belongs to the company. Instead of limiting employees' ability to work like a non-compete agreement, the non-disclosure spells out what behavior constitutes stealing secrets. Courts support these agreements because they don't like theft. Non-disclosure agreements are discussed in Chapter Eleven.

Following the trend of many CPA firms, Young and Bryant has begun offering management consulting services to complement its tax practice. Scott was subcontracting with one of Young and Bryant's retail firms on a loss management program. While sharing business stories with another consultant, Scott unintentionally revealed confidential financial information about how much a client had lost due to employee theft and the cost of the retail client's new security system. Little did Scott know that the other consultant was working with a competitor of the retail client. This leak in information was passed on by Scott's consultant friend, hoping to look good in the eyes of his new client. The competitor used the information in an advertising campaign. Young and Bryant's client attributes a large loss of sales to the competitor's advertising campaign. The client points to the first decline in business in ten years, which began the day after the advertising began. The competitor's slogan was "How can you trust a store when the store can't trust its own employees?" Scott says he didn't know the financial information was confidential. Young and Bryant is being held responsible by the retail client and can't provide any documentation proving that they informed Scott that the client information is confidential and must be protected.

Commentary

This CPA firm is in a world of trouble. Not only is there a breach of the duty to keep information confidential, the client can show actual money that it lost because of this leak of information. The money lost is called the company's "actual damages." Ultimately, the CPA firm is liable because it had the contract, the relationship with the client, and found the subcontractor. Young and Bryant may be able to force Scott to pay some of the costs, but most subcontractors don't have large cash reserves. Probably the most important loss, however, is the public loss of respect and trust suffered by the retail store, Young and Bryant, and Scott.

Alternatives to Non-Compete Agreements. There are other ways to protect against subcontractors' marketing directly to your clients. Some firms provide a list of strict guidelines to which subcontractors agree before performing any work. Other firms stay in close contact with their clients regarding subcontractors' performance issues and directly arrange future work during those conversations.

Other primary consultants rely on a subcontractor's sense of ethics. However, if you rely only on another consultant's ethics, you should be warned. Everyone's values and ethical lines are drawn differently. Notifying subcontractors of the expected guidelines from the start is a better practice. Come to a clear understanding in the beginning about what you deem ethical, what behavior is permitted, and what is not allowed.

SCENARIO

Tony was never really successful as an independent consultant. He wasn't good with details, had difficulty staying organized, forgot to invoice clients for his work, and never did balance his checkbook. But he was a great talker! And clients loved him. He had lots of ideas—he just couldn't put the plans together to make them happen. Tony had his weaknesses, but he had strengths that were hard to find elsewhere. That's why his new arrangement as a subcontractor for Kathleen was such a great idea. However, Tony never quite accepted the idea that having a lady boss was appropriate for him, so he sometimes played a larger role than was appropriate as a subcontractor. One day in a client meeting he had a brilliant idea! It was so brilliant the entire group got excited and started sketching out plans on a flip chart. When cost was questioned, he stated that it was within the boundaries of the present contract limits. He wasn't going to let anything interfere with this idea. Now Tony is on his way back to the office. He knows this idea will exceed the parameters of the project and involve a great deal of extra time. Also, Tony is wondering how he is going to explain to Kathleen what he has done.

Commentary

One way for Kathleen to get out of this mess is to throw it back on Tony. He was the one who invented the problem, let him derive a solution for it. He is creative and a good talker. He may just need to own up to the truth and admit he didn't know that the budget would not hold this additional piece, but that the present contract could be amended for a nominal cost.

Perhaps the project can take on a new focus and the client can choose what to eliminate or reschedule into additional time at additional cost. Maybe Tony feels so strongly about the project that he wants to do it at no additional compensation.

Can the company hold Kathleen to additional work with no additional cost? Maybe. Kathleen should have informed the client that Tony is an independent contractor, not an employee, and that any project changes need to go through her. If Tony appears to be Kathleen's agent, however, Kathleen may be bound. Of course, she could place the additional time and cost on the subcontractor, Tony, but in the end it is her reputation that is on the line.

Limiting Authority for Subcontracting Consultants

The problems that can occur when dealing with agents are most apparent when working with consultants as subcontractors. First, a primary consultant wants to present a united front when performing work for clients. Many clients become uneasy when they believe a group of independents—a hodgepodge of consultants—are working on their delicate issues.

However, presenting the subcontractors as employees can also create the issues discussed in the preceding chapter. In addition, you cannot let your subcontractor appear to have authority or represent the ability to make decisions for you without actually ceding that authority.

Instead of implying that a subcontractor is a consultant or even a partner, a better approach is to state the truth. Tell your client that as the primary consultant you pull in experts in different areas when the work at hand requires them. Just as a doctor gains trust by referring to specialists as needed, your consulting abilities will be held in higher esteem if you bring in people as needed. However, be clear that you will remain involved in supervising and achieving the desired result. If the client has any concerns or wants to address any issues, the client should discuss the work with you.

It is also important that any subcontractors clearly understand their relationship to the client and the primary contractor. Subcontractors must understand they have no authority to act or make any commitment of any nature on behalf of the primary consultant. Also, subcontractors should not make any representations that they possess any greater authority than they actually have.

Making Agreements. Subcontracting consultants must understand the limits of what they can agree to on behalf of the primary consultant. Contractual issues, changes in the delivery, or questions regarding results should be turned over to the primary. Also, subcontractors should never discuss money with the client.

Using the Primary's Name. The primary's name, like other business assets, belongs to the primary. Without agreement, your subcontractors should not use your name in representing themselves to clients other than yours. If they have questions about using your name, they should come to you.

SCENARIO

Sally's consulting business had been in a slump for over a year. The primary industry she served was depressed, but she was certain it would come back soon. In the meantime she decided to subcontract her services to Tequin. Although she had always been jealous of Tequin and couldn't understand why their professional association seemed to provide more recognition to Tequin than to her, she thought she could set that aside during their working relationship. Sally has become friends with one of Tequin's clients and has told the client about numerous occasions when Tequin has taken advantage of Sally. Over dinner one evening Sally tells the client about a new instrument she has been using with her own clients. The client is interested and Sally suggests that her instrument could take the place of the data-gathering process Tequin has introduced to the client.

Commentary

If you don't respect a consultant, don't work for him or her. It appears Sally's ethics need a tune-up. She shouldn't be bad-mouthing Tequin in the first place. Somewhere she has forgotten Tequin is *paying* her. Sally shouldn't recommend using her process over one Tequin has used with the client. It appears Sally is trying to take Tequin's client away from her. Does this type of situation occur? Sure, all the time. No matter how many protections you establish, you will face this type of situation with others you thought you could trust.

Upholding the Primary Consultant's Standards and Decisions

As a primary consultant, you have a right to accept or reject the work of your subcontractors if it is not up to an agreed-upon standard. You have a right to expect a subcontractor to operate under the same set of ethics as you do. Clarify your expectations by giving a copy of your ethics statement to your subcontracting consultant. You also have a right to expect your subcontractors to be both positive and supportive of you and your decisions.

Subcontractors need to support in word and deed the delivery of services. The subcontractor's responsibility is to enhance the primary's performance. Discussions regarding alternative methods or different courses of action should take place out of the client's presence. You don't want to create a plan of action for your client only to have your subcontracting consultant later attempt to outguess you in front of your client. Once again, any proposed deviation from the plan of action in place should be directed to you, the primary consultant.

To maintain a good relationship, both the primary consultant and the subcontractor must agree to uphold certain guidelines. Exhibit 7.3 provides a list of these guidelines for the subcontractor.

💾 Exhibit 7.3. Guidelines for a Subcontractor.

- Represent yourself as a united team with the primary.
- Do not represent or discuss your own firm.
- Be positive and supportive of the primary.
- Enhance the primary's performance.
- Do not market yourself to the client.
- Report any offers made by the client to the primary.
- Do not represent yourself as the primary's agent.
- Do not speak for the primary.
- Refer contractual issues to the primary.
- Refer changes in delivery to the primary.
- Do not discuss money issues with the client.
- Return all materials, files, computer disks, and other information to the primary consultant at the end of the project.

RESPONSIBILITIES TO A SUBCONTRACTOR

Your expectations of the subcontracting consultant represent only one side of the story. Primary consultants have responsibilities to their subcontractors as well.

- *As the primary, you shall clearly identify all issues of pay, time, and performance expectations up front.* Make sure there is a clear arrangement of how profits will be divided and how expenses will be paid or shared. Also, identify any potential problems as soon as you are aware of them. Has the client been slow in paying? Do you predict the job may extend past the initial completion date? Does this job have a tight deadline? State doubts you may have about any aspect of the project, even if it has not been stated by the client, and is still just your gut feel.

• *Make sure that the subcontractor has a clear assignment of work and expectations.* A subcontractor needs to know what the assignment is as well as how to judge when the assignment meets the standards of both you and the client. Is this client notoriously picky? Do you have standards that might be difficult to meet? Be completely honest and candid about what you expect from the subcontractor in terms of performance and what support you will commit to make that performance happen.

• *Keep your subcontractor informed.* The primary must have open lines of communication with the subcontractor. Your door must always be open for questions, observations, and opinions. In some ways, subcontractors are similar to employees and clients. You have the same ethical responsibilities to keep them informed and involved in changes and concerns about the plan of action. A boss with an unapproachable personality, an inflated ego, or limited time availability may miss out on valuable information. As a primary consultant, you risk the same loss. You must make yourself available for feedback as well as forecasting.

• *Identify a method of dispute resolution for disagreements.* If at all possible, come to an agreement on how disagreements will be resolved before entering into a joint consulting relationship of any kind. Your worst scenario is to involve outsiders in a professional disagreement. Agree that you will abide by a neutral consultant's decision or that you will use a local mediation center if a dispute arises. Specify what will happen and how it will happen before any disagreements occur.

• *Provide a method to dissolve the relationship.* Just as in the discussion regarding business entities, have a method to dissolve a consulting relationship that is not working. Have a trial time period and review the services provided to that point.

Exhibit 7.4 identifies a list of guidelines to keep in mind when you are the primary consultant.

💾 Exhibit 7.4. Guidelines for a Primary Consultant.

- Clearly identify all issues of pay, time, and performance expectations up front.

- Be completely honest and candid about the project.

- Give clear assignments of work and expectations.

- State any doubts you may have about the project.

- Keep the subcontractor informed.

- Let a subcontractor know if a project will be extended or shortened.

- Have a dispute resolution process for disagreements.

- Provide a method to dissolve the relationship.

Client Issues

Matt, an architectural consultant, assists architectural firms in installing the latest and best computer equipment and software. Matt has been very cautious about including everything in contracts with his clients—until his last contract. He neglected to include a statement that allowed the contract to be revised if new technology is developed during the project. The statement would have allowed the client to choose between technology available at the contract's signing or a renegotiated price for new technology created after the date of signing the contract. Newer items became available after the contract was signed and the client forced Matt to provide the new items and comply with the contract. The cost of providing the latest and best new computer equipment was too much. Now Matt has filed Chapter 11 and is looking for a job.

Commentary

Matt, like all consultants, is human. A clause regarding new technology should have been used. Also, another clause regarding resolving disputes might have been helpful.

One statement that should be in all contracts is that the prices are quoted for the services or projects available as of the date stated in the contract. If additional work is required or changes to the materials are necessary, the cost will be agreed upon before adding anything new. If additional compensation can not be agreed upon, the consultant will be paid what has been earned to date and the contract will be terminated.

CONSULTANT'S AGREEMENT

You have a good relationship with your client. Do you actually need to put your consulting arrangement in writing? One answer states, "only if you want to be paid." In reality, however, consulting work is performed on a handshake every day. The solution to avoiding legal problems is not legalizing an agreement as much as making sure all parties understand the agreement. Putting an agreement in writing enables understanding.

Most clients will see written agreements as a positive step. A written agreement provides tangible evidence of the project that your clients can take to the people to whom they report. A written agreement that clearly defines the consultant's role and the client's expectations goes a long way to increasing communication. Also, the very act of clearly spelling out the arrangement forces you to think through what services you will provide and how you will provide those services. Do those contracts change as projects and relationships progress? Of course they do.

Whether you use letters of agreement or proposals or contracts, the secret is putting the agreement in writing. Many contractual terms are used interchangeably by consultants and clients. For purposes of knowing what agreement you have when you are looking at it, it helps to understand the different formats and when a contract is actually created. So, what's the difference between all these agreements?

Letters of Agreement

Typically, a letter of agreement is a letter sent by a consultant to the client. The letter confirms and documents the basic terms of the consulting arrangement. If the letter reflects the client's understanding of the agreement, the client signs and returns a copy of the letter to the consultant.

Proposals

A proposal may be prepared for a potential client in any number of ways. First, a client may have a formal process, a Request for Proposals (RFP), or an announced opportunity to receive bids. A bid advertisement or RFP may give specific standards and may require any response to be in a standard format. The more formal process is usually employed to enable a client to compare services, implementation processes, or proposed results offered by several consultants. Government consultants and consultants in very structured environments are familiar with this process. Usually, the bid will be accepted or rejected as drafted—the client will provide limited opportunities for a consultant to clarify. Usually counteroffers and revisions are not part of this process.

Proposals are also used as an initial plan offered by the consultant to perform a certain project. Proposals are usually submitted after researching an organization. They address the basic issues encountered, the means or method proposed to address those issues, the time and effort it will take to implement those methods, and the results a company should experience after the consulting process is complete.

In either case, the proposal is actually an offer by the consultant to the client. If the client accepts the consultant's proposal as written, the parties then have a contract. However, if the client makes changes to the proposal or asks for additional services, the client has made a counteroffer that the consultant can either accept (forming a contract), revise (creating another counteroffer), or reject.

Contracts

Some organizations have standard contracts prepared by attorneys that are used with all vendors and service providers. Contracts created in this manner cover all types of issues and come in as many forms as there are organizations. When working with these organizations, it is always a good idea to take what they have written to your attorney for interpretation. If you decide to revise the contract or to supplement it with your own language you can expect delays in starting the work. Most corporate legal departments prefer their contract form. A sample contract can be found in Exhibit 8.1. With all the different contracts in the consulting arena you can bet that this one looks nothing like the ones you will receive. However, it may address some similar issues.

💾 Exhibit 8.1. Sample Contract.

AGREEMENT

Agreement made and entered into this 3rd day of January, 2010, by and

between _____ (Client) of _____
(address)

(hereinafter "Client") and CONSULTANT of _____
(address)

(hereinafter "Consultant").

In consideration of the mutual covenants and promises contained herein, and for good and valuable consideration, the parties hereby agree as follows:

I. PROJECT RESPONSIBILITIES & OBLIGATIONS

Consultant will develop and implement a Member Services Staff Training and Intervention plan as further detailed in Exhibit A to this contract, which is hereby incorporated by reference. Implementation of said plan will be based upon input and guidelines provided by the Client. Implementation of said plan will include, but will not necessarily be limited to, the following components:

A. Gathering Information and Data;
B. Designing Three Training Courses;
C. Conducting Training Courses;
D. Designing Training Materials; and
E. Providing Consultation Services.

These are detailed further in Exhibit A herein. Delivery of services shall reasonably conform to the "Timeline" set forth in Exhibit B.

Exhibit 8.1. Sample Contract, Cont'd.

Responsibilities for each party shall be as follows.

Client:

1. Provide one contact person who is knowledgeable about the project and who understands the goals of this effort. This individual will assist with establishing meetings, scheduling interviews, copying and distributing information, and completing other coordination tasks.
2. Provide copies of the participant materials for the last four sessions of "Member Services Staff Training."
3. Provide training space and all audiovisual equipment for the training sessions. This includes an overhead projector and two flip charts for all sessions. A video camera, monitor, and tape deck will also be required for the two-day "Train-the-Trainer" session.

Consultant:

1. Complete all aspects required to implement the plan outlined above, including, but not limited to:

   • fulfill all planning and coordination

   • gather and compile all data and information

   • fulfill all interview preparation, coordination, and facilitation

   • design a one-day session "Member Services Staff Training"

   • design a two-day Train-the-Trainer session for six to ten individuals

   • design a one-day Coaching session for supervisors

   • develop the training materials for Member Services and Coaching sessions

   • develop a training guide and outline for the Train-the-Trainer session

   • provide participant materials for the pilot of the Member Services session, the Train-the-Trainer session, and the Coaching session

   • develop and provide audiovisual materials.

2. Provide materials ensuring the Client's self sufficiency following the implementation including, but not limited to:
   • a master of "Member Services Staff Training" participant materials
   • a master of "Member Services Staff Training" overhead transparencies
3. Provide arrangements for Client to use Consultant's copyright for all participant materials used in this project.
4. Invoice monthly for work completed plus travel expenses.

II. CONSIDERATION

In exchange for Consultant's services, as set forth in Par. I above, Client will pay Consultant monthly, total compensation not to exceed thirty-eight thousand two hundred dollars ($38,200). Consultant will be paid as services are rendered in any given month as set forth in Paragraph I excluding 5 percent ($1,910) which will be held until completion of the full engagement. Final payment will be made within thirty days of receipt of a bill itemizing charges incurred to complete all services.

III. TRAVEL EXPENSES

In addition to the consideration set forth in Par. II above, Client will pay to Consultant reasonable and necessary expenses as specifically set forth herein. Reimbursement of expense under this Paragraph shall include charges incurred for travel (airfare, mileage, car rental, and/or train fare), lodging, and meals for trips to the Client's site. All travel expenses shall be procured at the lowest cost available. Travel dates are outlined in Exhibit B. Reimbursement for travel expenses shall be paid within thirty days from invoice date by Client upon submission of receipts, evidencing out-of-pocket expenses incurred by Consultant.

IV. TERM

This agreement will take effect as of the date indicated in the introductory paragraph above and shall extend until Consultant's completion of all services set forth in Par. I unless earlier termination by the Client upon the giving of 30 days written notice. Upon any such notice of termination, services by Consultant shall be discontinued and compensation will cease to accrue.

V. CONFIDENTIAL INFORMATION

A. Upon being notified that a party to this Agreement considers information confidential, each party hereto agrees not to disclose the confidential information of the other party, directly or indirectly, under any circumstances or by any means, to any third person, without the express, written consent of such party, obtained in advance. Each party hereto agrees that it will not copy, transmit, reproduce, summarize, quote, or make any commercial or other use whatsoever of the other party's confidential information, except as provided herein. Each party agrees to exercise the highest degree of care in safeguarding the confidential information of the other party against loss, theft, or inadvertent disclosure, and agrees generally to take all steps necessary to ensure the maintenance of confidentiality.

B. Upon termination of this agreement, or as otherwise requested, each party agrees to deliver promptly to the other party all confidential information of that party, in whatever form, that may be in its possession or under its control.

VI. NO TRANSFER

This Agreement shall not be assigned or transferred by either party without the express written consent of the other party, obtained in advance.

VII. TAXES

Both parties shall promptly pay all applicable taxes of every kind, nature, and description arising out of the establishment, nature, and operation of its business in connection with the event described in this Agreement.

VIII. CONTRACTOR RELATIONSHIP

The parties to this agreement agree that Consultant is an independent contractor. Nothing contained in this agreement should be construed to create either a partnership between the parties or an employment relationship with Client. No employment benefits shall be paid by either party to or for the other.

IX. NOTICES

All notices to be given and communications in connection with this Agreement shall be in writing, and addressed to the parties at the following addresses:

CONSULTANT   **CLIENT**

_____   _____

CONSULTANT   CLIENT
(name)   (name)
(address)   (address)
(address)   (address)

X. MISCELLANEOUS

The parties intend to create and be bound by a valid agreement. If any provision of this Agreement is held or declared by a court of competent jurisdiction to be void, invalid, or illegal for any reason, such provision shall be deemed to be altered to the extent necessary to conform it with applicable law, and such actions shall not in any way invalidate or affect any other provision of this Agreement.

💾 Exhibit 8.1. Sample Contract, Cont'd.

Consultant and Client agree that: (I) this Agreement and all matters pertaining thereto shall be governed by and construed according to the laws of the State of _____; (II) this Agreement has been
(consultant's state)

entered into in _____ County, _____, and it
(consultant's state)

shall be deemed for venue and all other purposes to be performable in

_____.
(consultant's state)

XI. ALTERNATIVE DISPUTE RESOLUTION

To avoid the expense and time of litigation, Consultant and Client will attempt to resolve all disputes outside of the court house. If the parties cannot reach a resolution of the matter through their own efforts, they agree to then employ more formal dispute resolution methods. Any disputes connected with this agreement, services, or duties will be brought to mediation within thirty (30) days of the date either party requests mediation in writing. If a mediator cannot be agreed upon, the parties elect to have one provided for them by the American Arbitration Association (A.A.A.) or by Judicial Arbitration and Mediation Services (J.A.M.S. Endispute). If mediation is not successful in resolving the dispute, both parties agree that the matter shall be taken to binding arbitration by a single arbitrator mutually agreed upon by the parties or by an arbitrator selected through A.A.A. or J.A.M.S. Arbitration shall occur within 60 days of the mediation.

XII. EFFECT OF PARTIAL INVALIDITY

The invalidity of any portion of this Agreement will not and shall not be deemed to affect the validity of any other provision. In the event that any provision of this Agreement is held to be invalid, the parties agree that the remaining provisions shall be deemed to be in full force and effect as if they had been executed by both parties subsequent to the expungement of the invalid provision.

XIII. MODIFICATION OF AGREEMENT

Any modification of this Agreement or additional obligations assumed by either party in connection with this Agreement shall be binding only if placed in writing and signed by each party or an authorized representative of each party.

BY THE PARTIES:

_____   _____

Name, Title   Name, Title
CLIENT COMPANY NAME   CONSULTANT COMPANY NAME

_____   _____

Date   Date

Source: Adapted from Biech, E. *The Business of Consulting.* San Francisco: Jossey-Bass/Pfeiffer, 1999, pp. 114–117.

There is a misconception regarding contracts. It is believed that contracts are very detailed agreements created by attorneys and written in complicated terms that no one understands. While some contracts are filled with legalese, basic contract law encompasses a lot more. For instance, a contract may be oral. Once accepted by the client both the letter of agreement and proposal discussed previously become contracts.

BASIC ELEMENTS OF ALL CONSULTING AGREEMENTS

Proposals and contracts should contain basic information regarding the parties involved and the role each is to play. The proposed approach that the consultant will take should be spelled out. This may include data gathering, designing of materials, content of program, delivery of services, and implementation. There should be a time line as well as a set of measurables to determine completion. The agreement should also identify the investment required to complete the plan and the steps to take if parties have a dispute. Some questions that all agreements should answer are found in Exhibit 8.2.

Since proposals are offers until they are accepted by the client, consultants may want to add their qualifications, marketing materials, and testimonials. Remember, proposals serve to promote the consultant as well as to suggest options for the work. Sample proposals are shown in Exhibits 8.3 and 8.4.

Exhibit 8.2. Basic Questions All Agreements Should Answer.

- Who is involved?
- What role does each play?
- What is expected of each party?
- What work will be done?
- How will it be done? (Methodology)
- How will you know if it has been completed? (Measurable)
- When will the work be done?
- What consideration will be exchanged for the work? (Payment)
- What payment schedule will be used?
- What will the parties do if the agreement is not working?
- What must occur if the contract must be changed?
- How will disputes or conflicts be resolved?

February 6, 2000

Mr. John Doe
Manager, Organizational Development
Good Business Company
123 Main Street
Any Town, USA 12345

Dear John,

Great to hear from you again! And your offer to get out of the blizzard state that we've been in most of the winter is music to my ears!

As you know most of the work that Consultants Inc. conducts is custom design work. As promised, I have provided an overview of how we would approach this project: the process, possible topic areas, a time line, and the investment. If you need more detail, I'd be happy to provide it for you.

The Process

Data Gathering. Since all our work is custom designed, we need to meet with you, interview your employees, gather data, review your materials, learn your jargon, and talk to your training staff. To do this we will send two people to work onsite for two days. I will be one of the individuals and the second person will be a designer.

Design. Based on the data-gathering process, we will develop a training session and materials that address your needs and are customized to fit your culture. We will develop graphics appropriate for your industry and create scenarios, critical incidents, role plays, and other interactive training exercises and materials for your corporation. You will have a chance to review the materials before we conduct any training. The materials will include a session guide as well as job aids that will be easy-to-use reminders that the participants will keep after the session to ensure they apply the skills they acquired in the session.

Training. We will conduct three sessions of twenty people each. We would like to conduct the first session one full week prior to the next two sessions (which could be back-to-back to save air fare) so that we have an opportunity to tweak the materials if anything unexpected happens during the first session.

Possible Topic Areas

Although it is not possible to pinpoint the specific topics for your Meeting Management training session, there are certain basics that are typical in many organizations. We generally think in terms of what must be done prior to a meeting, during a meeting, and after a meeting. These topics break down as follows:

Advance Preparation:
    Ensuring you need a meeting
    Determining the type of meeting needed
    Establishing an agenda
    Notifying and preparing participants
Managing a Meeting:
    Time management
    How to keep a meeting moving and focused
    Dealing with difficult people
    Processes to generate ideas, make decisions, solve problems
    Meeting facilitation skills
Meeting Follow-up:
    Meeting evaluation
    Tracking progress

💾 Exhibit 8.3. Sample Proposal: New Project, Cont'd.

Getting commitment to act
How to improve your meetings

We will address meeting management from two perspectives: the meeting leader's and the participants' viewpoints and responsibilities.

Time Line

Early March	Data Gathering	2 days onsite
March to Early April	Design Materials	
April	Conduct 3 Sessions	6 days onsite

The Investment

The investment includes all activities listed in preceding paragraphs. It also covers the cost of the materials for training 60 of your employees in 3 sessions of 20 each. It does not cover travel, which is always billed at cost and provided at the lowest rates possible.

The investment also assumes that you are interested in a shared copyright. This means that you will be able to make as many copies of the materials for internal use as you wish, but that you cannot sell them outside the company.

You also mentioned that you might be interested in a train-the-trainer so that your staff could provide training for the program at a later date. I always think this is a wise investment. While I have not included the cost of an actual train-the-trainer in this estimate, I encourage you to have a couple of trainers in the room as I conduct the training. Then I would be happy to meet with them informally following each training day to answer their questions.

Exhibit 8.3. Sample Proposal: New Project, Cont'd.

The investment for the Meeting Management Training as described above will be $_____.

John, if you have any questions, please give me a call. I look forward to working with you again.

Sincerely,

Elizabeth Smith
Consultants Inc.
123 Main Street
Anywhere, USA 12345

Exhibit 8.4. Sample Proposal: Extending a Contract.

To: Mr. John Doe
From: Elizabeth Smith
Date: 29 September 1999
RE: Modification to existing contract:
        Contract/Purchase Order No.: PO–1234–99

Proposal

Under the original contract, Office of Government Work (OGW) requested Consultants Inc. to assist a team of top-level managers to identify and streamline existing OGW business processes. This modification to the existing contract is requested to extend the work period for six months and to add additional funds to cover the scope of work. Consultants Inc. will continue to make two employees available to OGW on a weekly basis to continue the process of examination, recommendation, and improvement of the business processes.

Scope of Work

Actual work tasks will include but not be limited to those listed below. Consultants Inc. will work with OGW employees to:

- Continue to facilitate weekly Reengineering Business Strategy (RBS) meetings for the full six months.
- Provide feedback for improvement to the RBS steering team.
- Coach and support RBS leaders on a one-to-one basis regarding meeting management, communication skills, team-building skills, etc.
- Assist with the development of commandwide communications plans for each implemented process.
- Initiate, facilitate, and complete at least four new process improvement or other Reengineering Business Strategy Steering Committee (RBSSC) chartered teams.
- Complete implementation of at least three reengineered processes.
- Meet weekly with all process improvement teams.
- Facilitate all meetings, supporting the chartered teams' efforts.
- Coach the team leaders of each team.
- Support the teams with agenda development and efficiency processes.
- Create independence and provide learning opportunities for the teams by encouraging team members to learn new skills and practice them, e.g., gather data, complete documentation, lead meetings.
- Finalize OGW business structure.
- Develop agendas for and attend progress meetings with the RBS and Ms. Caroline Martinez, Director of Acquisition Department.

Period of Performance

The expected six-month period of performance for this statement of work is October 1, 2000 to March 31, 2001. (It may be decided at a later date that additional time is required to complete the total project.)

Investment

Given that the efforts described are ongoing and continuous, we will invoice the work in six equally divided portions.

Facilitator Fee:	$34,400 per month x 6 months	$206,400.00
Travel:	$3,950 per month x 6 months	$23,700.00
TOTAL:		$230,100.00

Terms Approved By:

_____   _____

(Name)   (Title)

FEE ARRANGEMENTS

Regardless of which type of agreement you use, it is a good idea to provide a fee schedule that outlines specific dates for payment. If that fee schedule is a separate document, you can add it as an attachment to any contract or use it as an exhibit with a proposal, bid, or letter of agreement. Just make sure you reference it in the other document as part of the agreement.

Some agreements call for retainers. Attorneys and consultants have different definitions of the word *retainer*. While in both instances a retainer is a set amount of money given by the client, attorneys have an ethical duty to keep a retainer or trust account separate from an operating account. They should not remove money from this retainer until it is earned or there are expenses or fees to be paid. Most consultants, on the other hand, consider retainers to be an "on call" fee for an established period of time. For example, a company may pay a $5,000-per-month retainer to a consultant. In exchange for the payment, the consultant is expected to hold a specified amount of time each month for the client. As with other agreements regarding payments, spell out the terms of your retainer agreement with your client.

NEGOTIATION POINTS

The phrase "everything is negotiable" is as true in consulting as it is in any negotiation. The points to be negotiated can range from time of delivery to methods employed. When negotiating with a potential client, especially one who is on the fence as to whether to use your services, try to keep the following guidelines in mind.

- *Make sure the client feels comfortable with you and your abilities.* Client relationships are built through time with empathy, understanding of the client's needs, and your own integrity. Client relationships are rarely begun when your competency, integrity, or authenticity are an issue. Make sure that a client has enough information about you and your skills in order to make a judgment. A well-written bio, company information, and client references can greatly increase your negotiating power.

- *Make sure the client feels comfortable with the process.* Most clients may not be as familiar with the consulting process as you are and may have heard horror stories about underestimation of completion time or overestimates of success rates. Worse yet, the potential client may have experienced unethical consulting firsthand. If so, you may have to generate some safety nets for the client to feel comfortable. Some consultants offer a 100 percent guarantee. Others have calendar review time for the client to give feedback as to the project's progress. The importance of clear communication about your proposed services cannot be stressed enough.

- *Be prepared with the essentials, concessions, and the benefits to all parties.* You have to know what is essential to make the project work well. You should also know what can be temporarily delayed or eliminated. Also, be prepared to discuss all the benefits to all involved.

- *Use questions and active listening to clarify a party's real interests.* As a consultant, you know that when faced with objections or roadblocks, you start asking questions and really listen to determine where the true interest lies. The same consulting techniques should be used when negotiating with potential or existing clients.

- *Be creative, generate options, and collaborate on delivery.* Be prepared to generate the lion's share of the options on delivery or performance. Most clients can tell you what they don't like, but not how they want the issue remedied.

- *Remember to involve a client in the planning stages.* People support what they create. Make sure the client collaborates with you in planning.

- *Know your bottom line.* Knowing your best alternative for reaching an agreement with this client is powerful for you. If you cannot effectively perform the job unless certain criteria are met, then any agreement that requires elimination of those criteria is unacceptable.

- *Know when to quit or give it a rest.* Some agreements just need time to simmer. Be prepared to suggest some time to consider what the client has presented and have the client reflect on your thoughts. Also know that some agreements won't be developed, no matter how hard each party tries. Don't be afraid to walk away from business that does not meet your standards or that you cannot properly fulfill.

When should you not negotiate? When you are only negotiating the amount of your fee for the sake of the fee alone. Many consultants believe it is unethical to state one fee and then reduce it for one client but not another. Clients talk. They will find out if they are charged different prices for the same service.

SCENARIO

Brett has just left a meeting with his client in which they told him they would not pay his last invoice. Brett is two months behind in developing the communication plan as outlined in their agreement. Although he has little documentation and no contract, he believes there are extenuating circumstances that have prevented him from completing the work. First, he has often arrived for meetings only to find no one available because they have all been called in to an emergency meeting regarding the launch of the new product. Second, he is frequently asked to work on other projects not outlined in the agreement and he believes he is adding value to the organization by completing what needs to be completed. Third, the organization is behind in compiling the survey results upon which the communication plan will be based.

Commentary

Brett has quite a dilemma on his hands. Does he quit the project, take the loss of one invoice, and learn never to work with clients that don't follow through? Does Brett now finance this project until he can get back on the client's timetable? Or does Brett realize that it is rare that a client will ever do all of its assignments and that he should set in place a plan both to communicate as well as bring the project and his invoice current?

So, what should Brett have done? At the first inkling that the project was off schedule, he should have been in contact with his liaison and come up with a new plan of action. Next, he should have a paper trail documenting in writing the meetings missed, the projects he completed that were beyond the scope of the agreement, and the survey results needed. Before proceeding with the additional projects, he should have received signed permission to begin those projects. When the survey results were not forthcoming, he should have spoken again with his liaison before proceeding, perhaps documenting the discussion in a memo.

WHAT IF YOU DON'T HAVE AN AGREEMENT IN PLACE?

Even if you do not have a contract, a proposal, or even a letter of agreement before beginning work, you can still commit your agreement to paper. You can provide your client with a summary statement that outlines what you are doing, when you will do it, and what the continued cost is to the client. It's best if your client then signs the summary. While a client's acceptance or agreement with the terms can be shown by continued payment of your invoices and the continuation of the relationship, a document with the client's signature eliminates that need.

COMMUNICATING WITH YOUR CLIENTS

It is amazing that consultants who impart such incredible business suggestions to their clients often do not follow their own advice. As you know, one of the strongest skills consultants bring to the table is their ability to communicate and help others in organizations communicate. However, those same consultants don't stay in touch on a regular basis or may avoid communicating when a business rift arises between themselves and their clients.

If you address issues as issues arise, continually apprise clients on the status of your work, and continue to receive confirmation on your direction, you are far more likely to avoid lawsuits and receive timely payments.

One way to keep your clients apprised of your work is through your billing statements. Make sure statements are detailed, including dates, work performed, and names of participants. Place a sentence at the bottom of the statement that tells the client to contact you if there are any questions.

Another way to stay in touch with your clients is through status letters. At the end of every client meeting or important phone call, briefly summarize the action steps you and the client have committed to. At the end of the letter you could add a statement along the following lines: "If any of the information presented here does not meet with your understanding, please advise me immediately." Or, "If this confirms your understanding of our agreement, please sign and fax or mail back so that work may begin."

Also have a specific place to put handwritten notes of your phone and office conversations. For instance, you might keep a legal size paper of a different color in the front of a client's file folder. Make it a practice to write down dates, the person you spoke with, the issues discussed, and any conclusions reached.

Documenting your conversations serves more than one purpose. Not only is it a great way to make sure that your next steps are understood and approved, it also covers you if the client later questions your actions. If you unfortunately find yourself in court regarding your performance or attempting to collect your bill, that documentation can also be introduced to support your position. The rules regarding introducing evidence in a trial can make it difficult to present all the information you have regarding your case. However, when you maintain notes or records as part of the regular course of your business, those business records or documents are usually allowed into the trial as evidence.

DOCUMENTS REQUIRED BY ORGANIZATIONS

An organization may request that you sign an agreement to keep information confidential or that you not reveal business or trade secrets. To have an effective consulting result, you will need your client's complete honesty and some disclosure about things such as financial situations, competitor's advantage, corporate errors, and other delicate issues. These nondisclosure or confidentiality agreements can be straightforward and discuss exactly what must be kept confidential. However, make sure you understand the terms. What one company may consider confidential may be information already available to the public or within your expertise. By signing such an agreement you are subjecting yourself to liability. For instance, if you tell one prospective client about a solution that you performed for a company with whom you signed a nondisclosure agreement, you may be in violation of that agreement.

Another agreement that some companies may attempt to have you sign is a non-compete agreement. Non-compete agreements are not unusual in consulting practices. As discussed in Chapter Six, some consultants have subcontracting consultants sign non-compete agreements before beginning projects.

Some consultants have a self-imposed noncompetition policy. For example, a consultant who works for one soft drink company may consider it unethical to perform work six months later for a competitor. Non-compete agreements tend to be unpopular with the courts when used with employees—the government likes people to have the ability to continue working. As an independent businessperson, however, you can sign noncompetition contracts that are enforceable. It is assumed that independent business people have more options and negotiation power than employees. Therefore, businesses can more easily decide to agree to contract terms or walk away from the deal without facing termination of employment. Make sure you are aware of the terms you are agreeing to before signing any noncompetition agreement. If the non-compete is so restrictive you will not be able to work in the future, find another client.

Some companies may require you to sign a waiver of ownership of all inventions or work product produced for their project. Be very careful with this type of arrangement. In the strictest sense, you could be forfeiting the right to use the tools or product you develop while working for a specific client. Most consultants customize solutions for companies but also have standard methods or tools that are used with all clients. Also, if you are training, these agreements mean that after you create the materials, the company can take the program in-house. If you agree to this type of arrangement, make sure you and the client specify what constitutes client property, what is off limits, and how much more you will be paid for producing property you can't use in the future.

CONSULTING AGREEMENTS WITH A FORMER EMPLOYER

Many consultants made the decision to become consultants because their company made the decision for them. When organizations are downsized, employees may opt to set up consulting arrangements with their former employers. Severance packages may even offer a consulting arrangement as part of the benefits. In this situation, most of the legal concerns rest with the former employer. For tax reasons, the company must make sure it now treats you as an independent contractor and not an employee. A more in-depth discussion on the differences between employees and independent contractors has already been covered in Chapter Six.

Some items to negotiate if you find yourself being downsized are the amount of business that you can depend on the company giving you and the rate of pay you will receive. Make sure you calculate what self-employment taxes, benefits, and costs of doing business will be when negotiating your consulting fee. See if the company will assist you in the form of secretarial support, someone to answer your phone, copying capability, or access to a computer or other office equipment, supplies, and amenities. Sometimes, companies can provide you with equipment or services at low or no cost to the organization. Those same low-cost services are worth many dollars to you. However, companies may be reluctant to do anything that might put your independent contractor status into question.

Also, see if you can be released from any non-compete or nondisclosure agreements that you signed as an employee or at least have them revised. Many of these agreements are written very broadly. You do not want to limit your ability to consult in your field to just your former employer. Also, review these agreements with your attorney to determine whether the agreement is written so broadly that it cannot be enforced against you.

DEBT COLLECTION

What if you have performed as agreed, achieved admirable results, and are not receiving payments in a timely fashion? One of the realities of the consulting business is that consultants are service providers. People who provide services are at a slight disadvantage when they are not paid. Service providers do not have the ability to retrieve a piece of equipment or hold some inventory until they are paid. Just knowing that there is a possibility that a client will not pay you, or pay you on time, puts you ahead of the game.

Here are some effective collection techniques which may help you get the money out of accounts payable and into your pocket.

- *Don't let receivables get out of hand.* Make sure your invoices go out in a timely fashion. At the very least, bill and collect on a monthly basis. If your client is holding your invoices before paying, begin billing more frequently. For that matter, who says you have to send bills monthly? Send bills weekly or semi-weekly or immediately after you have performed some work on a project. Bill when the good work is fresh in your client's mind.

- *Add a sentence that tells when payment is expected.* Some clients automatically add an additional thirty days when bills state they are due upon receipt. If you state that the invoice or statement is due within seven or fifteen days of receipt, it gives clients a specific time to pay.

- *Avoid sticker shock as much as possible.* Break large receivables into smaller amounts. The larger the bill, the more difficult for a client to justify in a budget and the more difficult for you to collect. It is far better for the client's psyche and your cash flow to have smaller, consistent payments on a regular basis.

- *Be sure to contact your client as soon as the first payment is late.* Don't let a past-due payment go even a day without at least a phone call. It becomes more and more difficult to collect late payments as the time from your completed work increases. Remember, the value of your services greatly decreases when you have solved the problem or when the client no longer needs you. Wait too long and the client may have more pressing needs or other alligators to fight.

- *If possible, be prepared to stop or slow work on a project until you are paid current.* Also, watch out for big companies who actually invest and earn money by holding payments to small companies and vendors.

- *Don't be afraid to take the matter up the food chain to someone with more power over the checkbook.* Do not avoid the problem because you don't want to risk appearing desperate. It is the client's problem they are not paying, not a reflection on you.

- *Make sure you have the right person making those collection calls.* Someone who avoids controversy or is uneasy asking for money is not your best bet. To be most effective, the phone caller may have to be you, the consultant. Remember to remain friendly as you inquire about payment.

- *Ask helpful questions like these:*

  "How much can you pay me today?"

  "When can you have the rest of the amount?"

  "What type of payments can you begin making?"

- *Be ready if the client stalls.* Here are two responses to the ever-popular "The check is in the mail" or "The check is being written right now":

  "Great, I'll be by to pick it up at 2 P.M."

  "Please fax me a copy of the check for my files."

Go ahead and prepare for instances of nonpayment now. Have a standard policy and time line regarding when you will make phone calls, what letters you will send, how you will track your contracts, and when you will turn the matter over to an attorney or collection agency. For example, you might make a personal phone call at thirty days late and then call once a week thereafter until paid. All work may cease until payment at forty-five or sixty days late. A letter may go out at sixty and ninety days. Do not wait longer than 120 days to get your attorney or collection agency involved.

Be prepared for the cost of using a collection agency. A collection agency will want a percentage of any amount collected. That percentage may be as high as 50 percent. If you plan on using an attorney, see if the attorney can draft standard letters for you to send first before turning the matter over to the attorney. Also, see if the attorney will represent you for a flat fee for all collection matters. A sample collection letter is provided as Exhibit 8.5.

Interest or Finance Charges

Some consultants charge finance or late charges to encourage clients to pay on time. If you are going to charge finance charges or interest fees, make sure those fees are in writing and comply with state law. For instance, if you are charging 1.5 percent interest per month (18 percent per year) and your state only allows 6 percent interest unless in writing, your client could then claim you are charging too much interest. The charging of excessive interest, called *usury,* usually carries extremely high penalties and may cost you in the long run. Also, some time limits may apply as to when those late charges may begin. For example, you may have to wait thirty days before you can add late charges.

💾 Exhibit 8.5. Sample Collection Letter.

Mr. De Adbeat
ABB Services
P.O. Box 123
Anywhere, USA 12345

November 27, 2000

RE: Past Due Balance of $3,000.00

Dear Mr. De Adbeat:

Please be advised that your account in the above-referenced matter is past due. Our records indicate that the sum of $3,000.00 is past due and owing. As you are aware, we have discussed this matter with you by phone on three previous occasions. Each time, you have stated that the payment would be sent. It has been ten days since our last call and payment has still not been received.

You have told us that you have no questions regarding this amount. However, if any of this amount has been paid or is in dispute, please contact us within thirty (30) days. If payment has not been received or arrangements have not been made for payment, we will be forced to proceed with our other legal options.

Thank you for your immediate attention to this matter.

Very truly yours,

Cindy Consultant
President
ABC CONSULTING COMPANY
123 Main Street
Anywhere, USA 45678

Financial Danger Signs

Watch out for signs of declining business or decreased contact from the client. Some signs that a client may be in financial trouble include laid-off employees, emptying warehouses, loss of a major customer, or failure to return your phone calls. The persistent or "squeaky wheel" creditor does get paid, but usually only if that creditor is necessary to the continued business of the company or if someone at the company feels obligated to pay you.

If you want to be paid when a company is going through tough times, there are a few things that will improve your chances. First, have a written agreement that you have followed. Be friendly in all your contacts with the company. Finally, if it looks like full payment is out of the question at present, indicate that you might be willing to take the amount owed you in payments or at a reduced rate.

Taking Your Client to Court

What if your efforts do not work? What legal options does a consultant have when dealing with clients who don't pay for work received? Sue the deadbeats!! Not so fast. Lawsuits are serious, expensive, and time-consuming.

Before plunging into a lawsuit against your nonpaying client, there are special considerations. If the client has even a minor issue with your work you may lose. The client may file a counterclaim arguing that you did not do as promised. A client might argue that you fraudulently misrepresented your abilities or breached your contract. Then you will be fighting two battles.

It's also likely that the client is a larger company than you are, with more resources to pursue a legal battle. This means it has deeper pockets and can afford to stay in court longer. It also means it may have the resources to force your attorney to spend hours reviewing documents, drafting responses, and going to court. And don't forget your time. You will be spending time reviewing documents, in depositions, and in court instead of consulting.

Also, you could get publicity, whether you win or lose. Unfortunately, this publicity will most likely do more damage than good to your reputation, even if you win. New clients may be reluctant to get involved with you.

If at all possible, you should avoid lawsuits with your clients. However, if bringing a lawsuit is inevitable, make sure you review Chapters Fifteen and Sixteen before proceeding.

Clients Outside
the Corporate Arena

Consultants have a wide variety of clients. When you're working with an organization that has a heightened duty to report finances and be accountable to a constituency for monies spent, the consulting relationship takes on a new dimension. Not only are methods and results scrutinized, but the consultant has many more people to please and may be required to follow a more formalized structure in one or more parts of the assignment than when working with a for-profit client. A good rule of thumb with all the entities described in this chapter is to balance out your practice with other sources of income. With the unique management and characteristics of these organizations, payment may be slow, sporadic, or, in extreme cases, not forthcoming.

THE GOVERNMENT

No matter which agency or branch of government is involved, consulting projects should be designed to benefit the taxpayer in some manner. That benefit may fall under a wide range of categories such as creating better relations with the public, providing more judicious use of funds, increasing information sharing among departments, improving resources, or creating partnerships with foreign countries.

If your consulting firm is minority or women-owned, you may qualify for contracts that would otherwise go to larger or more well-established firms. Usually, certification is required to prove that the majority ownership is held by women or minorities. However, once that process is complete, you can compete for a percentage of the contracts that are held out to be granted only to those designated businesses.

Before entering a contract with the federal government, you should be aware of the differences between government and private industry. In most cases, the government is required to hire the lowest bidder for the work, unless a justification such as "sole source" can be made. That is, a higher bidder must offer something that ensures more value or increased results over a lower bidder.

Like local and state governments, the federal government has a well-deserved reputation for late payment. To address this, the Prompt Payment Act requires government agencies to pay their bills in a timely manner—in most circumstances within thirty days. The thirty days is usually counted from the time of receipt of a "valid invoice." This can be tricky, because if you have forgotten a piece of data or have a typo, the invoice will be returned to you and the thirty-day countdown will start over once the agency receives the corrected invoice. While many agencies have corrected or greatly improved the process over the past few years, payments may still take more than thirty days. Although long delays are becoming more the exception these days, an invoice may be outstanding for a significant amount of time—even longer than one year. There are numerous reasons payment can be delayed. You should be aware that on occasion, you will face similar situations.

If you intend to respond to a Request for Proposals (RFP), read the fine print! RFPs can be more than a hundred pages long. However, if you are going to go through the trouble of submitting a proposal, do yourself a favor and spend adequate time reading and understanding the task. In some cases, you will only be allowed to ask questions for clarity by fax or letter. The agency will compile all questions asked and then return all responses to all who requested information. This process ensures fairness by guaranteeing that everyone has access to the same information, at the same time, and in the same manner.

If you are considering conducting work with the federal government, you are strongly encouraged to get a copy of the Federal Acquisition Regulations (FAR), the rules that govern the purchase of goods and services for the federal government. You can request a copy by contacting the contracting specialist at the government agency with whom you are working. You can also check out the FAR home page at: http://www.arnet.gov/far.

Exhibit 9.1 discusses tips for dealing with the government.

Exhibit 9.1. Tips for Dealing with the Government (and Getting Paid).

- Read the RFP thoroughly.

- Submit invoices using the format you are provided.

- Be clear about what services will be invoiced—have it in writing.

- Invoice the same day you complete the work.

- Call your contact thirty days after sending your invoice to remind them about payment or see if they had any questions about your statement.

- Checks are assigned a date to be cut—ask when that will be.

- Keep a log to track your invoices.

- Never wait and hope the check is in the mail—call!

- Realize that government agencies begin the thirty-day countdown once they have received an *accurate* invoice.

- Resubmit corrected invoices the same day.

- Have patience.

Mia is in shock. She was recently awarded a large Department of Defense train-ing contract to train three thousand employees over the next ten months. She spent months writing her response to the Request for Proposals (RFP), which was over five hundred pages long. She hired eight trainers across the country who lived in the geographic areas specified by the organization. She conducted a week-long train-the-trainer session for the eight new employees. And most recently she has worked diligently at scheduling the training sessions at various sites. The first ten training sessions have been completed. Today she received a telephone call stating that the budget had been cut and with it, her training program.

Commentary

Mia has been given the assignment of a lifetime only to have it dissolve into thin air. What does Mia do now? She has eight new employees, has invested time and money in training them, and has invested time and overhead in scheduling ses-sions across the country. As long as she was following her RFP, she should be paid in a timely manner for the work completed to date. Under the legal concept of *quantum meruit,* people should be paid for the value of the goods or services they provide. If Mia is not paid, the government will receive something for nothing or be "unjustly enriched."

It is rare that a government agency would refuse payment for work completed. More likely than not, a government agency's failure to pay in a timely way is a func-tion of inefficient pay procedures rather than a violation of the law or of a con-tractual agreement.

However, most government contracts give the government the right to cancel work. Had Mia been working in the private sector, she could have included a pro-vision in her contract for "liquidated damages" or a sum that both parties agreed would be fair compensation if the contract were canceled. For example, such a pro-vision might state that if the client cancels training after a certain date or after cer-tain events have occurred, the cancellation fee will be the same as that for a specified number of training sessions or a percentage of the estimated cost of the entire contract or even a specified amount of money.

While Mia could have tried to include such a cancellation provision in her agreement with the government, it is very unlikely that it would have been ac-cepted. As a consultant, you should, however, be sure that your proposal clearly outlines the scope of work and the amount that will be invoiced. Remember, employees of the government must report to a number of individuals and ultimately the taxpayer. If there is payment for work that is not completed, the payment may not be a popular expenditure of funds.

What about collecting for the work Mia is losing? Mia probably will have difficulties if she tries to sue the government because of a little doctrine called *sovereign immunity.*

Sovereign immunity historically meant that one could not sue the king or the sovereign. In modern times, sovereign immunity protects the government or ruling entity. The immunity was created to eliminate the effects civil actions would have on the government's decision making and the time available to devote to running the country.

Collecting a judgment that has been granted against the government is also difficult. The money to fund the judgment has to be budgeted and creditors can be stalled through the bureaucratic procedures in place. Even settlements where both parties agree that the government will pay usually have to go through some sort of approval process. An approval process may involve the head of a department, the leading official, or a committee or council of leaders. For example, a state department may simply require the stamp of approval from that department's head. However, local entities may require a vote by city council approving the amount.

NONPROFIT ORGANIZATIONS

The rewards of working with nonprofit organizations often exceed the fees that consultants may be paid. Although a nonprofit may be unable to pay a consultant's normal fee, it offers the personally fulfilling opportunity to provide services to an organization that funds research for curing deadly diseases or advocates on behalf of those in our society without power. However, consultants still face legal issues when contracting with nonprofit organizations. Like the government, nonprofits have a duty to show expenditures of finances as well as results to donors, volunteers, board members, and the government. This close scrutiny makes a consultant's bookkeeping and documentation even more important.

Exhibit 9.2 discusses some possible solutions if a nonprofit indicates it cannot pay a consultant.

Exhibit 9.2. Alternative Forms of Compensation.

- Part of the fee can be considered a contribution to the organization with public recognition as such.

- Space could be given the consultant to promote his or her services in the organization's next trade fair or printed advertisement.

- Letters of recommendation could be drafted for other nonprofit organizations.

- The consultant could be recommended to corporate members for services in their organization.

- The consultant could be granted membership in the association or organization.

Note: Check with your tax adviser to understand the tax implications of any barter or advertising benefits exchanged.

SCENARIO

Sean belongs to a professional association that is run by a volunteer board of directors. Several months ago Sean was contacted by one of the board members to gather data from the local chapter units. The two of them verbally agreed upon a fee for the work and Sean moved forward. The member who invited Sean to complete the work has since rotated off the board. Sean has contacted the new board president to get on the board meeting agenda to present his findings.

Sean's findings have touched a nerve in the organization, one that the association has been avoiding for years—lack of partnering with its chapters. Several of the board members know that to open this can of worms now would be disastrous. Instead they tell Sean that the board member who asked Sean to complete the work did not have the authority to do so, that the work was not authorized by the board, and that no money has been set aside for the project. In addition, since there are many consultants with Sean's skills in the association, the typical process is to request that the work be completed by volunteers for the cost of the expenses incurred only. The board has told Sean that they will not continue with the project and have requested that he take a large reduction in his fee.

Commentary

One of the problems when dealing with nonprofits is determining if your services will be valued by the next board of directors. Should Sean have determined that there was an internal group of volunteers that could provide the same services as a consultant? Maybe. If the goal of consulting is to help clients become self-sufficient, then identifying existing services within the organization would certainly be part of a well-structured approach. Should Sean have required the board of directors or its president or chairperson to sign the contract? Again, it is a good practice to make sure you have authority before proceeding.

What about bringing a lawsuit against the individual volunteer who contacted Sean or against those board members who knew of his work? With the new laws protecting volunteer service, it will be difficult to sue the board of directors to try to recover the cost of the services provided. In addition, any benefits of working with the nonprofit would be greatly diminished by the publicity both within the nonprofit arena and among volunteers of the organization.

There are alternatives. Sean could appeal to the decency of the board members for payment. In return for payment, he could offer an additional service, such as helping to get volunteer advisers up to speed on his findings if, of course, the new board is willing to tackle the issue.

Sometimes a consultant has to be creative in inventing solutions if it looks like a client is not going to pay. Part of the consultation fee could be considered a contribution to the organization, with public recognition as such. Always check with your tax advisor to determine the tax implications of any barter or advertising exchange, as well as to help you choose your best option. Space could be negotiated for the consultant to promote his or her services in the organization's next trade fair or printed advertisement. Letters of recommendation could be drafted for other nonprofit organizations—preferably, organizations that pay. The consultant could be recommended to corporate members for services in their companies. There may also be an opportunity for membership in the association or organization.

ASSOCIATIONS

Most associations are set up as nonprofit organizations. Therefore, the legal issues are similar. Like nonprofits, many professional associations have an executive director, a paid management team, or even a large staff hired to handle the day-to-day operations. When performing services for a professional trade association, your performance is scrutinized not only by a board of directors, staff, and volunteers, but by members of a specific profession. As with other business entities, there are pros and cons when dealing with associations. One obvious pro is the visibility and credibility you receive when working for an association. If an industry association says you're the expert, you're the expert. One of the greatest cons is that the client may want you to provide services at a reduced rate or at no cost due to its limited budget. In addition, you may have collection problems similar to those encountered with nonprofits and government agencies.

SCENARIO

Kyle was hired by his industry association to establish the skill standards for copier repair technicians. Since Kyle was the noted expert and consultant in the field, the association members were confident that Kyle would pull together a team of other experts and manage the multifaceted assignment with success. Unfortunately, a week after accepting the project, Kyle ran into some personal problems with his spouse and family. Determined to complete the project, Kyle did not tell anyone about his personal plight. Kyle has accepted payment for almost six months of work, although his results are far from what the association expects from him. The national conference where the skill standards will be unveiled is scheduled for next month and the board of directors has asked Kyle to attend their board meeting next week to discuss his results.

Commentary

Kyle has a big problem right now. Not only is his personal life in turmoil, so is his professional life. If Kyle does not produce the skill standards that the association expects, he breaches his contract. He also ruins his professional reputation. Kyle's acceptance of the funds to date has basically said to the board that the project is proceeding as promised.

So what is Kyle to do? Well, the good news is that he has a week. Kyle also has a few options. If this is a project that he can complete alone if all of his energies are focused on it, he can use the week to create a time line and accomplish as much as possible during the time. If he needs to bring in others to complete the work, he can use the week to prepare his game plan for completing the assignment with other consultants and show how the plan meets the association's expectations and how he will pay for the costs of the additional consultants.

What happens if Kyle can't complete the project under any circumstances? Well, he can offer to return the entire contract amount. He can come to an agreement on what would be a fair compensation for the services he has provided to date and return any monies exceeding that amount. He can negotiate an extension providing both extra value as well as assurances and defined checkpoints to show that the project is completed within the new time frame.

One thing is certain. Whatever option he chooses, he needs to be up front with the association. While details are not required, he does need to state that personal matters have kept him from focusing his entire attention on this important issue and that these are the solutions he has generated.

RELIGIOUS ORGANIZATIONS

Religious organizations offer a twist to the nonprofit management style described. In an environment where charitable causes are championed, paying for consulting services may seem a contradiction to some members. Some may think it is a consultant's duty to provide services free of charge. With smaller organizations, priorities ranging from paying the water bill to building a new chapel or installing a stained glass window may take precedence over payment of your consulting bill. Lawsuits have been brought successfully against religious organizations, especially the parent or religious governing body. However, some religious organizations do not have the funds to satisfy a judgment brought against them. When dealing with a religious organization, you can either make certain that all parties involved understand that you are entering into a business relationship and that the funds exist for the project or you can make the determination that you are donating your services. As with all clients, be clear with the organization about your arrangement, any payment terms, and the scope of the project instead of having those decisions made for you by the religious organization.

Nina, a marketing consultant, was hired by her church to put together an outreach and marketing plan. She agreed to do the work for half her regular fee and had a contract for the work drawn up. Nina has invoiced the church twice. Her second invoice indicated that she would begin charging interest on the unpaid balance. Last week she started leaving messages for the pastor and the church treasurer. No one has returned her calls. She is certain her work was satisfactory, but she also knows funds are tight in the church.

Commentary

What's Nina to do? She has cut her fee in half and been patient with payment. Nina is in a tight spot. She probably doesn't want to bring a lawsuit against a church and she knows funds are tight, so payment might be unlikely even if she did receive a judgment.

Some consultants have only two fees, full and free, for just this reason. If a fee can be discounted, it can be argued that it is too high in the first place. And if a partial write-off is justified, a client might wonder if the entire amount can be written off as well. Also, adding an interest charge that was not in the contract at this late date can be dangerous. If Nina exceeds the allowed interest in her state, she could be accused of usury and face significant damages.

If no payment is forthcoming, Nina might try contacting one of the more powerful members of the congregation to advocate her position. She might also impress upon the pastor that she has already discounted her fee and that a reputation of a church as accountable and honest is as important as that of a consultant. Unfortunately, the only way Nina will probably see her money soon is if the pastor or the congregation feels it is a priority.

Unique Consulting Situations

Consultants are brought into organizations for a wide variety of reasons. Some of the situations in which consultants find themselves also present unique legal concerns. In some of the situations, insurance or a well-drafted contract can decrease liability risks. In others, just knowing a risk is present can help in choosing whether to accept the assignment or in thinking through the manner in which you will handle a unique issue when it arises.

As a consultant you will want to be aware of the many consulting liabilities that may be raised in unique consulting situations. You will want to be aware of the ways that you can structure your assignments to limit your liability.

SCENARIO

Karen Anne's computer consulting company advises the fashion design industry in implementing systems that are compatible with a variety of buyers. She prides herself in finding unusual solutions that require a minimum amount of downtime for her clients. Because of Karen Anne's foresight, her clients did not experience the Year 2000 problems faced by others in the industry. However, the buyers that purchase her clients' merchandise were not prepared for the effects brought on by the Year 2000 changes, resulting in huge delays and mistakes in purchasing. Karen Anne has just received a letter from a client who wants to know why their business wasn't warned that the relationship with buyers could still be affected.

Commentary

Could Karen Anne actually be held responsible for her clients' relationships with their buyers? Maybe. Remember, Karen Anne's specialty is to provide consulting to ensure that her clients' computer systems are compatible with their various buyers. It could certainly be argued that Karen Anne's scope of consulting should have included warning clients that their buyers might not be taking the same precautions and what problems could result.

Karen Anne may want to take a look at the Year 2000 Readiness Disclosure Act, which was passed in 1998, and the state statutes that followed. This act was designed to encourage communication and may give her some protections for statements made in good faith about compliance.

SCENARIO

Fredrich was excited about his new venture. Two years ago he presented his ideas about increasing innovation in the workplace at an international conference in Orlando. One of the individuals in the audience, Nyuk, asked him to present at a conference in Asia the following spring. The conference designers would pay for all his expenses.

Nyuk advised Fredrich that he could avoid much of the hassle involved with getting a work visa if he simply said that he was entering the country for pleasure rather than work. Nyuk assured Fredrich that this process was appropriate since Fredrich was not getting paid a fee, but simply having his expenses covered.

Fredrich's presentation at the conference in Asia was successful and led to several offers from those in his audience. Fredrich accepted one offer from an electronics firm in which he would oversee the language translation of his reference book and workshop materials. In addition he would license the rights to his materials for internal use only to the firm on an annual basis. Fredrich made several trips to the country, each time citing his reason for travel as "pleasure."

When Fredrich's publisher attempted to negotiate the rights to his book with a publisher in the Asian country, the publisher found that Fredrich's book was already available in the bookstores—available through the firm that had done the translation and was presently paying Fredrich a small licensing fee for using the materials internally!

Commentary

Foreign licensing agreements in Europe and Japan are usually adhered to. Many countries honor trade secrets and intellectual property just as the United States does. However, in parts of the world—especially some Asian and South American countries—the focus tends to lean toward protecting the user, not the inventor. While consultants may see the behavior as misappropriating or "ripping off" books, CDs, videos, and other materials, in these countries the behavior is just not seen as wrong. In fact, there the belief is that it is more natural that the materials become owned more by the user than the developer. Regardless of the country's overall approach to intellectual property rights, there is usually something that can be done to protect a given piece of work—but the attempt is always more difficult and less likely to succeed if the consultant can be shown to have ignored other aspects of the country's laws.

Fredrich should have completed the visa forms appropriately right from the start. Had he followed the country's legal requirements, he would have been in a better position to have his materials protected. As a consultant, you can have the client assist with this. Many times, clients will help complete forms that state the specific skill the consultant brings, the time frame the consultant will be working, and the reason this consultant is being brought in from outside the country. The process then becomes a simpler one for both the client and the consultant to receive permission for a time-limited work permit.

SCENARIO

Clay had been hired by a Toronto firm to present information about the use of new heart scan equipment that he helps clients install. He also trains clients in the use of the equipment. When he arrived at the border, the overhead transparencies he intended to use for his presentation were confiscated when he refused to pay taxes on them. The Canadian officials classified them as a "product," which they assumed Clay would sell.

Commentary

Generally a consultant who is selling advice doesn't need to worry about sales tax unless the consultant is selling a product. When crossing the Canadian border you can expect to be questioned and detained when carrying things that may be sold, such as Clay's transparencies. Make sure you find out what laws the country you are visiting may enforce that differ from those in your own country. A solid partnering and building a good relationship with a client or potential client is imperative to help you through these surprises.

Clay's problem is similar to the situation faced by Karen Anne in this chapter's first scenario. Once again, a lack of knowledge about how others conduct their business has resulted in a problem. This time, the confusion was caused by a lack of understanding foreign laws and procedures.

SCENARIO

Byron provides consulting with regard to human resource and employee relations issues. Byron is often consulted regarding termination procedures, government hearings, and the language to be used in drafting severance packages. Byron has just received a letter from the State Bar Association informing him that he is under investigation. Apparently, an attorney claims that Byron, a non-attorney, is making recommendations that constitute legal advice. The attorney has filed a complaint with the State Bar for Byron's alleged unauthorized practice of law.

Commentary

Byron is facing a common problem. Many issues a consultant deals with have some legal aspect. How does Byron draw the line between explaining good business practices and offering legal advice?

Byron now has to prove that something did not happen. Think about it—it is much harder to show that legal advice has never been provided than for an attorney to show the one time it has. Also, attorneys have a strong interest in making sure that non-lawyers do not give legal advice. Many people would say that this interest is purely financial and attorneys want to avoid the competition. In some cases that may be true. However, just like doctors, attorneys want to make sure valid information is presented. They also want the ability to "police their own" and make sure that everyone giving legal advice is bound by the same legal standards and ethical rules.

One of the easiest ways for Byron to avoid this problem in the future is to tell his clients to have their legal counsel review his suggestions before implementation. Both orally and in writing, Byron should remind them that he is not an attorney and that nothing in his consulting services constitutes legal advice.

WHAT'S A CONSULTANT TO DO?

The scenarios described thus far in this chapter share one common thread. There is a failure to define responsibilities and limit the scope of the consultant's work. If an organization is not aware of a consultant's limitations, the organization cannot prepare or acquire additional consulting regarding those areas. As you are probably aware from your own experience, one of the hardest lessons to learn is when and how to admit to things you do not know.

There are some clear ways to define your scope as a consultant in a unique situation. Make sure you clearly define the project so everyone knows his or her duties and responsibilities. Provide a statement that nothing the consultant does will constitute legal advice and that all legal matters should be reviewed with legal counsel before implementation. Make sure to point out where advice from other professionals is required. Also, identify in writing any particular dangers or unusual concerns presented by the assignment, including instructions regarding those concerns. The ways to define your scope as a consultant are provided in Exhibit 10.1.

**Exhibit 10.1. Tips for Limiting
Your Liability by Defining Your Scope.**

There are some clear ways to define your scope as a consultant in a unique situation:

- Clearly define the project so that every party knows his or her duties and responsibilities.

- Include a statement in your contract that nothing the consultant does will constitute legal advice and all legal matters should be reviewed with legal counsel before implementation.

- Point out where advice from other professionals is required.

- Note any particular dangers or unusual concerns of the assignment and include instructions regarding those concerns.

Carlton is an energy consultant in the oil and gas arena, helping companies with their safety concerns. Carlton sees a corroding pipe that could potentially pose a dangerous situation. He points out the pipe, as well as other violations of OSHA and EPA regulations, to the safety coordinator and plant operations manager. They ask Carlton to rank the most immediate dangers and provide a time line for each. Carlton ranks other dangers more immediate than the pipe problem in his action plan for correcting safety concerns. The company uses Carlton's ranking in assigning a time line for remedying the problems. Unfortunately the pipe was in worse shape than Carlton suggested. It broke within the month, causing property damage in excess of $1 million. A lawsuit is brought against the oil and gas company by property owners for the damaged property. The company in turn sues Carlton for his bad advice.

Commentary

Carlton is in a unique consulting field requiring specialized knowledge. Carlton's safety advice affects not only employees of oil and gas companies but also private citizens. He faces liability risks similar to those of consultants who advise regarding safety equipment, health needs, and hazardous environments.

Hopefully, Carlton conducted the safety review under a well-written agreement that clearly stated his job was to find the problems and the company's job was to fix them or hire someone to do the work. Ideally, this agreement places the liability on the oil and gas company for failure to correct any potentially hazardous situations. Carlton's agreement should also include an "indemnity and hold harmless" clause that states that the company will pay for the costs of defending a lawsuit against Carlton and not look to him to pay any part of a judgment against the company.

If Carlton doesn't have an agreement that covers these points, there are some other things he could have done to decrease his potential for liability. First, Carlton could have had a catch-all section or standard protection language in his report regarding the limits of his assignment. Construction contracts or appraisals often have a section or paragraphs of standard protective language. Carlton is facing what could have been an insurable risk. However, indemnities are not favored by the courts and should always be drafted by your counsel.

While every report will reflect differences in industry, a report can be drafted to protect a consultant like Carlton. A report should state that the inspection results presented are based on standard guidelines as provided by federal, state, and local law and as generally known in the industry and that the results are accurate only to the date of the report and to the extent that the consultant has been provided access to the site, the people involved, and all documents concerning the matter. A consultant's report should state that it is strongly recommended that the suggestions provided in the report be implemented immediately. If a suggested time line has been provided at the client's request, the consultant should reiterate that all recommendations should be addressed as soon as possible. The consultant should also disclaim any liability for the client's failure to implement the recommended measures or for improper implementation of the recommendations. A list of recommended provisions can be found in Exhibit 10.2.

Exhibit 10.2. Protective Clauses for a Report.

- The job to be performed consists of [provide a clear summary of proposed work]. For example, the consultant is to find the problems and the client's job is to fix them or hire someone to do the work.

- The client company is liable for failure to correct any situation that has been detected.

- The inspection results presented are based on standard guidelines as provided by federal, state, and local law and as generally known in the industry.

- The results are accurate only to the date of the report.

- The results are accurate to the extent that the consultant has been provided access to the site, the people concerned, and all documents concerning the matter.

- It is strongly recommended that the suggestions provided herein be implemented immediately.

- A suggested time line has been provided at the client's request, however, all recommendations should be addressed as soon as possible.

- The consultant assumes no liability for failure to implement or for improper implementation of the recommendations.

At the very least, Carlton should be able to show the notes he took while making his determinations, standards he used, and notes or letters regarding all conversations with the oil and gas company.

UNIQUE CONSULTING SITUATIONS WHEN TRAINING

For many consultants, part of their job is not only to identify issues but also to aid in addressing those issues through training. If the job includes training, there are additional liability risks to consultants.

SCENARIO

Judye has been teaching a creativity session for five years. A recent seminar that she conducted for a professional association was truly the worst situation she'd ever been in. The group included several participants from the same company whom she silently called "stick-in-the-muds." They refused to use the colors or modeling clay. When it came time for the "toy break," they were unwilling to toss a ball, jump rope, or blow bubbles. And no amount of prodding or coaxing would get them to make finger-print animals or close their eyes during the visualization exercise. Their evaluations showed their displeasure with the day. The participants pursued the matter following the session by filing a complaint against the company for forcing them to attend the training session. Judye was accused of harassing the participants.

Commentary

Not only was Judye unable to work her creative magic with the stick-in-the-mud participants, now she must respond to a not-so-fun complaint. The good news is that it does not appear from the scenario that Judye singled anyone out for a reason other than nonparticipation. Unless Judye publicly embarrassed these company participants by calling them names or discriminated against them in terms of age, race, sex, national origin, religion, or disability, Judye is probably off the hook legally. For example, nowhere is it said that Judye discriminated against the participants because they were older or of a certain race or national origin. Instead, members of the same company are mad at the company and Judye for "forcing" them to attend the training session. Judye may lose the company's future business and the company may demand a refund, but further legal action seems somewhat limited.

Rochelle's ropes course for team building has been operating for almost a year. Established teams arrange to use her outdoor facilities to climb walls and solve problems that lead to better teamwork. Patricia's team has contracted with Rochelle for a team-building experience. Patricia is six months pregnant. Her team is told that they have to figure out a way for Patricia to scale the wall. Although Patricia has participated in all the events on the ground, she has quite clearly told her group that she will not be scaling any wall. Rochelle tells Patricia that the team should have been given the opportunity to resolve the issue and that she prevented natural teaming to occur. Patricia tells Rochelle that team building does not start with tearing down one of the team's members. Patricia then turns and walks out leaving the team, the wall, and Rochelle.

Commentary

Rochelle had a golden opportunity to show that not all team members participate at the same time or at the same frequency and she blew it. Rochelle may also have exposed herself and Patricia's company to pregnancy discrimination and gender bias claims from Patricia. A good rule of thumb is that if someone does not want to participate in a certain exercise for a health reason of any kind, allow the person to sit out or find a creative alternative in another activity.

Rochelle learned a valuable lesson with Patricia and does not plan to repeat the same mistake twice. About a month later, Trey, who has a mobility impairment and uses crutches to walk, is a participant in her team leadership training session. When Rochelle gets to the wall portion of the course, she stops the group before the exercise to announce to Trey that no one expects him to climb the wall.

Commentary

Well, Rochelle just doesn't get it. Now she may have exposed herself and Trey's company to an Americans with Disabilities Act (ADA) claim. Unless Trey tells her that he needs special help or an "accommodation" to perform the exercise, Rochelle needs to back off.

HOW CAN YOU LIMIT LIABILITY
AND ALSO APPEAR SENSITIVE?

In school, children are given permission slips to participate in certain events. Adults sign releases. In Rochelle's situation, she needs a good release form explaining the physical challenges and releasing her and the company from liability. Rochelle also needs a clear orientation that occurs before each training session and that reflects the issues contained in her release. During this orientation, Rochelle needs to explain the rules and the challenges and to give each participant the permission to ask for additional help or to be allowed to sit out if the participant desires. Rochelle also needs to explain that she can stop or redirect an exercise as she sees necessary. In addition, Rochelle can ask participants to leave the premises if they are involved in reckless behavior or horseplay. It is imperative that all expectations are clear prior to the event.

SCENARIO

To end the sexual harassment that Gary has observed running rampant in the course of his duties with a certain company, Gary convinces his client to conduct a diversity and sensitivity training course. Gary begins the training session by asking the class what they consider to be sexual harassment. In response to his inquiry, a participant grabs a coworker, swings her around, gives her a big hug and plants a kiss on her lips. Immediately, Gary has visions of an EEOC claim being filed against him and his client.

Commentary

Gary's example hammers in the point that you never know what participants in a training session will do. How could Gary have known that his question would elicit such a response? Unless he was warned ahead of time about individual participants, Gary probably couldn't foresee such a response. What's more important, however, is how he handles the situation now. This is one of those nightmare issues that require both finesse and diplomacy. One method might be to immediately break the participants into small groups to list on paper as many examples of harassment as possible. While that exercise is occurring, Gary could speak privately with the female participant and ask if she wants the male participant to leave the room or if there is further action she wants taken. Next, a private conversation should occur with the male participant regarding his behavior. It would be appropriate to ask him to leave the session or to outline expected behavior in the future.

Further, Gary probably has a duty to report the incident to someone from human resources, his contact for the session, or a manager so that proper procedures can be followed. While Gary and his client may still be technically liable for the sexual harassment, immediate attention and corrective action is what most people who file complaints desire.

One way to help curtail unexpected behavior might have been to set up some ground rules before beginning the session. For example, Gary might have said, "During the session today, you will be asked to discuss many issues relating to harassment and diversity. The purpose of the session is to become more sensitive to others' feelings and encourage teamwork. If your comments or actions are not in keeping with that position, you may be asked to leave. Also, if anyone feels uncomfortable, you should inform the session leader immediately."

SCENARIO

Yukio had dabbled in meditation and positive thinking techniques for years. When she was laid off from her teller's position at the bank after a merger, she decided to offer training in the techniques she espoused in her community college's adult education program. Yukio's techniques included first getting everything out on the table and then taking people out of their comfort zones so that they could unleash their maximum potential. Yukio's session was filled from the first day.

One of Yukio's first participants was Sally, the training manager for a local utility company. Sally invited Yukio to lead a mandatory two-day off-site meeting with the utility managers. Sally explained to Yukio that recent changes in top management had led to negativity, low morale, and increased turnover. Yukio accepted the job and facilitated the two days, leading the managers through exercises in which they listed all the problems they were having with top managers, assigned animal names to top managers, performed a skit as these "animals," imagined that they were in charge of the company, and used Far Eastern meditation techniques to reach their potential and "true self."

Yukio has just received a letter from the attorney for the utility company. It seems two of the participants are requesting monetary damages stating that the off-site session infringed upon their religious beliefs and caused emotional distress. Both participants took medical leave as a result of the events that took place at the off-site session.

Commentary

Yukio's first response may be that these participants' actions just confirm how much more consulting is needed for the company's negativity, low morale, and increased turnover.

Although unusual in her training technique, Yukio probably didn't interfere with anyone's religious rights until she started with the Far Eastern meditation techniques. The fact that the off-site training was mandatory supports the employees' contention that this training was a condition of their employment. Yukio would be in a better position if she gave her participants the opportunity to opt out of any part of the training that made them uncomfortable. Although this is not an extreme case of religious discrimination, religion is a very personal issue and a protected right under federal and state law.

SCENARIO

Josh consults regarding performance issues within organizations. Josh's great results speak for themselves. He has always believed that you must help address individual problems before you can repair the organization's problems. Josh draws on his education in psychology, his years of on-the-job experience, and his belief in a spiritual awareness. To increase his own self-awareness, Josh studied Eastern religions, Judeo-Christian beliefs, and a more modern approach known as SEIS. SEIS stands for "The Power of Six." Followers of SEIS believe that you must accept signals beyond what your five senses tell you. The ultimate goal of SEISers is to become at one with their sixth sense to reach a true sense of peace. One of the tenets of SEIS is to witness those who are not at peace and help them follow the path beyond the physical world.

During a one-on-one fact-finding session, Josh spoke at length with an employee who was facing some major life problems and was overly stressed. This employee had been identified as a key player in an important project. Josh felt moved by the employee's condition. Josh told the employee that unless some of the personal issues were corrected, the employee would never rise to the level the employee was capable of in the organization. Josh then shared how much SEIS had comforted him and empowered him when he faced similar situations. Josh explained exactly how to start down the path to SEIS and seek internal peace.

When the employee left, Josh felt he had once again been given the opportunity to aid another employee begin the path of inner peace. Upon leaving, the employee did begin a path. However, this path led to the company's human resources department to file a complaint against Josh. The complaint reads that this New Age teaching and talk of the SEIS religion violated this employee's freedom of religion. The complaint also states that Josh implied that if the employee did not convert, a recently discussed promotion would not come to fruition.

Commentary

First, Josh's comments about this employee not rising to the level of which the employee was capable could have been interpreted by the employee as a threat that he would not receive the promotion. If the promotion is not forthcoming, for example, if someone better qualified is promoted, it may appear that the employee was treated adversely because of his religious beliefs.

But why is Josh being persecuted? Josh had the employee's best interests at heart and was really attempting to better another's life. How could someone actually consider Josh's behavior as unlawful? Josh has forgotten his role as a consultant for an organization. The company hired Josh to work on performance issues, not convert employees to his religion. As a consultant, he is still the company's agent. Companies have a duty not to treat employees differently on the basis of religion. If Josh feels strongly about his calling to speak about his religion, there are appropriate forums outside of the business setting.

Protecting Work Product, Trade Secrets, and Intellectual Property

As a consultant, you are selling your education, your experience, and your knowledge. You do not have a piece of equipment or a tangible item that you can repossess or lock up for safekeeping. Instead, the information you create, your processes, and your reporting method are the things of value that you have an interest in protecting.

SCENARIO

Eileen discovered a system from a study of infant versus adult humans and apes that helps adults discover their strengths by recalling actions from their childhood. Through the Applied Patterns of Emotional Survival (the A.P.E.S. method), individual responses as a child can be used to assess strengths of adulthood. Eileen is actively seeking funding so that she can professionally print and distribute her assessment system. She is worried that someone who acquires her system could beat her to the marketplace.

Commentary

Eileen is ahead of the game. She knows that the description of her system and this designed assessment are private information with a value of their own. Through protections discussed in this chapter, she can protect her system and the documents she has created.

THE VALUE OF INFORMATION

Although your knowledge, information, and systems are not tangible material goods, they do have value. Protecting your systems and other secret information decreases the risk and the ability of others to misappropriate or take all or portions of the information you've spent time and money to develop.

If an explanation of your consulting programs and a description of your individual systems were copied, your ownership interest in this private material might decrease. Even if the value does not decrease, the person who takes that information has acquired at no cost material you spent years developing. Basically, your information may bring someone up to speed on your special consulting process with little to no investment on that person's part. You may not have exercises or checklists or models to protect, but most consultants do.

Once it is determined that you have information that has some value, you need to decide what you can lawfully protect. These secrets are called intellectual property. As long as you work to keep them secret, they enjoy a special legal status—as *trade secrets*—and have some protection under the law. In addition, the formal protection available for intellectual property are copyrights, trademarks, and patents.

TRADE SECRETS

Information that is not known to your trade, that gives you an advantage over your competitors, and that is held in confidence, is known as a *trade secret*. A trade secret can consist of proprietary business information, financial information, a manufacturing process, blueprints, computer programs, customer lists, chemical compounds, and patterns for a machine.

There is no formal trade secret registration available. However, trade secrets are protected by common law, state statutes, and contract law in the United States and in most other countries. Words that show that documents relate to trade secrets include *confidential, proprietary,* or *restricted.*

Treating Confidential Information as Confidential

Disclosing any of your secrets will potentially prevent you from protecting the value of your information. To protect trade secrets, you have to show you took reasonable steps to keep the secrets confidential. Since maintaining secrecy is the key to protecting trade secrets, how do you do it effectively? You should secure information both physically and legally. Lock information in filing cabinets and protect secrets on computers with passwords. Restrict access to information to a need-to-know basis only. Make sure that people who do have access have signed a written agreement that spells out their duty to keep information confidential. For instance, do you leave documents showing out on your desk for anyone to see or do you lock them in a drawer? Do you tell your employees that no one should have a copy of your special design without approval or do you have them send a copy to anyone who shows an interest in hiring your services? Do you mark documents confidential and keep them covered or are they faxed without a cover sheet?

It is common knowledge that you should not talk in public places about private matters and that you should mark private information "confidential" when sending it through the mail. However, protecting trade secrets has become more complicated as technical advances have occurred. Although laws protect privacy, some claim that sending information by e-mail or discussing it on a cellular phone invalidates secrecy, since neither of these communication systems is considered secure.

For example, if you e-mail an employee your customer list without protecting or encrypting the message, it could be argued that the list is not protected if another person acquires your e-mail message. If you disclosed a part of your consulting process while talking on a cell phone and another person intercepts the conversation, you may have failed in keeping that part of your consulting process a secret. While these are unique cases, the potential exists for your messages to be intercepted. Be careful when you are communicating in any form about your trade secrets.

How long are trade secrets protected? As long as you keep them confidential. Also, the protection is only good against misappropriation or obtaining them through an improper means. If someone discovers the information or process independently, the trade secret is not protected.

While placing such notices on your materials does indicate ownership, it does not show that the item is registered under law to you or that unauthorized use is not permitted. Therefore, the notices alone are usually not enough protection for most consultants.

Some of the more formal ways you show that the information is owned by you can be reflected on documents and writings. As discussed, your statement of ownership may be incorporated by clearly marking materials "Confidential," "Proprietary," "Secret," "Restricted," or "All Rights Reserved."

Some more formal ways of protecting ownership are through registering materials with the Copyright Office, registering service marks and trademarks, and by applying for a patent with the Patent Office. All of these options will be discussed later in this chapter.

You may also want to use confidentiality or nondisclosure agreements or a licensing arrangement.

Agreements with Potential Partners or Others on Joint Projects

Your trade secrets are at risk whenever someone learns of the confidential information. However, when you are considering joining forces with other consultants or companies or are interested in discussing a joint project, it may be necessary to provide others with trade secret information. In connection with negotiations or discussions, you may disclose ideas and concepts that must be maintained in confidence. This need for secrecy is critical if you are revealing trade secrets or client information. One way to contractually bind a person to secrecy is through the use of a nondisclosure agreement. In a nondisclosure agreement, you and the other person agree that the information is important and valuable, that it will be maintained in strict confidence, and that all materials will be returned if an agreement cannot be reached. Once the project is completed or the parties decide to part ways, the two of you must agree that the information will not be used by the other person and that any materials used will be returned. These agreements are also used when someone is seeking financing but does not want the ideas or trade secrets made public in the process.

Contractual Agreements with Subcontractors

You might also elect to work with another consultant in a subcontracting arrangement. As discussed in Chapter Seven, working with other consultants presents some special legal risks. In protecting your trade secrets and proprietary information, some of the clear agreements you should reach are that your subcontractor will agree to the following:

- To not contact clients directly
- To not make agreements for other work
- To direct all inquiries to you
- To not discuss your arrangement with the client
- To maintain the confidentiality of all client materials and information
- To maintain the secrecy of all your systems and materials unless authorized to reveal them

Use of Licensing Agreements

One of the ways consultants limit the use of their materials is to grant permission in the form of a license. Licenses provide a way for an organization to rent the materials or system for a specified time and at a specific price. During that time, the consultant may offer to provide updates, train people in the company, or answer questions as they arise in using the material. Licensing arrangements are also used when working with other consultants and companies. Other consultants and companies can be licensed to present or consult with material owned by you.

Licensing enables you to ensure licensees are trained properly and are using only the materials that meet your standards, and enforces the concept that the information is protected and not to be copied. One additional benefit is that, by their very nature, licenses show ownership belongs with the owner and specifies the permitted use of the material. Therefore, licensees cannot later claim that they did not know the materials were protected or that certain uses were not permitted.

Protecting Confidential Information When You Have Employees

Once again, the way you treat confidential information is as important as any document you could have an employee sign. Your duty is to constantly educate employees on the serious issue of protecting your trade secrets. Remind your employees of your policy both in writing and orally, especially if you see or hear someone not acting in a confidential manner. Make sure computer software contains an initial screen that states the disk or material is not to be copied. Have confidential stamps to mark those documents you consider private. Place notification or *trailers* on every document that could be considered proprietary. These trailers can be placed on the bottom of every document and state, "Confidential Information. All rights reserved. This document should not be disclosed or copied in any form without the express written permission of the owner." (Note: A copyright notice could also be used here. Copyrights are discussed later in the chapter.) Have a confidential warning on client lists, procedures, rate sheets, and memoranda.

Make it a policy to shred confidential documents. Also, implement an employee policy that every document and all company information must be returned upon termination, including materials at home, and that company computer software must be deleted from an employee's home computer. Change passwords and entry codes immediately upon an employee's termination and confiscate entry passes and office keys. Employees also should be made aware that all client information must be kept confidential.

Protective Agreements with Employees

Employers are usually worried about three things when dealing with trade secrets:

- That an employee will use information and begin directly competing with them
- That the employee will leak secret information
- That an employee will keep an idea or invention created while employed and not turn the ownership over to the employer

In addition to acting as if your information is confidential, you may wish to enter into written agreements with your employees. While agreements may be used in a court, a more important purpose of these agreements is to serve as an educational tool. The agreements show how serious the company is about protecting trade secrets, they describe the information that is protected, and they identify the behavior that is expected from the employee.

These agreements usually cover a combination of the following eight items, depending upon what you are protecting. It is important to remember that no agreement alone will protect your secrets. You must have policies in place and train employees constantly. Here are some elements of a nondisclosure agreement:

- *A description of the technical information that is to be protected.* This might include, but not be limited to, software, electronic equipment, technical drawings, or specifics regarding products.

- *The business information that is to be protected.* Information about how you run your business is also a trade secret. Your client list and how you deal with clients is proprietary information. However, it is just as crucial to protect secrets regarding your costs, profits, marketing, and sales.

- *The information affecting future development that is to be protected.* You don't want the money you have invested in research and future marketing used by your competitors.

- *The nondisclosure of the company's trade secrets and proprietary information.* If your company has a trade secret, such as a formula or special process, that information should be identified to your employee as confidential and not to be revealed.

- *The nondisclosure of clients' and others' secrets and information.* Not only does an employee have to protect a company's confidential information, there may also be a duty to protect others' information. A clear example would be an employee working with a client's financial information.

- *Directions for how to treat and protect company and client property.* Not only do you need to tell employees that information is secret, you need to give them specific steps on how to keep that information confidential.

- *Clarification of who owns inventions or new developments both during and after the employee is employed.* If the employer acquires the ownership of an employee's inventions and new developments (and most of the time the employer does), the employee should be informed of the company's ownership rights.

- *The method for returning company documents and property and deleting software upon termination of employment.* Once the employee is no longer under your control, you want your protected information returned. You do not want the employee to think that now that the employment relationship is over the employee is no longer bound by the duty to protect your trade secrets and proprietary information.

Former employees can also interfere with your business relations. Your employees gain specific knowledge regarding your company's special processes, marketing techniques, and services. An employee who does your marketing and builds business relationships on your behalf is a prime example. If you fire the employee, what may happen? The employee may try to go to another consulting company or open his or her own consulting business with your clients and even your employees. To safeguard against this you should make sure you remain in contact with clients, that clients have more than one contact within your organization, and that if necessary you ask employees to sign confidentiality agreements, agreements not to compete, and non-solicitation agreements. The employment relationship is discussed more thoroughly in Chapter Six. Suffice it to say that if people understand your business, you run a risk that they could use that information to interfere with you.

Non-competition Agreements with Employees

Some companies also have their employees sign a non-compete agreement that limits who employees can work for in the future (e.g., non-competitors), cites specific locations where employees can work, and identifies the time period when they are prevented from working in certain areas. As noted in Chapter Eight, non-competes tend to be difficult to defend in court as the courts want people to have the ability to work—the public interest favors anything that keeps unemployment low and reduces the need to pay unemployment or welfare benefits.

To be able to enforce a non-compete, you must make sure it is "drawn very narrowly." This means that the agreement must be written to avoid too broad a geographic area, too long a time frame, and too general a description of prohibited employment. Also, an employee already working for the company usually must receive something of value besides a continuing paycheck as a consideration for signing the agreement.

SCENARIO

Last year Svede and four of his friends wrote a proposal to provide computer consulting services to their local university. Much to their surprise, their proposal was selected. The other team members are employees working for companies; Svede is the only self-employed consultant. Therefore, much of the day-to-day work of scheduling, client discussions, and billing has become Svede's responsibility. The team has developed a computer program that Svede has started to use with other clients. One of his teammates has now told Svede that the copyright belongs to the group and that Svede must share his income from the use of the program with the entire team.

Commentary

When a consultant works with other consultants, problems like copyright ownership do occur. It appears that all of the members created the program, so all hold the copyright and probably a right to have an accounting of the amounts paid Svede. All members would need to approve Svede's individual use. This is a time for Svede to negotiate. Svede could remind the group of his internal duties and the benefit his continuous presence plays in the survival of the consulting practice. Also, the teammate wanted Svede to share his income. The amount is not mentioned. Svede may be able to pay a small percentage of his profit to the group as a sort of royalty in exchange for the group's approval on the use of the software.

COPYRIGHTS

When you copyright materials it serves as additional protection from people who may try to use your work as their own. While it would be impossible to copyright ideas, the works in which an author expresses those original ideas are eligible for copyright protection. These works can be dramatic, musical, artistic, or literary. A few examples of copyrighted material include computer programs, architectural drawings, advertisements, newscasts, performances, books, music, and other forms of intellectual expression.

When you own the copyright, you own and control the right to

- Reproduce the work
- Prepare derivative works based on the work
- Distribute copies or phonorecords of the work to the public either by sale or by renting, leasing, or lending
- Perform the work publicly, as in the case of musical or dramatic presentations or motion pictures
- Display the work publicly
- In the case of sound recordings, perform the work publicly by means of a digital audio transmission

Many consultants are worried about original literary pieces they author or written exercises they create. Under the 1976 Copyright Act, materials actually have protection from the moment the work is "fixed in a tangible form of expression." This means the material must be written or recorded or somehow preserved. Believe it or not, just typing out an original proposal or writing an article gives you copyright ownership in those documents automatically without doing anything further. So why do people put the word *copyright* on their writings? This is good practice because it reminds others that the materials are protected and informs them of who owns the information.

A copyright protects the information for the life of its author, you, plus an additional seventy years. When there are joint owners, the protection extends an additional seventy years after death of the last living author. If the work was created under a work-made-for-hire arrangement, the copyright protection stays with the owner for ninety-five years. Work made for hire arrangements are a big issue for consulting firms. It is important to be clear at the outset if the consulting firm is being asked to give up its ownership rights in the materials created. If so, the ownership rights are worth much more than the company's right to use the material. The notice requirements include the copyright symbol (©) or the words *Copyright* or *Copr.*, the first year the copyright was filed, and the name of the owner of the copyright. For example: "© 1999 Training Associates Inc. All rights reserved." You may want to include the words "Printed in the U.S.A." for international distribution.

This notice must be placed in a highly visible location on the material, such as on the bottom of a worksheet or on the first page of a multipage document like a book. Some authors, especially those using material for training or in a newsletter, place the copyright notice on every page in case the pages become separated. Phonorecords, which include CDs, cassette tapes, and LPs, use the symbol "P" and have slightly different rules.

Registering Your Copyright

As noted, copyright protection exists from the moment the work is created and put into a fixed form, whether the copyright notice is used or not. However, there are strong advantages to registering the material with the U.S. Copyright Office in the Library of Congress. By registering, you

- Create a public record that the materials are protected

- Have evidence of a valid copyright and proof in the certificate of registration of what is copyrighted

- Have complied with the filing requirement that is necessary before you can file a lawsuit for infringement

- Can seek damages provided by statute as well as attorney fees, instead of just actual damages and profits, if you registered before the infringement

- Can record your registration with the U.S. Customs Service to protect against exporting the material

It is fairly easy to file a copyright registration. You complete an application, pay your filing fee (currently $30) and send a deposit copy of the work that you want protected.

The checklist in Exhibit 11.1 provides you with the steps to take to ensure copyright ownership rests with the appropriate owners and that you can complete the process properly the first time.

Exhibit 11.1. Steps for U.S. Copyright Registration.

Follow these basic steps when registering your material with the U.S. Copyright Office:

1. Request an application form from the U.S. Copyright Office. Both forms and circulars describing the process are free. You can request information in a number of ways:
   - By calling the twenty-four-hour Copyright Office forms hotline: (202) 707-9100
   - By writing to the office:

     Library of Congress
     Copyright Office
     Publications Section, LM-455
     101 Independence Avenue, S.E.
     Washington, D.C. 20559-6000

   - By visiting the Copyright Office Web page: http://www.loc.gov/copyright. To view or download documents, your computer must have Adobe Acrobat Reader, which you can download free of charge from http://www.adobe.com.

2. Obtain the proper application form for your need. (Note: there are forms for different uses. For example, the form for literary works is different from the application for sound recordings, which is different from the application form for dramatic works.)

3. Properly complete the form (handwritten in black ink or typewritten).

4. Send a nonrefundable filing fee (currently $30). Do not send cash. The $30 should be in the form of a check, money order, or draft from a U.S. bank for U.S. funds, and should be made payable to Register of Copyrights.

Exhibit 11.1. Steps for U.S. Copyright Registration, Cont'd.

5. Send a nonreturnable "deposit" of the work you want copyrighted.
   - If the work has not been published, send one complete copy. Published generally means to distribute copies or phonorecords of a work by sale or other transfer of ownership, or by lease, and so on.
   - If the work was published in the United States before January 1, 1978, send two complete copies of the work as it was first published.
   - If the work was published in the United States on or after January 1, 1978, send two complete copies of the best edition. (*Note:* there are exceptions for trade secret manuals and computer programs. Review and understand these exceptions if you are attempting to complete the copyright process with these items.)
   - If the work was published outside the United States, send one copy of the work as it was first published.

6. Mail the properly completed application, filing fee, and your deposit copy or copies to:

   > Library of Congress
   > Copyright Office
   > Register of Copyrights
   > 101 Independence Avenue, S.E.
   > Washington, D.C. 20559-6000

7. Don't leave any of the three items out. If you don't mail all the requested elements, your application may be returned to you. You also run the risk that it won't be returned. Then you have to complete another application and submit another copy with a filing fee.

8. After you submit your application, you will hear from the copyright office in one of three ways: a letter or telephone call requesting more information, a notice that your registration is rejected and the reasons why, or a certificate of registration.

9. A copyright registration is considered effective on the date an acceptable application form and all the required elements are received. Therefore, the filing date is your copyright date, not the date the registration process is complete and your certificate is sent.

Joy was delighted when one of the Fortune 100 firms asked her to develop a customer service training program. One of the corporation's training department managers heard Joy speak at a national conference and liked her easy-to-remember Customer Care system, which she called C^2. Joy had been in business a little over a year and this was just the break she wanted. Joy was overjoyed when she signed the company's agreement. The corporation hired her as an independent contractor to tailor the two-day training program to use their industry's jargon and then scheduled her to conduct the session at various locations around the country. The corporation would print the material and ship it to the training site, where a room would be set up to Joy's specifications. Joy had a steady income, was training a system she had developed, and enjoyed the assignment immensely . . . until the day the corporation decided to provide the training in-house. The corporation claimed that it had paid Joy to develop the system for it. Joy claimed that the system was hers and, although the corporate materials did not display her copyright statement, she had not intended to sell the model to them. Joy is not sure that she has the time or money to take the corporation to court.

Commentary

Unfortunately for Joy, copyright cases can be expensive. If Joy registered her copyrighted materials she could get her attorneys' fees back. The company's agreement has language stating Joy's work is "work made for hire." Usually, in an employment relationship, employees give up the ownership to the employer when authors create something during the scope of their employment. In addition, independent consultants who sign work-made-for-hire agreements are stating that they are paid to give up ownership rights. However, the company would be hard-pressed to claim that it owned the original Customer Care system. Joy had already developed C^2 before she began working with the corporation. In fact, she was hired because of a speech presented at a national conference.

Unless the company can show Joy assigned or gave it all her rights in the original system, Joy will be able to continue to train using the standard system and can adapt it to other industries as appropriate. The big question should be whether Joy can continue to use the tailored material herself with others in the same industry, for instance, with the corporation's competitors. As noted, the company does appear to have legitimate ownership in the customized material through its signed contract. As the material is tailored to the industry, the chances of the company allowing Joy to use or even license the material are probably slim. Why would the company want to invest money to develop a program for its competitors?

So what does Joy do? Appealing to the corporation's sense of fairness and asking for additional money to license her original version as modified probably will not produce the outcome she desires. A licensing agreement with ownership rights held by Joy might have been acceptable had Joy presented it during the contracting phase.

Joy does have some other options. First, she might sit down with the corporation and determine if they want her to have a continued role in a train-the-trainer format. This would continue her ties, recoup some of her invested time, and ensure that the program was conducted uniformly and at a high level by the trainers. If she can continue her relationship in some manner, she can also offer new material as it is developed. Also, being a relative newcomer, she will want a reference and success story to prove her competency. Next, she could ask the corporation for recommendations of others who would benefit from her training. Which customers, contacts, and other industry folks could be referred for this type of training? In both these cases Joy is appealing to the corporation's sense of fairness, though the corporation is probably not legally obligated to do either.

Preventing Client Companies from Stealing Work Product

To avoid a situation like Joy's, you should obtain help in contracts. Your contracts with a client company should

- Define exactly what services are bargained for
- Identify pre-existing material
- Clearly state the ownership of the material after the services are completed
- Determine if a license arrangement is needed
- Specify the ownership of any copyrights
- Specify to whom the consultant can later market the materials

If your agreement is a work-made-for-hire, then you give up the copyright and ownership rights to the materials you produce under the contract. Ownership rights have value and you should charge accordingly.

TRADEMARKS

Remember, not only are your consulting services valuable, the marketing and goodwill that is identified or associated with your name or logo also has value. The main purpose of a "mark" is to show the source or who owns the mark and distinguish the goods or services of the mark holder from the goods and services of another.

There are four types of marks that can be protected:

- Trademarks
- Service marks
- Certification marks
- Collective membership marks

Trademarks and service marks function in essentially the same way, except trademarks are used for products or goods and service marks are used for services. A trademark identifies a word, symbol, phrase, or design of a product. A service mark identifies the source of a service rather than a product itself. For example, a soft drink's name or logo would be trademarked "™" and a dry cleaner's name or logo would have a service mark "SM." As a consultant, you would probably have a service mark beside your logo because you provide services. However, if you also have a product you created, you may have a trademark symbol by that product's name.

Certification marks indicate that the products or services meet the requirements of the owner of the mark, for example, "Certified by the American Heart Association." Collective membership marks indicate the membership in an association. For example, use of the logo for ASTD indicates membership in the American Society for Training and Development, SHRM means the individual or organization is a member of the Society of Human Resource Management, and MPI means membership in the Meeting Professionals International. For simplicity, the term "trademark" will be used for all the protectable marks listed.

Trademark rights are obtained when the mark or logo is actually used or when an application to register a mark is filed with the U.S. Patent and Trademark Office. For example, if your consulting business uses a logo, you may already have certain trademark rights even though you have not applied to register the mark. However, these common law rights usually only protect the mark in the geographic area that you do business.

SCENARIO

Dave's marine biology and preservation consulting firm has just discovered that Bob's Fishing Store is using Dave's logo, an endangered rainbow flying fish leaping underneath a rainbow. Dave is outraged that a fishing store would use a picture of an endangered fish as its logo. He is even more enraged that someone would copy his logo. Dave wrote a scathing letter to Bob and told him to lose the logo and fast. Bob sent back a response, on logo letterhead no less. Bob told Dave that he has had the logo for years prior and it is a registered service mark with the U.S. Patent and Trademark Office.

After Dave's nasty letter, Bob says that he won't let Dave's infringement pass. Dave must discontinue use of the logo immediately and destroy all copies of the improper logo, and Bob expects Dave to sign an injunction that says Dave won't use the mark again. If Dave does not comply, Bob will pursue money damages against Dave. Dave has heard of trademarks but not service marks. Besides, Dave thought that trademarks were only for nationally sold products like tennis shoes and shampoo.

Commentary

Whoops. Dave has just learned a lesson most businesspeople have learned. While scathing letters can make the author feel better when writing them, they usually have a different effect on the reader. Dave also learned that he'd better make sure he has all his facts straight before writing his next letter. But what about the use of the logo? The courts look to whether there is a likelihood of confusion regarding use of the mark. Will people be confused if Dave uses a similar mark with his marine biology firm and be unable to distinguish the firm from Bob's fishing store?

If Bob was using the mark first, the answer is clear. Bob wins the right to use the logo. He used it first, he registered the mark, and he is able to enforce his ownership rights.

If Dave can prove he used the logo first, the situation becomes muddier. If neither had registered the mark, Dave would be able to use the logo. Since the two are in different businesses, there may be a way for two unregistered mark holders to have the rights to use the same trademarks as long as they are not in the same geographic area. If they are in the same area, a court would have to determine the "priority of right" or the first person to use the mark in that area.

In the scenario, however, Bob has registered the mark. If Bob was not the first to use the service mark, he is not the "senior user" of the mark but the "junior user." Even if Dave has used the mark longer than Bob, he sat on his rights by not actively protecting his mark.

But wait, you say. That's not fair.

The government protects people who act, not those who sit around. Dave had many years to contest Bob's or anyone else's use of the mark by registering the mark with the government. Dave didn't think it was important to do so. Since Dave and Bob are probably dealing with very different services, channels of trade, and customer groups (consulting clients versus fishermen), there is not likely to be too much confusion among their consumers.

If Bob used an attorney when he filed his registration, the mark was probably researched. That means that a good-faith effort was used to determine that no one else had rights to use the mark. In this situation, Bob probably has ownership rights in the logo.

Registering Your Mark

Unless you register the mark with the U.S. Patent and Trademark Office, you have not securely protected all your rights and the benefits related to the mark. There are two types of trademark applications in the United States:

- Intent-to-use applications
- Use-base applications

An intent-to-use application is filed by an owner before actually using the mark in order to reserve it. The applicant must have a *bona fide* or genuine intent to use the mark in commerce and the trademark must actually be used before the intent-to-use application can officially be registered.

The use-base application is filed for a trademark that already has been used in commerce.

Normally, the first to use the mark has the right to register the mark with the U.S. Patent and Trademark Office (Trademark Office). Most attorneys will advise you to conduct a search to determine if the trademark is available and whether the proposed mark could infringe on any registered or existing common law trademarks.

A great percentage of trademark applications filed are initially rejected by the office. These are sent back to the applicant in a document called an "office action." The office action lists the Trademark Office's objections to the application or its reasons for rejecting the application. Then the applicant must file a response or make arguments to present evidence that the trademark should be registered. A common mistake made by trademark applicants is misclassifying their goods or services. The United States adheres to the International Classification System, which gives forty-two categories to classify goods and services. For example, chemicals, perfumes, and electronics all have different classifications.

Another common mistake is not correctly describing your goods or services in the application. Many applicants will describe their services narrowly and then later want to add a service. While the identification of goods or services in the application can be narrowed, it cannot be broadened from what was initially described.

If all goes without a hitch, the attorney's fees and filing fees will cost you a few thousand dollars, more or less. Like all government offices, the Trademark Office has set standards. Unlike many government policies, those policies can't just be "read up on" and it is difficult to learn some of the intricacies. It is to your benefit to get a knowledgeable attorney's advice up front; otherwise you may end up spending many more dollars in attorney's fees later to fix misunderstandings. You should also be aware that the entire registration process may take several years.

The checklist in Exhibit 11.2 gives you the basic steps for registering trademarks.

Exhibit 11.2. Steps for U.S. Trademark Registration.

1. Request a free application form and information regarding registering trademarks from the Assistant Commissioner for Trademarks. You can contact the Trademark office in a number of ways:
   - By calling the Patent and Trademark General Information Line:
     (800) PTO-9199
     Or the Trademark Assistance Center:
     (703) 308-9000
   - By writing the Assistant Commissioner for Trademarks:
     Box NEW APP/FEE
     2900 Crystal Drive
     Arlington, VA 22202–3513
   - By visiting the Patent and Trademark Web page:
     http://www.uspto.gov/
2. Complete the application correctly. If the mark is already in use, you must complete that section on the application form.
3. If the trademark or service mark is one you intend to use but you haven't yet started using it, you must complete another section of the application. Before the mark is officially registered you must file another form showing

---

Exhibit 11.2. Steps for U.S. Trademark Registration, Cont'd.

that you are now using the trademark in commerce. This form is known as an Allegation of Use for Intent-To-Use Application, With Declaration.

4. You must identify when you began using the mark and the name and title of the person signing the application.

5. Complete the information regarding your identity, address, legal status, and the description of the goods and services that are connected with the mark.

6. Submit a drawing of the mark on a separate piece of paper.

7. If the application is for a mark that is already in use, you must submit three "specimens" of the actual use of the mark with the goods or services.

8. Enclose the required filing fee. A list of fees can be obtained through the trademark office.

9. Mail the entire package to:

> The Assistant Commissioner for Trademarks
> Box NEW APP/FEE
> 2900 Crystal Drive
> Arlington, VA 22202–3513

Some General Notes:

- Attorneys can perform a search for similar marks before you file your mark.

- The form appears to be one any individual could complete. However, do not be deceived. A misclassification or incorrect drawing can create problems, as can an improper description of the goods or services associated with the mark. According to some attorneys, initial trademark filings require more information or need additional explanation approximately 85 percent of the time. If you have decided to invest your money in protecting your trademark, pay a little extra and use an attorney who knows about trademark registration.

- Also, once your trademark is registered, don't stop there. There is an additional filing between the fifth and sixth year to protect your registration. In addition, a federal registered trademark has a term of ten years and must be renewed. The renewal period begins six months before the trademark expires, so keeping track of deadlines is very important.

Trademark Protections

Applying for trademark registration means that you are actively protecting your investment in your name and the services you provide. It also means that you have placed others on notice of your rights. If a court determines that someone has infringed on your right to use your logo, then the court can make that person discontinue the use of the mark and possibly award you damages for the person's use.

What Does ® Mean?

The use of the service mark symbol (SM) or the trademark symbol (TM) shows that the owner is claiming common law trademark rights. Once the trademark process is registered, the owner can use the registered symbol (®). An owner cannot use the ® symbol until registration has been issued and is limited in using the ® only with the goods or services that were identified in the registration. What is interesting is that some companies never register their trademark or service mark. They just use the SM or TM symbols to show ownership. Even more interesting, some companies do register their trademark, but do not reflect their registration by changing the SM or TM to ®. The filing requirements can be tricky and require staying on top of deadlines. For instance, if you have used a mark and had registered it at least five years prior, you have the right to file a declaration of use and continued use between the fifth and sixth year to keep the mark.

Foreign Recognition of Trademarks

Most countries will protect trademarks and service marks, but not all. Some countries recognize common law rights or that the mark is being used, so an owner must show that the mark has been used in commerce before the country will register the mark. That is, these countries will only permit a use-based application and not an intent-to-use application.

In other countries, trademark rights are determined by applying for them and receiving a registration. In these countries, an owner's priority to the mark is usually determined by the person who filed first, the filing date. This means you could have used a trademark all over the United States and in other countries, but that someone could have superior rights in the same trademark in a country simply by filing there first.

While the use of trademarks in foreign countries is not at the top of most consultants' concerns, you should consider what steps you will take before entering another country. Just like a soft drink manufacturer or a fast food restaurant owner, you do not want to invest your time and marketing in a service that won't be identified with you. If your consulting takes you abroad, you will want to make sure you are not infringing on another's trademark rights and, of course, you do not want to end up providing advertising for a competitor who filed before you in a given country. The best way to make those determinations is to consult with an attorney who specializes in trademarks and intellectual property and who is familiar with the laws of the foreign countries you wish to enter.

Do You Need to File a Trademark Application?

You can develop a common law right to use your trademark or service mark in the geographical area where you do business. You don't foresee expanding outside the United States and you don't want to spend a lot of money in attorney's fees in filing a trademark application. You don't believe any of your potential clients would ever mistake you for another business.

Do you need to file a formal application for a trademark? Maybe not. What you do need to do is talk to your business attorney and determine what risks you run of infringing on someone else's trademark and what rights you have in the logo or name you are using. Not all names or terms can receive trademark protection. Some terms are too common and don't distinctly identify a particular good or service.

Filing a proper application for a trademark is tricky. Remember, this may be an area where your business attorney needs to refer you for consultation to an attorney who deals with intellectual property. Do not hesitate to ask for a referral if you are not getting the answers you need.

PATENTS

Another area in which specialized legal advice is required is patent protection.

Patents evidence a long-recognized relationship between the inventor and the government. The government wants to encourage technology but recognizes the research costs associated with that technology. Therefore, the government grants a patent to an inventor, thus excluding others from making, using, or selling the patented invention. In exchange, the patent owner agrees to disclose his or her invention to the general public. The power of Congress to give these rights of exclusion to inventors is actually provided for in the U.S. Constitution.

Under Article I, Section 8 of the Constitution of the United States, it states:

"Congress shall have power . . . to promote the progress of science and useful arts, by securing for limited times to authors and inventors the exclusive right to their respective writings and discoveries."

The drafters of the Constitution knew granting these rights of exclusion was necessary if they wanted to promote scientific and artistic development. Through a number of patent acts beginning in 1790, patent owners have been given the right to limit who makes, uses, or sells their invention for a limited amount of time. In this way, inventors are encouraged to develop new ideas and then given time without competition to reap the rewards of their efforts and recoup the money and time they invested.

Currently, there are three types of U.S. patents granted:

- Utility patents
- Design patents
- Plant patents

Utility Patents

Utility patents protect functional things or how things operate, such as pencil erasers, Post-it Notes, or light bulbs. During the time period of the utility patent, the patent owner can exclude others from making or manufacturing the invention, using the invention, selling the invention in the United States, and importing the invention into the United States.

An inventor must show three things before a utility patent is granted. The invention must be (1) novel or new (not seen before in public); (2) useful (has some sort of practical value); and (3) non-obvious (not obvious to one of ordinary skill in the art).

Once granted, utility patents are effective when issued and extend for twenty years from the *filing* of the application providing maintenance fees are paid.

Design Patents

A design patent protects ornamental features of a thing or how it looks. For example, a *patented design* would protect a special type of mop or a new type of zipper or a special file folder or a doll. Again, an owner of a design patent can keep others from making, using, or selling the patented design in the United States and from importing it into the United States. To be issued a design patent, the inventor must show that the design is (1) new (not seen before in public), (2) original (not copied or derived from another design), and (3) ornamental (involving visual characteristics of the article, for example the way a lamp is shaped or the special "leather look" achieved by processing plastic in a certain way for seat covers or a different design for a letter opener).

Design patents are granted for fourteen years from the date the original patent application was *granted* (the issue date).

Plant Patents

Unless your consulting practice involves farming, agricultural research, or horticulture, you will probably not need a plant patent. A plant patent is used for new strains of plants, such as new types of roses, various fruits, or drought-resistant grain. To receive a plant patent, an inventor must show the plant is (1) distinct, (2) new, and (3) asexually reproduced (originally produced in a method other than a seed, for example, budding, grafting, etc.).

Plant patents are effective when issued and give protection for twenty years from the date of filing the patent application.

Obtaining a Patent

Perhaps you've seen products marked "patent pending" or "patent applied for." These phrases mean that there is a patent application on file and put others on notice of the intent to protect the invention.

Obtaining patent protection can take a couple of years. You must, however, file an application promptly. An application for a patent may not be granted if it exceeds the one year bar, which means it has been more than a year since the invention was

- Patented previously (Again, an original owner sat on his or her rights and took no action to apply for patent protection during the years the patent was pending and the year after the patent was registered. The government is not likely to protect patent ownership rights for someone who does not take his or her own interest in those rights.)
- Described in a printed publication (in the United States or in a foreign country)
- Put into public use
- Placed "on sale," meaning used commercially

The checklist in Exhibit 11.3 describes the steps in obtaining a patent. The Patent and Trademark Office stays busy. According to figures provided by the U.S. Patent and Trademark Office, approximately six million patents have been issued. In addition, more than 200,000 patent applications are filed each year and the Patent and Trademark Office receives over five million pieces of mail each year. (Statistics provided in *General Information Concerning Patents,* reprinted 1997, U.S. Department of Commerce and Patent and Trademark Office.)

Once a patent has been issued, products covered by the patents should have the word *patent* or *pat.* and the patent number marked on the article. This gives notice that the goods are covered by a patent. It also provides stronger protection rights for the patent owner. For example, if the patented product is sold without the marking, a patent owner's damages are limited to when the infringer knew of the patent. If an item is not marked, you can see the difficulties of proving that the infringer knew of the patent. The patent owner must show that the infringer had actual knowledge of the patent, for example if the infringer is the owner's former employee or associate and knew of the patent application.

Applying for Foreign Patent Protection

Patent laws protect the invention inside the United States. To have protection in other countries, you must make a timely application in those countries. A "timely" application is usually within one year of filing your application with the U.S. Patent and Trademark Office. This depends on public disclosure or sales of the invention.

Do You Need a Patent?

In the industries in which you consult, you may have an incredible invention that could solve a common problem. You may have computer programming or an invention that would help your own practice and other consultants as well. Does that mean you need to patent the invention? You may if you think the invention would be popular and your time and money investment would be compensated. Once again, these are questions for attorneys who practice intellectual property law and know about patents.

Some basics about patents:

• *Do not use a service that advertises to inventors.* You want someone who has an attorney-client privilege and your best interest at heart.

Exhibit 11.3. Steps for a U.S. Patent Application.

1. Obtain brochures, and other information regarding patents from the U.S. Patent and Trademark Office by:
   - Calling the PTO General Information Services:
     (800) 786-9199 or (703) 308-4357
   - By writing to:
     Commissioner of Patents and Trademarks
     Washington, D.C. 20231
     Attention: General Information Services
   - Or by accessing the Patent and Trademark Office Web site:
     http://www.uspto.gov
2. Make sure the application is drafted to suit your needs. There is a provisional application for patent that only provides a date and usually does not give you the protection you need. Also, make sure that you choose the proper patent protection: utility, plant, or design.
3. Have a search made to make sure your invention is "novel" and patentable.
4. Include drawings where necessary. It is usually a good idea to have those drawings prepared by a patent draftsman.
5. Have a written document with the specifications (description and claims) and an oath or declaration. It is also a good idea to have the specifications and claims prepared by a patent attorney. The attorney must be registered to practice before the U.S. Patent and Trademark Office.
6. Mail all with filing fee to:
   Assistant Commissioner for Patents
   Washington D.C. 20231

Note: In much of the Patent and Trademark Office's literature, there are warnings about unscrupulous services offering to patent and/or promote an inventor's inventions. Be careful with these services. You could waive your rights or pay a great deal of money for nothing. The government publications tell you to thoroughly research any service. The materials also strongly advise you to obtain legal assistance from an attorney who is registered with the U.S. Patent and Trademark Office. The U.S. Patent and Trademark Office has a list of those attorneys it has registered, which is available by request.

- *Keep the invention a secret.* Patents are granted to new inventions, not ones that have been released to the public. Remember, your patent application will not be granted if you wait more than a year after your invention is described in a printed publication, put into public use, or used commercially. Also note that patent protection outside the United States may not allow the one-year period before applying.

- *Don't trust most people with the secret.* Usually, patent rights are granted to the person who invents the product and who files the application in a timely manner. Make sure your invention remains secret until the application is filed.

- *Know if you have any contractual duties to give patent rights to someone else.* If you are an employee and you create the invention as part of your job, your employer probably owns the invention. If you have reached an agreement with a consulting client that any patentable ideas you derive during your consulting with the client become the client's property, you may be contractually bound to give the client the patent rights to your invention.

Giving Credit Where Credit Is Due

C hapter Eleven discussed the importance of protecting your work product. What happens, however, if you want to use someone else's work product?

Calvin was asked to speak at a convention about consulting in the security industry, especially about guarding computer secrets. When Calvin was asked about his most difficult computer protection project, he revealed the client's name, the secret project they were developing, and how easy it was for people to break into the system. As an aside he mentioned the company had to terminate two people for looking at pornography sites, but said that they were told their firing was due to performance issues.

Commentary

In this situation there are a wealth of issues even if we discount the potential slander suit the two employees have regarding the termination for viewing pornography. (Remember, if the consultant can't prove the termination was for the misconduct, and here the employees were given a different reason, there is a potential suit for slander.) An even greater problem is that Calvin appears to have revealed his client's proprietary information. If he had signed a confidentiality agreement with his client, he probably just broke it. Also, finding additional work may be a bit more difficult once other potential clients find that he can't be trusted to maintain confidentiality.

USING INFORMATION AND MATERIAL
THAT DOES NOT BELONG TO YOU

People and organizations own information just as they own tangible assets. Using that information without authority or permission is as bad as taking someone's physical property without permission. Misappropriation of trade secrets occurs when there is an unauthorized disclosure of private information. A trade secret owner can bring an injunction to stop the use of the material as well as file a lawsuit for the misappropriation under a number of legal actions including tortious interference with business relations, unfair competition, and, if an agreement is present, breach of contract. Also, many states have enacted the Uniform Trade Secrets Act, which states what actions are not permitted and what remedies are available.

Criminal charges may also be filed. Misappropriation of trade secrets is considered a theft of property under state criminal laws and a newly enacted federal law. If found guilty, an infringer faces fines and even imprisonment.

HOW TO AVOID INFRINGING ON OTHERS' PROPERTY RIGHTS

You know that you don't want your hard-earned work to be presented as another's. You agree that you don't want to infringe on someone else's property rights. But as a consultant, you can't be expected to think of everything. What if you are not creative? Can't you use a quote or a cartoon that depicts the situation perfectly? What about copying a personality test or an assessment to use as an example with a client? What happens if you are training and want to use music to create a mood or atmosphere?

How do you go about obtaining the right to use something that is not your own and use the material in a way that is allowed by law? When dealing with protected information you have several choices. First, don't use it. Instead, invent something yourself that can serve the same purpose. A second choice is to use it and hope that you are a small enough fish that the creator won't ever find out or won't consider you worthy of attack. This is not an option an attorney or any reasonable person would advise you to take. Third, obtain the creator's permission to use the materials. You might be surprised to find how easy this is as well as how readily people will give you permission. Or fourth, you could acquire permission through a service or agent that represents the creator.

S C E N A R I O

After years of teaching, Stacy has become a consultant and trainer. During her years of teaching, she used portions of articles and cartoons with her classes. Although moving from the school environment to the corporate arena, Stacy still feels she is teaching . . . just at a much higher pay rate. Stacy is still using cartoons and portions of articles. One of her participants, the client's in-house attorney, asked her if she had permission to use the information she presented. Stacy told the lawyer that she was educating and therefore her use fell under the "fair use" exception. At the time, she was certain the attorney was just trying to show her up and show off his knowledge. Now, she is trying to remember what she learned in college about the fair use exception and whether it still applies to her.

Commentary

While Stacy is right that fair use is an exception to the copyright laws, it probably does not apply here. Fair use was created to protect librarians, teachers, students, and researchers, not consultants making a profit through training.

Stacy is making money in consulting. She is responsible for requesting permission for use of the materials and for paying whatever fee the author may charge. Failure to do so may expose her and her employer to a copyright infringement lawsuit.

WHAT IS FAIR USE?

Fair use was created as an exception to the copyright holder's rights in ownership. The "fair use doctrine" was created to provide balance between owners' rights and the public's need to have a free exchange of ideas.

The idea of fair use is that you are allowed to utilize a limited portion of another author's work without seeking permission first as long as you clearly acknowledge who wrote the material and where to find the copyrighted original. What constitutes a "limited portion" varies from work to work. To make this determination, you can consult with your attorney or request information from the U.S. Copyright Office.

The copyright fair use doctrine excepts use for nonprofit educational purposes. Without the fair use exception, students couldn't cite research unless written permission was granted. The fair use provision of the copyright law also protects use of materials for criticism, comment, and news reporting.

Although financial situations may be tough at times, consulting is not characterized as a nonprofit enterprise but a commercial one. Thus the fair use doctrine does not apply.

SCENARIO

In her informational packet, Peggy sends out copies of an article that featured her consulting practices. She also sends copies of other articles about the problems encountered by organizations that did not use consultants. Peggy likes to highlight one of the articles' titles, "Failure to Plan Costs Companies Big Bucks," as well as the statement inside the article, "A good consultant can help." Peggy just sat in on a lecture that discussed copyright law and wonders if she should edit her marketing packet.

Commentary

Peggy probably should edit her marketing packet. Luckily, this situation isn't too difficult to fix. First, she should contact the magazine that published each article to ask for permission to reprint the article. If the magazine does not own the rights to the article, the magazine's representative should be able to tell Peggy who she needs to contact. If Peggy has a few dollars, she may even be able to purchase some nice reprints of the article in which she is featured. Since magazines are interested in additional exposure, it is rare for a magazine to refuse someone permission to republish an article. However, it does occur. Once Peggy is granted permission, she should put the words "©[year]. Reprinted with the express permission of [copyright holder]" (or whatever wording is given to her by the magazine publisher) at the bottom of each page of the article.

SCENARIO

Carlos added humor to his training sessions to ensure that his audiences stayed interested and remembered the points he was trying to make. He frequently made overhead transparencies of cartoons and comic strips he found in newspapers and magazines. He would intersperse them throughout his presentations. Last month he presented at his association's annual conference. He used numerous comic strips to make his point about communication difficulties. Today, he received a letter from the attorney of a newspaper syndicate holding the rights to the work of one of the artists whose comic strips Carlos presented. The letter tells him to cease using the artist's work, to make a public apology to the association's membership, and to pay the syndicate past royalties for the cartoon's use. If Carlos does not comply, the letter states he will be sued for copyright infringement.

Commentary

Carlos should stop using the artist's work and try to negotiate a small royalty payment. But what constitutes a "public apology to the association's membership"? Maybe he could take out an advertisement in the association's newsletter or journal. Maybe he could mail a letter. Maybe the attorney will settle for an apology to the artist and the syndicate. In truth, Carlos got off easy. All he has to do is stop using an artist's work, pay the back royalties, and make a public apology. Carlos could have been facing something far worse, such as a lawsuit and statutory damages of up to $100,000 per infringement. In the future, Carlos should be sure to request permission to use this (or any) cartoon from the appropriate syndicate and pay the royalty fee associated with the use.

GAINING PERMISSION TO USE OTHERS' WORKS

Gaining permission to use another's work begins with your request. When requesting permission to use materials, you must make sure to keep clear records. If your use of the material is ever questioned, you want to have the documentation to prove that you submitted a request, received a grant of permission, and used the material appropriately.

When requesting permission, you must first determine who owns the copyright. Requesting permission to reprint a portion of a published book is usually one of the easiest processes because you need only contact the permissions department of the publisher. In other cases, determination of ownership can be more complicated. Does the cartoonist or the newspaper syndicate own the cartoon, or both? Does the recording artist, the group of musicians, the lyricist, or the studio's technical staff own the rights to a song you wish to use—or a combination of any or all of them? Obtaining permission to use music is very complicated and will be covered in greater detail later in this chapter. Your request for authorization to use material should be made in writing. The request should specifically address why you want to use the material, how and where you plan on using the material, and how many times you want to use it. You should also send a copy of the material in question.

An example of a letter requesting permission for a quote is shown in Exhibit 12.1.

💾 Exhibit 12.1. Sample Letter Requesting Permission for a Quote.

Ms. Sybil Light
Peale Center
66 East Main Street
Pawling, NY 12564

Dear Sybil,

As we discussed during our telephone conversation, my book, *The Business of Consulting*, will be published by Jossey-Bass/Pfeiffer in September, 1999. It has fabulous endorsements from Peter Block, Margie Blanchard, ASTD, *Training Magazine*, and two dozen other CEOs, executives, and consultants.

Each of the chapters opens with a quote—as many books do. I am writing to request permission to use a quote that is attributed to Norman Vincent Peale. The quote was in the book *Whatever It Takes*, published in 1994 by Compendium, Inc. The quote is, "If you put everything off till you're sure of it, you'll get nothing done." I would like to use it to open Chapter Four, which is titled "Starting . . . "

My publisher needs written permission to use this quote. For your convenience, I have enclosed a self-addressed stamped envelope. Please call me at (608) 742-5005 and let me know how to proceed. I look forward to your response.

Again, Sybil, thank you very much for your help.

Sincerely,

Elaine Biech
P.O. Box 657
Portage, WI 53901

An example of a letter requesting reprint rights for a cartoon is shown in Exhibit 12.2.

💾 **Exhibit 12.2. Sample Letter Requesting Reprint Rights for a Cartoon.**

Natasha Cooper
Reprints Rights Manager
United Media
200 Madison Avenue — 4th Floor
New York, NY 10016

Re: Reprint Permission for Dilbert Cartoons

Dear Ms. Cooper:

It is my understanding that United Media controls reprint rights for Scott Adams's cartoon "Dilbert." I am a consultant who presents training seminars on the legal aspects of consulting. Mr. Adams captures the essence of the ethical problems faced by consultants in the two cartoons enclosed. Please consider this my request to use both of these cartoons in future training seminars.

Over the next eighteen months, I will present this topic at approximately twenty functions at locations in the states of Texas, Florida, Georgia, and Virginia. It is anticipated that the attendance will range from fifty to four hundred participants at each session.

Of course, the proper acknowledgment will be placed at the bottom of each transparency.

Please let me know what fees are associated with this use and advise whether the artwork can be sent to me on a computer disk.

Please contact me at (972) 416-3652 if additional information is needed or another action should be taken on my part. Thank you for your help.

Very truly yours,

Linda Swindling, Esq.
The Peacemaker
1120 Metrocrest Dr., Suite 200
Carrollton, TX 75006

Enclosures

Don't forget that photographs also fall under copyright protection. The photographer's permission should be granted before you use a picture. Also, be careful with the Internet. Pictures placed on the Internet were taken by a photographer. Downloading a photograph from the Internet for your use may require permission from the photographer. Additionally, if there are people in the photo, you may also need to get a release from each individual.

You may unintentionally violate a copyright when you provide a photograph of yourself to another company to reproduce for publication, in marketing materials, or on the Internet. While the subject matter of the photograph is you, the photographer may own the publication rights so permission may still be required. Luckily, most photographers are only concerned that you return to them for reprints of the photo. This especially is true if the photographer knows the photo is made for marketing purposes.

Many times magazines and newspapers will take their own photograph of you to avoid infringing on another photographer's ownership rights. Other publications may request proof of your photographer's permission to allow you to use a photograph before the publication will reprint it.

If you are given permission to use another's work, you must still acknowledge the copyright holder's ownership. For instance, if you are reprinting cartoons on overheads, each transparency should state the date of copyright, the name of owner or owners, and the permission to use the material. For example: "Copyright © 1999 United Media International. All rights reserved. Used with permission of the copyright holder."

The use of the Internet has made copying text and information as simple as highlighting and copying. Be careful when using others' work to follow the permission stated in the legend. Don't forget to record your source while you have it on the screen. Also, spell out what your ownership interest is in information you put on your Web site or give in an e-mail.

In the consulting field there are many occasions when one consultant wants to use an instrument developed by another consultant. If you find yourself in this position, you must obtain either written permission or a license to use such an instrument. If you obtain a license, you must follow the terms of the agreement. A license is a contract. If you break the contract, you are subject not only to a copyright infringement claim but also a claim for breach of contract. In addition, it will be much easier for a copyright holder to show that you intentionally infringed upon the copyright because you knew to ask for a license to use the material. Willful or intentional infringement can subject you to some pretty hefty fines and damages.

Tim knew about copyright infringement and was not about to fall into the trap of copying information without permission. The only place Tim used work that wasn't his own was when he conducted exercises with small groups. In all of the various exercises Tim used, he was careful not to reproduce the work, either as a handout or on overhead transparency. Instead, Tim read the instructions to the participants.

Commentary

By reading the exercises, Tim is still infringing on the author's rights. Without authorization, Tim is "publicly performing" the written work by reading it. The copyright laws assign to the author the right to reproduce, display, publicly perform, create derivative work, and distribute the original work. Thus Tim is not permitted to perform this material without first obtaining permission from the author.

As part of his consulting services, Parker offered training to ensure that his clients' employees knew how to properly implement the quality management system he designed. To aid in his participants' receptiveness, Parker liked to use music during his training sessions. Usually, the selections were from various CDs that he played over a portable player. Parker found the perfect song that supported his theme of quality. Parker began using this song, "People of Quality," by the popular singer Jenny T. He has just been contacted by an attorney representing Jenny T. Apparently, Parker's latest training videotape, which was taped live and then edited, has the "People of Quality" song playing as Parker closes his talk. Parker did not contact anyone for permission to use the song.

Jenny T and her lawyer have filed for a temporary restraining order to prohibit Parker from playing the song at any additional speaking engagements and to ban the future sales of the videotape of Parker's event. They are also threatening to pursue this matter under federal law and to seek actual damages and a hefty fine for copyright infringement.

Commentary

Parker may have thought he was paying Jenny T a big compliment by using her song—but he is in big trouble now. Parker has not only infringed upon Jenny T's ownership rights, but probably the rights of all the people associated with the recording. He has also put his own video at risk, a video in which he has invested a substantial dollar amount. Without authorization, he can't use the video or he infringes upon others' copyright ownership. In addition, he can't copyright his own video because he doesn't have the right to use the materials in it.

MUSIC AND SOUND RECORDINGS

Obtaining authorization for the use of a musical selection or sound recording is more complicated than for print materials because you need to get permission of everyone who played a part in the recording. These owners can be the performers, the musicians, the composers of both the words and music, and in some circumstances the technicians—the people who record, capture, edit, and process the sound.

If a recording artist, a company, or a performer hires people to record the sound the ownership rights may belong with the artist or to the company or individual paying the workers under a work-made-for-hire agreement. However, watch out. Make sure you are clear about those ownership rights before using the material.

There are options with music. Rather than seeking the owner, you may be able to work with a music library that has the right to authorize use on behalf of all separate owners of the copyright. Usually these permissions can be obtained through Broadcast Music Incorporated (BMI) or American Society of the Composers, Authors, and Publishers (ASCAP). If you choose to work directly with the copyright owner, you will have to submit separate written requests to composer, lyricist, performers, technicians, etc.

Another option is to purchase or rent the right to use certain music that is developed for reproduction. For instance, television and radio stations use music that is recorded with the intent that it will be mass distributed. Some trainers use this type of music or sound effects in their programs. People who develop videotapes, Web sites, audiotapes, and promotional CD-ROMs use music and sound effects that are distributed for multiple uses. These products are licensed for use in a couple of ways. First is a *buy out,* which means that the CD-ROM or tape containing the selections is purchased and the purchaser is licensed to use the music or sounds as much as desired. Another method grants a license to use the selections and the licensee pays an agreed amount each time a song or effect is used.

If you or a conference hires someone to tape you during a training session, the person or technical company recording you may retain rights, and you may have to get written permission to use the recording again. If you use others' material during your performance, it is especially important to have proper authorization to use the material. Without proper permission, you will not be able to copyright your own tape.

HOW CAN PERMISSION BE GRANTED?

A copyright owner may just send you a letter granting you permission to use the material in response to your written request. The copyright holder may limit your use. There may be a charge.

If you are granted a license, you are in effect renting the use of the material. The license agreement could set out a flat fee for a fixed number of times you are permitted to use the material. You could have an agreement that requires you to pay a fee each time you use the material. For example, you might agree to pay a $5 royalty every time you use an artist's cartoon. Also, you could have a multiple-use fee that either increases or decreases as the number of uses increases. If the author does not want the work overpublicized, the fee would probably increase per use. If the author wants the publicity, the fee would probably decrease as the use increases. In all of these license fee arrangements, it is important to keep records showing the actual use. If your actions are ever called into question, you want proof of the agreement as well as the dates and places and the circumstances under which you used the material.

WHAT CAN HAPPEN TO YOU IF YOU
DON'T OBSERVE PROPERTY RIGHTS?

Because the government has decided to grant rights to encourage creative works and inventions, it has also created ways for owners to enforce those rights. The owner's remedies against a person or entity who has infringed on property rights vary, but all are designed to show the seriousness of infringement.

Penalties for Copyright Infringement

Bad things can happen to you if you are infringing on others' copyrights. The copyright laws are federal laws. The federal government in particular does not have a sense of humor about violation of laws it feels are important. (The penalties for tax evasion are a good example of this serious treatment.) On the severe side, an infringer could be subject to criminal sanctions for infringement with large fines ranging from $10,000 to $50,000 and even imprisonment. A federal court may order the infringer to destroy the violating works and to pay restitution or compensate a copyright owner for what the owner lost due to the infringement.

There are also civil penalties. In addition to receiving an *injunction* (a court order restraining the infringer from selling or making the product or continuing an infringement), a copyright owner can seek money damages. The owner of a copyright can seek damages for the infringement, lost profits, possible statutory damages, costs, and attorney's fees. For example, people caught counterfeiting NBA or NFL apparel must stop producing the material, stop selling it, destroy what they have, and pay money damages to the owners, and may face criminal charges. These statutory damages can be pricey, up to $100,000 per infringement.

Penalties for Trademark Infringement

Good news. You won't go to jail for infringing on someone's trademark or service mark. However, you may face a civil lawsuit for some severe penalties, including monetary damages.

Typically these penalties provide injunctive relief to prevent further use of the trademark and may require destruction of materials with the mark on them. If the trademark holder can prove sales taken from it or monetary damages, an infringer could be required to pay those amounts. Usually, the damages, especially for an innocent use of a mark, are not large. However, there are exceptions.

If the infringer has taken a great deal of money away from the trademark holder, damages can be larger. If the trademark holder is a small business and the infringer is a big company, juries and judges tend to award larger damages. Also, if the infringer knew about the mark and there is a "bad faith" adoption, the damages awarded by a court can increase significantly.

Penalties for Patent Infringement

As discussed in Chapter Eleven, patent owners have control on the use of their patented materials for a limited time. Violate the protected patent holder's rights and you face steep civil damages. These damages also include injunctive relief and orders by the court to cease all further infringement on the patent. Sometimes, infringers are ordered to pay a royalty for the use of the patent. If an infringer is ordered to pay lost profits or is found to have intentionally infringed on a patent owner's rights, the court-ordered damages can be extremely high.

Protecting Assets Through Insurance

SCENARIO

Jarred has been a corporate trainer for fifteen years. On weekends he conducts activity-based corporate team building. During the summer months he holds his team-building sessions in a nearby state park. During the winter months he rents the local gym. All of his work occurs as a result of referrals from friends and colleagues. Last month one of the participants fell off a wall and injured her head. She is still in a coma. Doctors predict that she may never regain consciousness. Jarred has never bothered with insurance or having participants sign forms releasing him from responsibility. After reading about the incident in the local paper state park officials have sent him a letter asking for more information about his team-building activities.

Commentary

Jarred is probably in big trouble here. Without an insurance company to adjust and probably pay the claim prior to legal action, it is almost certain that a lawsuit will be filed against Jarred's company and Jarred individually. Not only is the participant injured, she is probably injured for life. This translates into huge medical bills, loss of her relationship with her family, loss of her wages, and a damage exposure of millions of dollars. While a lawsuit could include her company and the state park, Jarred will be the target defendant since he planned and controlled the activity.

REDUCING OR PREVENTING EXPOSURE TO LIABILITY

Jarred could have conducted a comprehensive safety review of his own operation. For example, he could have hired an expert in the activity he performed (sport climbing) to make sure the basic safety measures were covered and that he hadn't missed anything. Remember, you can be experienced in the consulting business but not even recognize all the risks of your planned activity. He could have had each participant sign an acknowledgment form where the risks were set out clearly. The form could have been a release, but most states will not allow these releases to be enforced. However, the benefit of having a release form is to show that Jarred pointed out the risks and that the participant knew and agreed to accept those risks. This acceptance of risk may help in Jarred's defense and certainly shows that the participant was warned to be careful. Jarred also could have done a risk analysis and obtained all the necessary insurance policies to cover the various aspects of his business.

WHAT ARE THE RISKS IN CONSULTING?

You are a consultant. It is not as though you engage in heavy construction or have people working around dangerous chemicals. What are the risks of a consulting practice? Here are some questions to help you decide where your potential liability might lie with people with whom you have a relationship, such as your clients, event participants, or employees:

- If you give bad advice, what damages will your client or other person suffer?
- Does any activity involve a risk of serious personal injury? Exhibit 13.1 identifies some of these activities.
- Does your consulting involve a risk of financial loss to your client or a third person? These activities may include investment advice, sale or purchase of a business, starting a new business, hiring employees who have access to cash or other valuables, and the sale or purchase of real estate.
- Is your consulting subject to review by a state or federal set of standards?
- Could your employees, vendors, or service providers injure a client or a third party?

- Could there be claims by contracting parties, employees, customers, or vendors that you have failed in some obligation to them such as a breach of contract?
- Do you have a fiduciary duty to treat your client or client's business in a special trust relationship?

A yes to any of these questions could lead you to decide to purchase insurance coverage.

Exhibit 13.1. Activities That May Involve Risk.

- Sport climbing
- Wilderness camping
- Boating
- Any activity involving extreme temperatures (hot or cold)
- Skiing or snowboarding
- Traveling by bus or auto during bad weather or late at night
- Any access to alcohol
- Any involvement by children under the age of eighteen
- Any physical activity that could trigger a heart attack or stroke
- Any physical activity where a head injury, serious bodily injury, or a broken bone could occur
- Any travel by auto or truck that occurs on a daily basis (e.g., delivery service, trucking, or outside sales)
- Scuba diving, parasailing, or other activities often offered at resorts as part of a business meeting or incentive package you may have put together
- Medical procedures or medication
- Food service or preparation
- Handling of any dangerous chemicals, explosives, or flammable substance
- Any event involving traffic or crowd control
- Any event where personal security for participants is at risk

---

Additional Risks or Exposure

What is your potential for exposure to the risks noted in Exhibit 13.1? As a consultant what should you really worry about? Here are some other questions to ask yourself:

- Could you face losses, claims, or investigatory actions resulting from a violation of law or regulation that directly or indirectly involved you?

- Could you injure a stranger or any third parties through your products or services?

- Could you damage the property of others, whether that property is tangible (equipment, lease space, etc.) or intangible (trade secrets, reputation, etc.)?

- Could your own property be damaged through fire, theft, vandalism, or flooding?

A consultant must analyze which situations present the most potential for risk. As a consultant, you are considered an expert in your field. In consulting, you help clients analyze problems and risks all the time. You help clients plan a course of action that achieves results but also limits their exposure to backlash, to an unacceptable return on investment, to business losses, and even the potential of lawsuit.

As a business owner, you also look at your own risk factors and act accordingly. You may need to obtain a second opinion on the potential risks and safety measures needed and add a release for some exercises. A safety policy may need to be developed as well as a detailed disclosure of risks in your contract.

Just as you might be negligent in not advising a client to correct business problems you have identified, not addressing the potential risks in your business is gambling with your ability to do business in the future.

SCENARIO

When Kurt started consulting, he was never concerned about the protections of incorporating or the need for insurance. Why should he worry about lawsuits? If he were ever sued, there would be nothing in the end to pay a judgment. Kurt knows attorneys aren't going to work for free and that people don't sue others just to get a piece of paper that says they win. People want money. Since Kurt didn't have any money in the beginning, he presumed that he would not be a very popular target.

Due to some smart business decisions, Kurt saw a large increase in business over the next three years. He was able to invest in some important equipment purchases that would serve him well in his plans for future expansion. He was also able to indulge his dream of putting money down on a lakeside home to be used on the weekends. Kurt has just returned from his attorney's office. Apparently, a former client is suing him for damages in the sum of $500,000 claiming that the client lost that amount of money on a business venture that Kurt advised the company to pursue. Kurt's attorney estimates cases like this cost between $35,000 and $55,000 to defend. Looking at Kurt's contract with the client and the facts, the attorney tells him that there is a good chance he will have to pay part of the $500,000. The real battle will be limiting the percentage Kurt does pay.

If a judgment is entered against Kurt, his attorney tells him that he could file bankruptcy and would be able to keep his house, some personal property, and his car.

Commentary

Fortunately, Kurt became very successful in consulting. Unfortunately, he never bothered to protect his assets through insurance. What happens to Kurt now? First he scrapes together fees for his attorney. After that he has three choices. He can determine if he can negotiate some sort of agreement to pay the client, he can try to stall the inevitable during the lawsuit, or he can wait to see if a judgment is taken against him and file bankruptcy. If a judgment is taken against him, he will probably have to sell his new equipment as well as his lakeside home to pay it. Remember, Kurt did not incorporate or limit the liability of his company, so many of his personal assets are fair game as well. Bankruptcy is almost never an easy way to solve a serious financial problem.

INSURANCE

Many risks can be addressed through proper insurance protection. Saving a few dollars in the short term and leaving your business without protection can be devastating to your financial future in the long run.

Is Insurance Necessary for a Consulting Business?

There are generally two schools of thought. One group will tell you that having insurance makes you a target for lawsuits. The premise is that if you do not have any large assets in the business and you do not have additional personal assets at risk, no one will waste the energy and expense bringing a lawsuit that is uncollectible against you. If you are "judgment proof," why invest in insurance that gives a plaintiff an opportunity to recover? On the other hand, do you feel obligated to provide for the losses you caused?

Of course, if you have any success as a consultant or were previously successful in a field that allowed you to accumulate any savings or property beyond your homestead, then you are not judgment proof.

The other argument is that if people believe they have been injured by a consultant's actions, they will attempt to obtain compensation for that injury as well as punish the wrongdoer. The premise here is that you should have insurance to protect yourself from the people who will sue whether or not you have it.

Many lawsuits are filed against businesses and individuals who do not have insurance. Those businesses and individuals are still responsible for their own attorneys' fees as well as court costs and the costs of litigation, even if the suit has no merit.

One of the advantages of many insurance agreements is that they cover the court costs, cost of litigation, defense attorney fees, as well as any agreed settlement or judgment. Insurance companies certainly have more resources to defend a suit as well as the expertise to settle claims that do have merit.

The need for insurance is best determined when you look at the risks involved in your particular area of consulting as compared to what you have (your assets) that you might be at risk of losing.

What Do You Have to Lose?

As evidenced by the preceding scenario, it is of the utmost importance to understand that you may not be as judgment proof as you think. Even so-called debtor-friendly states allow very effective and efficient collection of judgments from self-employed persons. Some debtors attempt to evade collection by giving up their checking and saving accounts and living on a cash basis in a constant attempt to keep the plaintiff's lawyer from finding where they work or live. Unless it is your choice to live in constant fear, always looking over your shoulder, it is best not to assume you are safe from judgments. Further, if you are an employee, many states will allow a court-ordered garnishment of your wages. In either case, the plaintiff will recover at least some of the money from you, cost you thousands of dollars to defend the collection efforts, and probably make your financial life quite miserable. Your lack of insurance may be a deterrent 1 percent of the time, but the other 99 percent of the time, it will be a legal and financial nightmare for you. The safest and most professionally responsible course is to have at least enough insurance to protect your property and compensate your own clients if you make a mistake.

What Types of Insurance Are There?

For every potential risk, there is also a possibility of finding an insurance policy to protect against it. You've probably heard of a singer insuring his or her throat or of insurance for the replacement of expensive jewelry.

In choosing the proper insurance coverage for your business, you have to weigh a few factors. You must determine the cost of the potential liability and the likelihood of the liability to occur and compare those to the cost and protection offered by insurance. To help sort your options out, here are some of the various types of insurance policies:

- Professional liability or comprehensive general liability for your professional errors in judgment, your failure to do something, or your omissions.
- Business liability (CGL) for accidents or injuries to third parties.
- Property insurance to cover the cost of damage due to theft, fire, or wind or other natural phenomena.
- General liability to cover injuries or damage to third persons occurring on or by your physical property.
- Health (PPO, HMO, group, or individual health) to cover the cost of illness or injury.
- Disability income to ensure an income when the insured is too ill or injured to work.
- Disability overhead for paying overhead costs like rent and utilities if you become disabled.
- Umbrella policies (excess insurance) for the liability and property policies in place.
- Automobile liability insurance for payment and protection against claims due to automobile accidents.
- Workers' compensation to cover cost of injury to employees due to work-related incidents.

What Does Each Type of Insurance Cover?

To help you determine what types of insurance may the most useful to you, here is a brief description of each:

Professional Liability. This is the most common and a valuable insurance for a consultant whose main product or service is advice. If your advice turns out to be bad and causes injury, the insurance carrier will provide a defense attorney, pay court costs, costs of litigation, and pay any settlement agreement or judgment up to the policy limit. Many of these policies require the professional to pay the deductible amount first, and some policies also calculate all payments in a calendar year so that the total paid by the insurance carrier cannot exceed the policy limits for which you paid a premium.

Business Liability Insurance. Business liability insurance is a policy commonly known as a Comprehensive General Liability Policy (usually referred to as "CGL"). This insurance covers a wide range of accidents, including premises liability claims and injuries to third parties, but does *not* cover your own employees or property.

Property and Casualty Insurance. Property and casualty insurance is a very broad term used to indicate insurance policies that protect your own property from fire, theft, storms, etc.

Health Insurance. Whether it is called PPO, HMO, group, or individual health insurance, a health insurance plan covers all insured members for treatment of a wide range of illness and disease. Beware that many of these policies specifically exclude on-the-job injuries. In most states, health insurance is *not* a substitute for workers' compensation insurance.

Disability Insurance. Disability insurance is a policy that will cover a percentage of the person's monthly income should that person become partially or totally disabled. Be careful when buying disability insurance. Many insurance companies have greatly restricted what conditions are considered disabling. In the past, many policies stated that you were able to recover lost income if you could no longer perform your livelihood of consulting. Now, the trend is to consider disability as being unable to perform any type of work.

Disability Overhead Insurance. Disability overhead usually refers to a policy that will pay a portion of your overhead, such as rent and utilities, should you become totally disabled. Again, check the insurance company's definition of *disabled*.

Insurance for Employee Claims. Some companies now offer insurance against employee lawsuits. These are relatively new and such a policy provision must be specifically requested and added to the insurance agreement by the inclusion of an "endorsement."

Umbrella Policies. Umbrella policies are a type of excess insurance that provides a large amount of protection over and above the primary liability policies.

Automobile Liability Insurance. Automobile liability insurance is required in all states, but the minimum coverage is essentially useless if a serious injury or death has occurred. Make sure you have at least $100,000 per person and $300,000 per accident plus a $1 million umbrella to have adequate protection. Incredibly, the cost for this extra protection is usually very reasonable. For example, a $1 million umbrella policy can cost around $10 per month.

Other Types of Insurance. As discussed earlier, there are many special risk insurance carriers who will tailor your insurance policy to cover the facts of your particular consulting practice. Beware that the language in these policies is usually not state regulated and a good attorney is essential to make sure the policy you get is what you told the insurance agent you wanted. Be careful when trying to use your personal insurance policies (car, home, and so on) to cover your business risks. Usually, these policies have exceptions for business-related claims. If you are in a low-risk business, your premiums will be minimal.

Workers' Compensation Insurance. Workers' compensation insurance protects your company from injury claims by employees for on-the-job injuries, large and small. It is a no-fault type of insurance that will pay the medical bills and a portion of the lost wages to a seriously or not-so-seriously injured employee. It will also pay some lump sum benefits to the most seriously injured, but does not allow recovery for "pain and suffering."

The most important benefits of workers' compensation coverage are twofold. First, it provides protection of your personal and company assets from a catastrophic loss or catastrophic legal fees or both. Second, it protects your employees with at least a safety net of insurance.

Workers' compensation allows the injury claim to be handled by professional adjusters and defense attorneys that know the specific laws and are being paid by the insurance carrier, not you.

This insurance is required for all employers in many states. You can contact your state workers' compensation agency or your employment attorney to determine your state's rules on workers' compensation insurance. If you have only office employees, your premium should be reasonable. If your employees are engaged in any high-risk activities such as construction, dealing with heavy machinery, handling chemicals, or working in a potentially dangerous job like window washing, security, or transporting flammable liquids, then your premiums will be higher. Workers' compensation insurance is strongly recommended, particularly in the latter case, even if your state laws do not require it.

Should consultants opt out of workers' compensation? Consultants should have workers' compensation insurance unless certain unusual circumstances apply.

These circumstances are if state law allows it, the premium is unaffordable, *and* the consultant's employees only do office work. Otherwise, a consultant is risking a very dangerous lawsuit as discussed in the upcoming scenario. Generally, if you can afford workers' compensation insurance, bite the bullet and buy it.

SCENARIO

Lovick consulted on cleaning up environmental problems such as asbestos in buildings and gasoline and oil spills. As part of his services, Lovick and his employees performed environmental site inspections. On one such inspection, one of Lovick's employees put a ladder on an uneven surface. The employee fell and broke his arm and collarbone and will be off work for at least eight weeks.

The employee has just called to ask Lovick what kind of pay he can expect during the time off and where the doctor's bills should be sent. In addition to being out an employee for the next eight weeks, Lovick can't believe that the employee thinks he should continue to pay his wages as well as the medical bills.

The ladder was not defective. The employee just didn't use it as instructed. When business was bad last year, Lovick canceled his workers' compensation insurance. Lovick calls his attorney, who says pay up, shut up, and hope that the employee doesn't want anything extra.

Commentary

Lovick decided to run the risk and unfortunately paid a price for not having workers' compensation insurance. Hopefully, when he made the decision he made specific arrangements for his employee health coverage to also cover on-the-job injuries. If so, most of the medical bills should be paid by that insurance. Since money was tight, Lovick probably didn't provide any other type of disability plan for his employees that would cover a employee's lost wages. (Some employers provide a short-term and even a long-term disability plan for their employees as a company benefit.) Another benefit of workers' compensation coverage is that it would allow Lovick to turn the matter over to the plan. There the employee would negotiate regarding what medical bills and pay are available. Now, Lovick faces a risk of a lawsuit and has lost negotiation power. He is probably willing to maintain the injured party's salary, just to keep the employee quiet.

Unlike many employees of consultants, Lovick's people are in hazardous situations. Even though the accident was mainly the fault of the employee, Lovick would have to show that he was not responsible at all for the injury if a lawsuit was brought for those bills. This will be difficult to prove. Although he probably doesn't feel lucky, Lovick should feel fortunate that the injury wasn't more serious.

The real risks of not carrying workers' compensation. In some states, workers' compensation is not required. If you are short of money, you may have decided not to pay for workers' compensation insurance. However, if you look at it from another perspective, you may realize that you cannot afford to go without it. Without coverage you lose the statutory protection of having workers' compensation insurance. You are then liable to your injured employee if any act of negligence by you contributed to your employee's injury. In many states, the employer loses the right to claim any negligence on the part of the employee. For example: In Texas, an employer without workers' compensation coverage who is one percent (1 percent) negligent is liable for 100 percent of the following damages:

- All medical bills, past and future
- All lost wages, past and future
- Pain and suffering, past and future
- Permanent disability
- Permanent disfigurement
- Loss of society and companionship in death cases or other severe injuries

In addition, you must pay your own attorney's fees and costs of defense, which can range from $5,000 to $100,000 or even more.

If you decide not to carry workers' compensation, there are some actions you can take to help reduce your exposure. First you should have a comprehensive health insurance plan that specifically includes coverage for on-the-job injuries. Oftentimes this is a suitable substitute for the medical exposure, but no other protection is provided. Second, wherever possible, hire genuine independent contractors—they are responsible for their own insurance. (See Chapter Six for information on the distinction between independent contractors and employees.) Third, insure all your commercial automobiles and trucks with personal injury protection and medical payments coverage. Make sure your policy does not exclude on-the-job injuries.

How to Protect Your Business from On-the-Job Injuries

No matter if you have workers' compensation or not, you want to keep your employees and contract workers safe. One of the best ways to avoid your employees' on-the-job injuries is to prevent dangerous situations before they occur. Stress safety first to all employees. Make sure there are safety policies and procedures in place and that you enforce them. All your employees should receive complete training on the proper tools and equipment. Employees should be instructed about how to lift properly. Employees should be taught to ask for more instruction if needed and to ask for help from other employees. Warning signs should be posted and instructions given whenever a potentially dangerous condition exists.

SHOULD YOU INSURE AGAINST THE ACTIVITIES OF YOUR CONTRACT WORKERS?

The simple answer is yes, if you can. However, you must make sure the insurance carrier is notified *when you buy the policy* that nonemployees will be performing various functions under your general direction or supervision. Make sure to put your request for any special insurance coverage *in writing* to the agent who sells you the policy and check your policy when it arrives to make sure your special needs are covered. Some contractors do not have insurance, even though it is to their benefit. When a client or third party sues both your contractor and your company for actions committed by your contractors, it is extremely helpful to have your contractor insured as well.

SCENARIO

Narva had been consulting ever since she stopped practicing internal medicine nine years ago. As a doctor, she knew the importance of protecting herself against risk. Early into her consulting practice, she established a relationship with an insurance representative. Since she was no longer practicing medicine, she replaced her expensive medical malpractice insurance with a more reasonable professional liability plan. Knowing the importance of dealing with people who know their way around insurance, Narva has maintained her relationship with her insurance agent, even when he changed companies—twice. She faithfully followed him and converted her coverage to each new company's similar product.

Narva has recently received a letter complaining about advice she gave on a medical procedure that went awry and injured an infant. While upset, Narva knew that these were the reasons she covered herself with insurance. She called her representative who put her in touch with the claims department. Narva was shocked when the claims representative told her that her coverage might not cover the claim in question. Although Narva obtained her coverage to consult with doctors, there is language in the policy that expressly excludes her giving medical advice. The claims representative thinks this claim might fall into the provision regarding medical advice. The representative tells Narva that even if the claim is covered, she is responsible for the first $10,000 in attorney's fees and court costs and the first $10,000 to satisfy any settlement or judgment.

Commentary

Narva did what a good consultant should. She thought through her risks and bought insurance to cover those risks. How could this happen to her? Narva is facing a problem a lot of insured people face: the policy they thought they were buying is not what they actually have. Narva relied on the advice of her insurance agent. While a valuable resource, insurance representatives are human. They do make mistakes. While most have your best interests at heart and want to establish a long-term relationship, they are paid to sell policies. Unless you are working with an independent agent, the pay is usually better if the representative sells the company plan of insurance rather than the best plan to suit your needs.

Narva should have had the policy examined by someone else, preferably her attorney and an independent adviser, to make sure that her risks were covered. Remember too, that Narva transferred her policy two times. Each of those policies should have received the same scrutiny.

What will actually occur in this situation may be different from what the claim representative stated. The claim representative may not know of additional language in other places in the policy or even have Narva's exact policy in front of her. In some cases, the insurance company may go ahead and pay for her legal representation under a "reservation of right" letter but reserve the right to determine whether the claim is truly covered when the matter is resolved.

CHOOSING INSURANCE COVERAGE

So how do you know what you need and from which company to purchase it? Ask other consultants what insurance company they use. Ask if others have had good results when they had questions or made a claim. It is easy for a carrier to give an insurance customer a lot of attention when he or she is purchasing something. From your perspective, however, it's more important to note how the insurance provider treats you when you are asking for help or filing a claim.

You will want to discuss your current coverage and the cost of any additional coverage with at least two insurance professionals you trust. At least one should be an independent insurance agent.

If you have a certified financial planner or a qualified financial adviser, use that professional to help you identify your true financial risk. Also, this is one of those important matters where you need your attorney's input. Only an attorney can explain your legal rights and responsibilities. Have your business attorney review not only your contracts but also your insurance policies—before you ever have a claim filed against you. If you have formed a good working relationship with your attorney, your attorney already has a good idea of your general business and can help you identify potential risks and dangers before they become a nasty surprise.

Exhibit 13.2 identifies some questions you may wish to pose to the insurance agents you interview as you determine the coverage you will need.

Accidents, mistakes, and injuries are going to happen. Claims and lawsuits are going to happen. Insurance is a cost-effective way for you to protect your hard-earned dollars and be able to sleep at night.

🖫 Exhibit 13.2. Questions to Ask Insurance Agents.

- How long has your agency been in the business?

- How long have you been an agent?

- Do you only work for one insurance company? (This question will answer whether the agent is independent and can sell insurance that best suits your needs or is a captive agent of one company.)

- If not, how many insurance companies do you represent?

- Can you handle all of my insurance needs?

- Who do you recommend to handle areas of insurance you don't?

- Do you refer to other independent agents?

- Have you ever written policies for consultants?

- Have you ever written policies in my industry? (If you are in a certain field of consulting like safety or medicine, the agent should be familiar with that field.)

- Do you have any customer references?

- Do you have any references in my industry?

- Can I review a sample policy of what you believe I should have prior to buying?

- What are the features of the policy and how does the policy compare to others?

- What is the rating for the insurance company you propose to handle my business?

- How long have you been writing business for this particular insurance company? (You are trying to determine the agent's experience with this company.)

- Do you have any special certifications or training? (Some agents have taken courses and passed tests to better advise you. For example, CLU for life insurance agents, CFP for financial planners.)

Buying or Selling a Consulting Practice

The ultimate goal for some consultants is to build a profitable business and sell it one day. For consultants just beginning in the business or looking for quick expansion, buying another consulting firm is often a solution.

GETTING A BUSINESS READY TO SELL

Even if you are considering a sale in the distant future, it is never too early to begin the process of organizing your business to sell one day. With all of life's unexpected events, from sudden disability to a fantastic job offer or relocation, just the process of placing your business in order will put your mind at rest. (This is the same pitch attorneys give you for drafting a will. By the way, do you have one prepared?)

You will find questions to help you get your business ready to sell in Exhibit 14.1.

🖫 Exhibit 14.1. Questions to Help You Get Your Business Ready to Sell.

- Do you have a business plan?
- Have you listed your step-by-step approach to different aspects of consulting?
- Is your Rolodex file in order?
- Have you computerized your Rolodex file into a contact management system?
- Do you have a place where you can record notes about clients?
- Are your financial records are up to date?
- What are your reputation as a consultant and your goodwill in the community and your professional circle?
- Have you collected your glowing client letters into a notebook?
- Have you placed your news clippings in the same notebook?
- Do you have a list of your awards and of the organizations you have served as an officer or a member?

Business Entity

The first thing to consider is your business entity, as discussed in detail in Chapter Three. If you are currently operating as a sole proprietor or in a partnership, this may be the time to consider incorporating or forming a limited liability company. The transfer of your ownership is easier to document if you sell something tangible to reflect ownership interests in a business, for example corporate stock or a certificate reflecting membership interest in a limited liability company. Some potential buyers hesitate to purchase a company without documents that prove the company exists in a more formal form.

Name Change

If desired, a name change could be phased in over a period of time before the anticipated sale date. Having a well-established name for your consulting practice adds value for a buyer. However, if your name is personally tied to the business and you will no longer be a part of the organization it may be more difficult to sell your business. For example, a company named John Smith and Associates may be more marketable as Consulting 2000 or another name that is not tied to its owner. You may want to begin that transition now, to allow the name's recognition to grow and be linked with your business reputation. Announcements to clients of a name change are common. For instance, "Our name has changed but our quality commitment to you hasn't. John Smith and Associates is now known as Quality Commitment Consultants, Inc. We look forward to a successful new year."

Determine Your Assets

Have you thought about what you have that someone would want to purchase? Do you own furniture? Do you have office equipment? Do you have computers or a fax machine? How about your reference library? Would you even want to sell these items?

The greatest value of your consulting business, however, is not based on equipment and furniture. Usually value is determined by the intangibles of your business. Your established client relationships, your database, your consulting processes, and your procedures are all more valuable to a buyer than your furniture or equipment. As much as you can, put these intangible aspects of your business into an organized structure. The more documentation you can provide, the more your intellectual property and intangible assets will be valued. Pull out your business plan—or, if you don't have one, go to Chapter Three and create one. List your step-by-step approach to different aspects of consulting.

Make sure your Rolodex file is in order. Better yet, computerize your Rolodex file into a contact management system where you can record notes about clients and your contact with each. Make sure your financial records are up to date and that you can trace the amount of business as well as the referrals attributed to each client. Have your accountant draft a profit and loss statement. Buyers prefer organized businesses where established procedures are in place. As much as possible, they want turnkey operations that allow them to pick up where you left off.

Just as important and often overlooked is your business name—your reputation as a consultant and your goodwill in the community and your professional circle. *Goodwill* is an intangible asset that basically means the positive image or favorable impression people have about your established business. Collect those glowing client letters into a notebook. Place your news clippings in the same notebook. Create a list of your awards and the organizations you have served as an officer or member.

Employees of the Seller

As the seller, do you have an employee or employees that will continue their employment and can help another consultant with their knowledge of the workings of the business? Could a buyer afford the salaries of the employees? Can the business be run effectively without them? If employees are terminated, who will pay their unemployment claims? This will probably be the new owner if the business continues under the same type of structure, unless agreed otherwise. Can the seller or buyer find another place of employment for workers during the transition phase?

Exhibit 14.2 provides questions regarding employees of the seller.

Exhibit 14.2. Questions Regarding Employees of the Seller.

- Are there employees who will continue their employment and can help the purchaser by sharing their knowledge of the workings of the business?

- Do you have any consultants or employees who are willing to teach the new owners your processes and introduce them to your customers?

- Will a buyer be able to afford the salaries of the employees?

- Can the business be run effectively without the current employees?

- If employees are terminated, who will pay their unemployment claims?

- Can the seller or buyer find another place of employment for workers during the transition phase?

How Do You Price a Consulting Business?

What is a consulting business worth? Start by determining what it has been worth in the past. How much did your profit and loss statement show in earnings for the last five years? What amount of accounts payable could you reasonably rely on receiving in the next two years? What are your known expenses?

The exact determination of the value of a consulting business is difficult. For example, if you are the only employee of your consulting business and you will no longer be a part of the business once you sell it, then the value of your business may only be that of your processes and your list of customers. However, if you have many consultants and many employees and you are willing to teach the new owners your processes and introduce them to your customers, then the value of the business might be greater.

To determine the value of your consulting business, you have to look at many factors:

- Customer base
- Accounts receivable
- Debts and obligations
- Transferable goodwill
- Assets of the business
- Established business procedures
- Continued participation of current owners
- Employees

Exhibit 14.3 summarizes what you need to know to put a price tag on your consulting business if you are the seller. The details of assessing the value are discussed later in this chapter, in the context of purchasing a business.

GETTING YOURSELF READY TO PURCHASE A BUSINESS

So you want to buy a consulting business. Here are some ideas to prepare you for such a purchase. First, how are your current finances? Do you have enough money in the bank to cover at least the essentials for the next six months? It is important

**Exhibit 14.3. Questions to Help
Price Your Consulting Business for Sale.**

- What has your business been worth in the past?

- How much did your profit and loss statement show in earnings for the last five years?

- What amount of accounts receivable could you reasonably rely on in the next two years?

- What are your known expenses?

- What do you have that someone would want to purchase?

- Do you own furniture?

- Do you have office equipment?

- Do you have computers or a fax machine?

- How about your reference library?

- Which things do you really want to sell?

- Can you trace the amount of business as well as the referrals attributed to each client?

- Has your accountant drafted your most recent profit and loss statement?

that you have some money put aside for the transition period. You will need these funds to cover the lost income when some clients choose not to stay with the firm and to meet expenses as you build the business.

How will you fund the purchase? Are you able to finance a purchase through family loans or savings? Are you going to approach a lending institution? If you have some credit problems, can you clear those up first through payment or negotiation before applying to a bank? Do you qualify for a small business loan? Have you considered owner financing? (Owner financing—where the owner agrees to accept part of the purchase price in deferred payments—is discussed in more detail later in this chapter.)

Exhibit 14.4 identifies the questions to ask yourself when getting ready to purchase a business.

💾 Exhibit 14.4. Questions to Assess
Your Ability to Purchase a Business.

- How are your current finances?

- Do you have enough money in the bank to cover at least the essentials for the next six months?

- Do you have some money put aside for the transition period to allow for some clients' not staying with the firm and to meet expenses as you build the business?

- How will you fund the purchase?

- Are you able to finance a purchase through family loans or savings?

- Are you going to approach a lending institution?

- If you have some credit problems, can you clear those up first through payment or negotiation before applying to a bank?

- Do you qualify for a small business loan?

- Have you considered owner financing?

How Do You Know That the Value Is Accurate?

A trusted accountant is a must in a business valuation. What do the numbers on the spread sheet really mean? Do they correspond with other financial data? Where are the hidden costs?

The value can be determined by several methods:

- An accountant or appraiser can value the business.

- A business can be compared with similar businesses and their value.

- The value can be determined by the going rate—the general price level at which businesses of a similar size and income level have been sold in the recent past.

Using an accountant to arrive at a value by examining the profit and loss numbers, finding other businesses for comparison, or determining that similar businesses have a going rate of three times the accounts payable are all valid ways of determining value. However, no matter what method or combination of methods you use, the value of a business comes down to two issues. First, what is a qualified buyer willing to pay? Second, what is the seller willing to accept?

If the three valuation methods point to a business value of $300,000 but no buyer wants to pay more than $250,000, then the market value of the business is $250,000. On the other hand, the market value may turn out to be higher than the valuation methods predict, especially when the services provided are in demand and the transfer of the practice will be a smooth one. If the seller's reputation and goodwill are well respected, the seller is willing to continue to provide support when needed, and the buyer's professional needs are met by the purchase, the value of the business may exceed $350,000.

SCENARIO

After Gregg agreed to purchase Michael's consulting practice, he was elated when Michael agreed to help in the transition. Michael had twenty-five years of consulting experience and a wealth of time-saving procedures that Gregg thought he could put into practice immediately. To Gregg's surprise, Michael seems to spend most of their time together reminiscing about past consulting experiences. Gregg has received little or no useful information regarding Michael's clients and has an idea that one of the greatest time-saving practices may be to ask Michael not to return. Also, Gregg has a sinking suspicion that Michael is not ready to leave the practice of consulting. In fact, Michael has mentioned on a few occasions that Gregg would have made a good partner. Gregg wants nothing to do with Michael or a partnership of any kind. He just wants to get to work.

Commentary

Sometimes good intentions do not bring good outcomes. Gregg could just grit his teeth and hope the situation one day gets better. However, Gregg is a consultant. He has experience with business relationships others might not. Gregg has an opportunity to practice his communication skills. He can tell Michael his reservations about how the transition is proceeding and ask for Michael's guidance about how to continue. Gregg could enlist Michael's help in drafting a proposed time line and schedule for the transfer of this information. Alternatively, Gregg could thank Michael for his time and tell Michael that he wants to work in the business for a while, and that he will call when he has questions. Michael may be having reservations about letting go. Maybe a nudge from Gregg to leave this chapter of his life will make any future meetings or phone calls more business focused.

PARTICIPATION OF THE FORMER OWNER

As in any situation, there are advantages and disadvantages of the continued participation of former owners in a consulting business that's been sold to new owners.

Advantages

From the buyer's perspective, the seller has unique knowledge that has been developed over the years since the beginning of the business. This may include nuances of the consulting processes used, idiosyncrasies of the clients, details that win contracts, special business development techniques that are uniquely effective within industries, or a host of other subtleties and distinctions that made the business successful. It might take the buyer the same number of years to acquire that knowledge. This learning curve can be reduced greatly if the former owner provides consistent coaching to the new owner. In addition, the former owner's presence in meetings, involvement in correspondence, or input in contracts may assure clients that they will continue to receive the kind of service they have become accustomed to with the former consultant.

From the seller's perspective, staying involved helps ensure that the reputation built by the company will continue into the future. This also ensures that the business will succeed—an especially important point if the sale involves owner financing, as it means the new owner will be able to continue to pay for the business. On the other hand, should the new owner not accept the advice of the former owner, the former owner would be a firsthand observer of the demise and would know what to do to pick up the pieces if necessary.

Disadvantages

Having the involvement of a former owner is not always an advantage. If you are purchasing a business that is on the downturn as a result of the previous owner's activities, it may be your primary objective to separate the previous owner from all aspects of the business. Also, if you are purchasing the business with the intent of revamping the business to your own style, you may not want to include the previous owner in any transition.

From the buyer's perspective, having the former owner constantly around for every business opportunity may get old. The buyer may feel constantly watched and judged for every move. Also, if the new owner has a new idea for the business, the former owner may squelch it out of a desire to do things "the way we've always done them." This could result in a lost opportunity. Finally, the buyer should consider the dynamics created by the presence of the former owner.

From the seller's perspective, it can be very difficult to watch your baby change and grow into something other than what you intended. Sometimes a clean break is the best move, especially if your personality is more the controlling style.

Usually it is best to weigh the options available and then determine the best choice for your circumstances. Based on the experiences of consultants interviewed, they suggest aiming for the shortest amount of time possible. It's easier to invite a former owner to stay longer than to ask a former owner to leave sooner!

OWNER FINANCING

SCENARIO

Micah sold his business to Edna two years ago. With the money his wife makes, his savings, and Edna's monthly payments, Micah took a sabbatical from work and returned to school to complete his master's degree. Edna had been making consistent monthly payments under the ten-year purchase agreement until three months ago. When Micah called Edna to ask where his last three months of payments were, Edna told him something he couldn't believe. She said that she was no longer working with any of the clients Micah gave her and didn't feel the business was worth his price. She said she had learned that Micah's reputation in the consulting community wasn't the glowing one he had portrayed. Instead, every consultant she has met who knows him says he is behind the times and an idiot. To support the sale, Micah does have a dated payment schedule that Edna signed.

Commentary

Ten years is a long time for a structured sale. Micah and Edna have entered into an agreement of sorts. There is a signed payment schedule as well as past checks showing payment from Edna. One of Micah's legal remedies would be to file a lawsuit and use the payment schedule and Edna's payments under the schedule as evidence of their deal. Unfortunately, Micah will make many trips to the courthouse because he probably won't be able to collect the future payments until each is past due. Micah doesn't have any "acceleration" language or an agreement in place that would make all the future payments due when one was missed. Edna may also be able to use the legal argument that Micah sold her a "false bill of goods" or that he misrepresented what his business was worth. Micah's best bet is to quickly reach some sort of agreement with Edna.

After two years, Micah should have finished that master's program or be mighty close. He may decide to simply go back into consulting, rekindle the client relationships that left when Edna took over, and start again.

Owner financing by itself is only as secure as the person who is purchasing the business. What guarantees does an owner have that the buyer will make a go of the business or turn out to be a good consultant? If an owner agrees to finance the sale, the owner remains tied to the former consulting business's success until the debt is paid.

With that said, owner financing can work and may be a valid option if the owner is dealing with the right person as a buyer. For instance, the purchase may spread the income from the purchase over a long enough time period to create some tax savings. Stock or ownership interest in the company could be purchased through a stock purchase plan. This would keep the majority of ownership in the seller's hands until the buyer paid a substantial amount. Also, owner financing may be the only method available to make the sale work. If the buyer doesn't qualify or the consulting practice is not valued at the amount a lender would finance, an owner wanting to pursue other interests or retirement may be forced to finance the purchase.

What happens when the business is sold but the buyer doesn't pay? You can always file a lawsuit. However, if the buyer is not paying you, there may be no money to collect if the judge finds in your favor. To avoid having to file a lawsuit, take advantage of contractual protections available to you as a seller at the time of the sale. You could have a provision that allows for a sum immediately payable or "liquidated damages" if the buyer defaults. Another contract might allow you to regain ownership if a certain number of payments are missed or if you buy back the buyer's interest at a nominal rate. The seller can also take a security interest in the assets sold and record the lien to provide collateral for the payment.

OTHER FINANCIAL CONSIDERATIONS

There are financial considerations other than financing the business and determining its value. These considerations are just as important.

Who Pays the Debts Outstanding?

Does the seller make sure everything is paid before the transfer or does the buyer assume the debts as well as the future profits of the business? If the buyer assumes the debts, is that arrangement approved by the seller's creditors? As a buyer, you do not want a surprise in the form of an overdue bill for a large amount of money as you assume ownership of the business. A formal sales agreement should list all amounts outstanding, accounts payable, and whether the seller or the buyer will have ownership or be responsible for each account.

Can the Seller Receive Future Profits from the Business?

The seller can do whatever is legal and the buyer and seller agree to do. A provision for a percentage of future profits may make both parties try harder to promote the business and make the transition smoother. If the seller has a vested interest in the success of the consulting practice, the seller will be more available for advice and the buyer won't have the feeling that questions are a nuisance.

INTERFERENCE WITH A BUSINESS

SCENARIO

Steve recently sold his small consulting practice that specialized in creating Web sites. As a part of that sale, he signed a non-compete agreement for the next eighteen months. A friend five hundred miles away has asked Steve to assist him with creating a Web site for his new catalog company. Steve is wondering what he should do.

Commentary

Steve has some options. He can refer his friend to the buyer and make a phone call asking the buyer to give his friend a price break. He can create the friend's site for nothing. Steve can call the buyer and ask if creating a site for a friend five hundred miles away is in any way a problem to the buyer. Or Steve can justify taking the job by telling himself that the buyer is not marketing to anyone five hundred miles away, the deal is for a friend who will swear to secrecy, and the buyer will never find out about it. Tempting as it may seem, this type of secret deal can really come back to hurt someone in Steve's position. It not only seems to violate the terms of the agreement, it looks like he thought it was wrong and hid his actions. Juries don't like sneaky behavior.

What Constitutes Competing Against a New Business Owner?

The purpose of a non-compete agreement is to allow the new business owner the benefit of buying the seller's business, the reputation in the community, and the name. If a seller opens shop just down the street, it defeats the purpose of the purchase and sets the buyer up for failure.

The parties may agree to limit competition in their purchase agreement. If the parties agree that competition means not contacting anyone for consulting work in a hundred-mile radius for two years, then such contact would be considered competition. Two independent consultants can agree to almost anything restricting competition. However, as discussed in Chapters Six and Eleven, covenants not to compete are much harder to enforce when the agreement involves employees.

SCENARIO

Amelia agreed to buy Tyrone's business. The papers are signed and during the next ninety days the two will be involved in the transition phase. During the transition, Tyrone determines that Amelia uses the DIPS personality assessment instead of the STOP method he has always used. Tyrone knows how undependable DIPS can be. He worries that the clients who have placed so much faith and trust in him over the years will now be misled by Amelia, a new consultant who doesn't even know to use the STOP method. Tyrone can't control the fear that all his work will be undermined. Tyrone begins calling his most loyal clients to suggest that once he is no longer available, they contact Victor, a reliable consultant who is a strong believer in STOP.

Commentary

Tyrone has clearly interfered with the success of Amelia's future business. Since Tyrone sold Amelia the business along with its clients, this interference could greatly decrease Amelia's potential profit. Amelia can do a few things. If she finds out about the phone calls before the business sale actually takes place, she may be able to back out of the deal. If she learns of Tyrone's interference after the transfer of ownership, she will have to prove the loss of business from the clients he contacted. This can be shown by a discontinuation of services or the client's increased use of Victor.

Tyrone had other options that would have been aboveboard. He could have told Amelia he had reconsidered the sale. He could have kept his mouth closed. He might have even tried introducing Amelia to the STOP method and selling her on its merits. Tyrone's phone calls were underhanded and sneaky and have probably exposed him to liability if Amelia decides to sue him.

How Does Someone Interfere with Business Relations?

Quite clearly Tyrone interfered with Amelia's business relations. If you contact people and try to convince them not to do business with another consultant, you have interfered with business relations. Another way of interfering with a business relation is using false information about a company in an attempt to disparage or discredit that company and gain a customer.

PUBLICIZING THE OWNERSHIP TRANSFER

If you are the seller, you want others to know that the buyer is now responsible for the debts and obligations of the business. You accomplish this notification in a number of ways. First, you make sure that any business filings with your state or county are changed to list the new owner as the contact person or the "agent of service." You should also advertise by filing a notice to creditors in the notice section of the local paper.

Also, if the buyer will occupy your leased space, you need to make sure the change complies with your lease and that you have the landlord's permission. The same is true for the transfer of leased office equipment or arrangements with other service providers.

Avoiding Legal Problems

onsultants could avoid most of the biggest legal problems they face. Most often, they fail to recognize that problems will arise. In any arrangement, there is a possibility for miscommunication and misinterpretation. Preparation for addressing items of conflict is imperative to prevent conflict from escalating and to ensure smoother business transactions.

SCENARIO

Yumeko landed a contract with a candy manufacturer several weeks ago. Up to this time the company has provided very little training in the communication and supervisory areas. A new plant manager wants to change all that. He expects the plant to improve communication, increase quality, decrease errors, and improve teamwork within and across departments. Yumeko's contract calls for her to custom design a comprehensive training program for all supervisors and managers in the plant. She has just started working with Anton, the director of human resources, to lay out the plan.

Yumeko and Anton were discussing these plans on the telephone last week. Just as they were saying good-bye Anton said, "and I'm really looking forward to my turn for one-on-one coaching." Yumeko hung up the phone not certain about what Anton meant. "One-on-one coaching" was not in her contract. The more she thought about it the more it bothered her. She called Anton several minutes later to clarify what he meant. Anton told her that, yes, one-on-one coaching with the top managers was a part of their agreement. Anton seemed to be a bit irritated that Yumeko didn't remember and chided her for forgetting such an important detail.

Yumeko knew coaching wasn't part of their agreement, but said, "Let me check our contract and look at my notes. I'll get back to you." When Yumeko read the contract, she confirmed that one-on-one coaching was not in the contract. When she read her notes, she saw that while the client team had discussed one-on-one coaching (an idea that had been presented by another consultant who was interviewed for the project) they decided to wait until later to decide if they would add it to Yumeko's work. Instead it was decided that a pre- and post-survey conducted before and after the eight training modules would determine if follow-up coaching would be required.

Yumeko faxed the contract and a cover memo summarizing the conversation based on her notes to Anton. Yumeko followed up the fax with a phone call to Anton to ask if he wanted to build in the coaching at this time. After reviewing the contract and the conversation, Anton remembered the course of events. Yumeko offered to prepare a proposal for the cost of one-on-one coaching and get it to Anton immediately so that he would have the approach and cost to consider as the time came closer to making that decision.

Commentary

This is an example of great diplomacy on Yumeko's part. Instead of reacting initially, she investigated the facts. She was organized and relied on documents and notes instead of memory. The result is a good one. The client was happy and not made to feel stupid for his mistake. The consultant maintained control of the situation and didn't end up adding services for free. Best of all there is a possibility for additional work if the proposal for one-on-one coaching is later approved.

The opposite result could have happened if Yumeko hadn't shown restraint and courtesy. She could have told Anton he was wrong during their first phone conversation. Yumeko could have relayed events of the meeting and described the conversation without going back for support. It appears Anton genuinely did not remember the change. After all, Yumeko was one of several consultants the team interviewed before hiring her for the project. Acknowledging Anton's position, referring to outside written materials, and giving him an opportunity to vent and cool down before the next conversation all helped her identify and correct a potential trouble area before it could grow.

This book has concentrated on ways to avoid legal problems in your consulting practice. In Chapter One, ways were presented to limit the use of lawyers. You can see that Yumeko followed the advice and employed several of the ideas, including these four that you will recognize from Chapter One.

- She responded to a client's complaints in a timely manner.
- She showed professional courtesy and concern for Anton's complaints.
- She kept notes of her conversation with the team that hired her.
- She confirmed their business agreement in a contract.

In addition, Yumeko went the extra mile and prepared an addendum for Anton. All of this turned Anton's initial chiding into a positive outlook and built a more positive relationship between client and consultant.

GOOD BUSINESS PRINCIPLES

Plan to conduct all your business following a few good business principles. This more than anything extra you can do will help you avoid legal problems.

- *Make sure your actions are perceived as fair.* Perception is everything. Even if your actions are legal or within the bounds of your contract, do you appear fair? If people perceive that they are being taken advantage of or that you are not playing by the rules, there is a greater chance that they will retaliate.

If you would not feel comfortable with your peers' hearing of your contemplated actions, without the benefit of your explanation, rethink your next move. Those same questionable actions may be discussed at dinner parties, meetings, and on the phone by other consultants who have heard of the situation without an opportunity for you to respond.

- *Stick with a process known to produce quality results.* Every successful business has a process that is guaranteed to produce quality. As a consultant, you have a set of procedures that has worked for you time and time again—whether it's a survey, an interview process, or a data-gathering procedure—so you stick with them.

If you are asked to try something new, inform a client that you will be willing to try it with a smaller group as a pilot test. Be honest with the client that you cannot guarantee the results. Also, build in time to evaluate the results with your client before moving forward.

- *Only do work you are qualified to do.* As a consultant you may be asked to perform work for which you do not feel qualified. At times you can become qualified by taking a class, reading, or working with another consultant. If that's the case, be honest with the client, get yourself up to speed, and then go for it.

However, there are other times when you need a particular degree, license, or certification before conducting work or giving advice. As a consultant you may at times come close to giving the same advice an attorney or accountant might provide. You don't want to be accused of the unauthorized practice of law or be held to the standards required of a CPA because you are considered to be giving tax advice. Ask your attorney if the services you are contemplating are services normally performed by an attorney or an accountant.

WORK WITH YOUR ATTORNEY

Often people think of attorneys only when there is a problem. A successful businessperson will also think of attorneys as consultants who prevent problems from occurring.

- *Involve counsel early.* For example, in a complex business transaction an attorney can point out tax concerns, potential regulatory risks, laws affecting the deal, risk exposure to your business, and alternatives—before you have committed your money and efforts to a proposal that won't work.

- *Review everything your attorney sends you.* You are a partner in your legal representation. The person ultimately affected by those legal contracts or attorney letters is you. You are in the best position to determine what is required and what might be missing. Read and review everything that is created on your behalf.

- *Don't ignore your attorney's advice.* Your attorney has your best interests at heart—and not only because you pay the bill. Attorneys have an ethical requirement to offer advice that represents their clients' best interests. If you disagree with the advice given or want a different course of action, begin asking questions. What are the reasons for this advice and what are the alternatives? People who ignore legal advice or choose a course contrary to the advice given often find themselves in exactly the situation they were trying to avoid.

- *Ensure that your contracts are clearly drafted.* Often your own contractual language ties you to something that you may not have intended. Are you clear about what services you are promising? Do you spell out what happens if additional days are required or information is not provided by the client as promised? Does the language state exactly when and how you are to be paid and what happens if you do not receive payment? You may think your agreement is clear, but you wrote it. You may assume some points that others won't. Make sure you have it examined by people who understand consulting contracts and by your attorney before you use the agreement.

- *Standardize your agreements where possible.* If you have a consulting agreement or a contract that you plan on using again or a trade secrets agreement you want people to sign, use your attorney to create some standard forms that need little customization for each job. As tempting as it is to tweak and revise forms as each occasion arises, avoid the temptation to change approved forms. Put that creativity to work in your consulting practice instead.

- *Make sure you understand the contracts you sign.* Perhaps you have told your clients that the only stupid question is the one that isn't asked. Follow this sound advice when signing contracts. Make sure you ask the client for clarification if you don't understand the contract or it does not accurately reflect your understanding of the agreement. After you receive that clarification, run it by your own legal counsel and determine if the explanation you are given is reflected in the agreement. If it is not, ask your attorney to draft the language needed so that you can present it as an amendment or revision to the agreement you were sent.

WORK WITH YOUR CLIENTS

You can avoid legal problems by ensuring that you work with your clients before and during the contracting process. Most important, be honest with your clients about your expertise and experience.

Kashita has provided consulting to a heavy equipment manufacturer. Although she has her four-year degree, she is continuing to work on a safety certification. She has been attending night classes but still hasn't received all the training necessary. At first the client didn't ask her to assist on the safety areas. After her second month, however, the client started having problems with hydraulic lifts and asked Kashita to help. Kashita knows that only people with safety certification should work on the lifts. Unwilling to admit that she still wasn't certified and believing she could do the job, Kashita agreed.

Unfortunately, something went wrong and three employees were hurt on the job. The incident might have happened anyway—even if Kashita had been certified. However, the special part that broke would have been covered in her safety certification course. The client learned that she wasn't certified and filed a lawsuit against Kashita. The client claims that it is impossible for anyone not trained to understand the intricate safety details of hydraulic lifts and that an expert would have prevented the accident.

A judgment is granted against Kashita. The judge determined that a person certified in safety for hydraulic lifts would have discovered the defect in the special part. The court holds Kashita to the expert standards she held herself out to possess. According to the judge, a certified safety consultant should have known about the defect.

Commentary

Kashita was sued for failing to perform the required duties of a specialized professional. Although she didn't specifically say that she had the certification required, she also didn't refuse work for which she wasn't qualified. She was probably surprised that she was held to the expectations that accompany the certification.

Don't hold yourself out to a certain professional standard if you lack the required training. Lying or misrepresenting yourself to others will stay with you the rest of your career. Just as honesty about your experience is important, it is just as imperative that you consider your potential client before forming a relationship. Don't be so quick to accept work unless you are certain that you know the client is one who will follow up on commitments made.

• *Select the right clients.* This could mean rejecting lucrative work with clients who may have dubious motives. Not all clients are good clients. Other consulting professionals like attorneys and accountants do not say yes to all the people who contact them as clients, so why should you?

• *Avoid pitfalls with clients before they occur.* Before beginning any project, it is important to have a discussion with the client regarding what potential problems could occur and a means for resolving them. (See Exhibit 15.1 for a list of questions to use during these discussions.) With dispute resolution methods in place before conflict occurs, both you and the client can concentrate on the issue at hand instead of the means to resolve the conflict.

🖫 Exhibit 15.1. Questions to Address with Your Client.

• If I have problems receiving information or cooperation as promised, to whom should I go?

• What problems have you had in the past with consultants?

• How did you resolve those problems?

• How could the problems have been avoided?

• Do you have any concerns with our relationship?

• How will we resolve issues if we can't agree?

• *Continue to communicate with your clients.* The same good communication skills that are a must as a consultant also will help you to avoid courthouse visits. Maintaining a calm demeanor, listening, and helping people reach a solution will help resolve more disputes than all the legal advice you could ever receive. Calmly asking an outraged client about the issues that need to be remedied—instead of responding in an angry fashion—will generally defuse the situation and promote a reasonable resolution. Although the services you provide and the business you run are personal to you, remember to practice those same communication skills you use with your clients when facing problems in your own practice.

• *Build a way to resolve disputes into all contracts.* If you plan to have a continuing business relationship with an organization or an individual, there's a good chance you will eventually have a dispute, a disagreement, or a miscommunication of some sort. Acknowledging that not every deal goes as planned and not every project works as well in real life as it does on paper is a big step to resolving disputes.

How can you plan for dispute resolution? Generally there are several steps. You could specify a contact person to be called as the first step. If that conversation does not resolve the situation, an in-person conference with the key people can be held in a specified number of days. If the conference does not settle the issue, a predetermined mediator could be called or the local mediation center could be contacted. If mediation is not effective, the dispute generally goes to final arbitration. Arbitration is a process where someone familiar with the industry or a panel of three people familiar with your industry or the problem at hand hear arguments and make a decision on who is right.

This dispute resolution process seems a little bit much to put into all of your ongoing contracts, right? You can't imagine having your client or another consultant sign a contract where the dispute process is spelled out like this. You can't fathom sending this type of language as an addendum or addition to a contract you receive, correct? For a moment, consider your alternatives.

If you could not reach an agreement through your own efforts in conversations, meetings, and mediation, who would you rather determine your dispute in the end? A judge who doesn't know you, a jury of people not qualified in your field, or some professionals who understand the nature of the matter before them? Put in another way, if you were about to invest $50,000 in a project that could either net you $500,000 or force you into bankruptcy, who would you want to help you make that decision? Would you go out and take a random poll of the next twelve people you see on the street or would you talk to a professional?

Or perhaps you see the need for a better way to resolve disputes out of the courthouse, but how do you get other parties to sign off on such a concept? Are they going to think that you plan on being a troublemaker? A presentation to others regarding a plan for dispute resolution might go something like this:

"I want to have an ongoing relationship with you as a client (vendor, consultant, or whatever) for a long time. While I do not anticipate any problems in the future, you and I both know that things can come up. I don't want any potential disputes or disagreements to slow down the process or harm the relationship we've established. Therefore, I'd like us to agree to a way we can handle disputes if any should come up in the future. I have some ideas and would like to know if this process is acceptable to you or if you would like to recommend another effective method."

What's the reality here? Are you or your attorney going to be presenting your side in front of an arbitrator any time soon? Probably not, but at least you have a process to which you and your client have agreed. If a dispute raises its ugly head, you might say, "Well, it looks like we are disagreeing on this point. This is the reason we have the dispute resolution process we do. We have a way to resolve this problem without affecting progress on the work. When is the best time for our first meeting?"

As a consultant, it is critical for you to be prepared for all the possibilities of miscommunication and misinterpretation. This preparation ensures that your business will run more smoothly, your clients will be more trusting, and you will be happier. Taking the time to develop processes to help you avoid legal problems will always be time well spent.

chapter SIXTEEN

What to Do When You Have a Legal Problem

The client won't return your phone calls, let alone send you a check for the money you are owed despite your many requests. The landlord refuses to tell the business next door that creating an advertising campaign for a stereo manufacturer does not give them the right to play music loud enough to be heard six blocks away. The employee you terminated for unauthorized possession of company property (funds from your checkbook totaling more than $2,500) is now suing you for race discrimination.

You've done all you can to avoid legal problems and yet a problem still exists. What do you do now? How do you enforce your rights and resolve these issues? Well, you first determine what those rights are. Your legal position may be better or worse than you think.

Marta and Carlos are both consultants. Marta has a clear contract with Carlos, who licenses Marta's material. Marta has just learned that Carlos has been making his own copies and using them with a new client for over a year without paying Marta the fee as stated in their contract.

Marta goes to see her lawyer who agrees that Carlos is in violation of their contract. Marta knows that Carlos will not be frightened off by a letter on attorney's letterhead because his spouse is a lawyer. Marta is really mad and states that she will show Carlos because it is the "principle of the thing."

Marta's attorney tells her that she has a right to sue under the contract and recover damages ranging anywhere from $20,000 to $30,000 depending on how the contract is interpreted. The attorney further tells Marta that filing fees are $150 and that it will cost an additional $50 for *service,* which means that the constable's office will officially hand the lawsuit to Carlos. The lawyer informs Marta that with the current caseload faced by the judges it will be approximately eighteen months to two years before the case is heard by a judge or jury. The lawyer estimates attorney fees to be $10,000 on a typical case of this nature and that at least two depositions will need to be taken, costing Marta another $750. The attorney feels fairly certain of a judgment for Marta if all the facts are as she is stating. However, the attorney tells Marta that a lawsuit is always a gamble and that a jury could find in Carlos's favor if they like Carlos or believe his testimony over hers. The attorney also says that most cases are settled before trial ever begins.

Marta reconsiders her previous desire to sue. She knows that Carlos has free legal advice via his spouse. Marta is also afraid of the backlash the lawsuit might create among Marta and Carlos's peers. Marta resolves to call Carlos again and see if they can resolve the matter. If her efforts don't result in a positive outcome, Marta decides that she will not pursue a lawsuit because her time and sanity over the next two years are worth more than the $10,000 to $20,000 she might clear.

Commentary

Good for Marta. She found out about her rights and her options. Only then did she make the decision about whether to pursue the claim or not. Marta has reached the conclusion that many people make. It appears that she will not pursue the suit. This does not mean that she is just walking away. Now that she is armed with the knowledge that she is in the right under the contract, she has also decided to make another attempt at resolving the issue herself.

THE COSTS OF A LAWSUIT

Financially, a lawsuit in a small claims court may cost you a few hundred dollars in attorneys' fees. It is not unusual to see larger suits have attorneys' fees well into six figures. Whether you win or lose the lawsuit, the costs and time compared to the possible recovery may make you a loser in the end. Not only are there monetary costs associated with lawsuits, your reputation, both with clients and in the consulting community, may be at risk.

Either way, you are probably not going to continue a business relationship with someone against whom you filed a lawsuit. Rarely do consultants go back to work for a company they fought. On the other hand, rarely should consultants go back to work for a client against whom they could have sued. Why would you want to do more business for someone who did not live up to commitments the first time?

SCENARIO

William and Tom have shared an office for the past nine months. Three months ago William asked Tom to partner on a new project with a new client. William had made promises to the client that were nearly impossible to keep and lied about his experience to both the client and Tom. In the end William told Tom that he would be unable to pay him as much as they originally agreed upon, because the project cost more and took longer than originally expected. Tom doesn't want anything more to do with William, including having to face William over the next few months in a lawsuit. Tom moves out of the office they shared and notifies others that he is setting up his own shop. Tom is pleasantly surprised by the response. One client calls Tom and requests a proposal ASAP. This client stopped doing business with Tom when he and William began sharing office space. A consultant friend of Tom's calls and congratulates him on the move. He tells Tom that William is renowned for big talk and little follow-through.

Commentary

Usually, a consultant, a company, or a service provider who has deceived you or failed to deliver has a history of similar behavior with others. Your continued adherence to professionalism, good record keeping, and quality work product can have surprising results. The decision to maintain your professionalism and divorce yourself from the bad situation can sometimes result in positive outcomes.

SCENARIO

Myra kept good business records. She always sent letters confirming agreements with all service providers. Recently she has had problems getting service for her copier. She has maintained her own service record and can show exact dates the service provider did not show up to repair her copier as promised. Myra files a suit in small claims court with a sworn affidavit supported by her business records. Myra's records also show how much it has cost her to use the services of a local printer and the number of trips she has made when her copier was down. The copier service provider doesn't have records and can't swear that Myra's are wrong. The judge finds in Myra's favor and awards her $2,000.

Commentary

Myra is glad she kept good records. The copier service provider probably now sees the value in good record keeping. Remember, the court can apply the law only to the evidence presented. Myra had the evidence through her business records; the copier service did not have the records to contradict hers. Myra wins. They lose. While there are exceptions, it is best to remember this rule, "If it isn't in writing, it didn't occur." Document, document, document.

TO FILE OR NOT TO FILE

Earlier in this chapter Marta made a decision to forgo a lawsuit. When is that the better route? The questions in Exhibit 16.1 will help you determine your decision whether to file a suit or not.

SCENARIO

Chekhov has completed his project with a large soft drink bottling company. The company has always been fifteen to twenty-five days late in paying his invoices, but Chekhov had always trusted them to come through. However, Chekhov's last two invoices are now forty-five and seventy-five days past due. He has called his contact repeatedly, but the contact has not returned the phone calls. Chekhov contacts his attorney, who writes a demand letter on law firm letterhead. Within

💾 Exhibit 16.1. Questions to Answer Before Filing a Suit.

- Did you do everything you agreed to do?

- Is the quality impeccable?

- What complaints has the client had with your work?

- Were the complaints legitimate? (Did they have merit?)

- Who else inside the company has been involved? How? To which side do they lean?

- What records have you kept? What do they document?

- What counterclaim might the client file? What proof would be produced?

- How legitimate are the client's claims or defenses?

- How will your reputation be affected? What will affect it?

- Will the effect on your reputation be different depending upon what the client does or the results of the lawsuit?

- How will your insurance rates be affected, especially if there is a counterclaim?

- Does your insurance policy cover a judgment against you?

- How supportive will your insurance company be?

- How much do you and your attorney estimate legal fees and expenses will come to?

- How much time does your attorney estimate will be involved (actual time, as well as extent of your participation)?

- How much money is involved? Is it worth it?

- What happens if you lose? Can you afford it?

- Is the potential of losing worth the risk?

- What can you do to prevent this from happening again?

ten days the client calls the attorney and a deal is worked out. Chekhov learns that the client has decided not to use all of Chekhov's books. Through his attorney, Chekhov and his client agree that the client will return the unused books and Chekhov will receive payment for the rest of the bill.

Commentary

Sometimes a well-drafted letter on an attorney's letterhead will get attention. That attention can be good and bad. Some companies will bristle at such a letter and put their attorneys on the matter. In some of those cases, the personalities can be removed and objective issues handled. In other cases, attorneys are paid to defend, not settle. It helps to know the culture of the organization you are dealing with before making the decision to send such a letter. Be sure you think through all the possible outcomes and your next step with your attorney before acting.

SCENARIO

Susan provided a one-time training session to a large organization. Several months later Susan found out that the organization had duplicated her protected materials and was using them in-house. Susan was in good legal standing. She had protected her materials by listing the copyright information on each page and had filed the material with the Copyright Office. Susan also had an agreement with the organization. When she pointed out the violation of the agreement as well as the fact that the entire course was available for purchase at a substantially higher price to her contact, Susan was repeatedly ignored. Susan reiterated her position to the president of the company in a demand letter. This time the message was heard and she was sent a check for the full amount of the program.

Commentary

Occasionally, lawsuits are avoided by going to the power source. Don't be afraid to continue upward in an organization with your complaint or problem. Your tenacity may be rewarded.

OTHER ACTIONS

There are many other actions you can take without filing suit. Let's explore some of these.

- *Ask your attorney to call your client.* Not only does the call show that you are serious about the problem, it also shows that you are willing to pay to do something about it.

- *Place a phone call yourself up the chain of command.* Sometimes the person who has the ability to correct the problem has not been made aware of it. Do not be afraid to continue to ask for someone who has knowledge of your situation or the power to fix the issue.

- *Send a well-drafted letter to the president of the company.* Once again, you show how serious you are about a situation and you send that information to someone with the power to correct the problem.

- *Negotiate for payments.* Mentally and financially, it is easier for people to handle smaller payments over a period of time rather than a large sum all at once.

- *Reduce the amount owed or services to be provided.* Face it. If you can get 80 percent or 90 percent of the amount owed to you, you might be better off than pursuing your legal remedies over a long period of time.

- *Conduct a face-to-face meeting.* It is harder to tell people no in person. Want proof? Think of how persuasive the good salespeople you know can be. Be sure to handle yourself professionally in any such meeting and don't lose your temper.

- *Offer to mediate before filing suit.* This is used to show you are trying to compromise, if necessary, and that you want to continue a relationship.

- *Request a respected peer or member of the community to listen to both sides and give advice.* Once again, you are open to being told you are wrong. You are working to keep the relationship with the person.

- *Find out what the other side needs from you in order to fulfill an agreement.* Sometimes just asking what the other side needs can help create an easy solution without much effort on your part.

- *Agree to take equipment or bartered services rather than money.* Sometimes there is no money to pay your bills. It is a fact of life. However, if your client has something you need or services you can use, take those instead and maintain the relationship. Check with your tax advisor on the tax implications of this method.

BRINGING A LAWSUIT

Before you ever consider bringing a lawsuit, you should visit an attorney. However, if the attorney quickly agrees that you should take on your nonpaying client or attack another consultant, you need to think twice. Don't get hooked on the "it's a matter of principle" argument or caught up in the emotional aspects. A lawsuit consists of many components, one of which is a significant amount of time.

Lawsuits are time-intensive. You can't just turn this over to your attorney to handle. You will need to devote time to depositions, preparation for depositions, document preparation, meetings with your attorney, document review, and even mental preparation. Lawsuits are inconvenient. One of the benefits of being a consultant is having some control over your schedule. As a litigant or someone involved in the litigation process, you work around the courts' and attorneys' schedules.

WHEN YOU ARE SUED

Probably, your first knowledge that a lawsuit has been brought against you will be when a constable or officer of the court hands you a copy of the paperwork. This delivery is called *service of process* or just plain *service*. There are all sorts of rules regarding how the lawsuit is served on you, but suffice it to say that if you're holding it, you have been notified.

The citation tells you that a lawsuit has been brought against you, by whom, and by what case number you will need to refer to it. The citation also has a document attached to it known as the *petition*. The petition tells you what you are being sued for and who is suing you. The person suing you is known as the *plaintiff*. The citation will tell you in which court the lawsuit was filed and the number of days you have in which to file an answer to respond to the things said in the petition. The number of days is important since you usually have a short time frame to file an answer.

What do you do now that you have been sued? You have just been handed this lawsuit, probably where you work, maybe where you live. Now what? First off, don't panic. While a lawsuit is scary, remember the only thing a person has to prove when filing one is that they have the money to pay the filing fees. Unfortunately, anyone can bring a lawsuit against anyone else for any reason. Later, the plaintiff has to prove why the suit was brought, but not when filing the original papers.

Now sit down and read the thing. Who is the plaintiff bringing this suit? What does the petition say is the reason? You may have suspected that the lawsuit was coming. If so, see what is actually being claimed. If this has taken you by utter surprise, figure out who the party is that is suing and try to determine your relationship to them and what they claim went wrong.

It is not uncommon to receive a lawsuit from someone you can't place immediately. An employee for a client company may sue you as well as the client company and the employee's coworker. Someone may have mistaken you for someone else. You may have known the firm's name that you worked with but not recognize the name on the petition, which might actually be that of an owner of the firm.

Next, call your attorney. No matter whether the lawsuit is valid or not, an answer must be filed on your behalf to protect your interests. Your attorney is the best person to draft this answer. What if you don't want to validate this frivolous lawsuit by filing a response? Well then, more likely than not, you lose automatically. If you don't file an answer and you don't appear in court, a default judgment can be taken against you and you will have admitted to the claims alleged.

What if you don't have a lawyer who could handle this litigation matter? You will want to find a lawyer—quickly! The best ways to select an attorney were discussed in Chapter One. You form a relationship. The attorney knows your business and you feel comfortable with the attorney's level of competence. However, what if you find yourself in need of immediate legal advice and you do not have an established relationship? Call the professionals you trust. Call your accountant. Contact consultants you respect and ask which attorney they use. You don't have to tell your peers the reason if you don't feel comfortable doing so. Despite your discomfort, the announcement that you have been sued probably would not come as a shock to anyone you call. In today's litigious society, lawsuits are common and are seen by many professionals as one of the known hazards of doing business.

PLEADINGS

After your attorney files an answer, it becomes part of the pleadings. *Pleadings* are the legal documents filed with the court; they are used each time a party wants to take an action with respect to the case. For instance, if the lawsuit is filed in another county but should be filed in your county, the attorney would file a pleading regarding moving the lawsuit.

Now that you have been sued, you are also subjected to *discovery requests.* More than almost anything, people don't like the discovery portion of litigation. You have to provide answers to questions or the *interrogatories* asked by the other side's attorney. You also have to dig through your records and provide the documents that are related to the case in response to *requests for production.*

Discovery is designed to level the playing field and ensure that each party has the same information as everyone else. In theory, providing the other side with all the information requested may help the party decide there is not enough information to proceed with the lawsuit or better yet, that your position, not the plaintiff's, is correct. More likely than not, you will feel that you are supplying the other side with information to help prepare the case against you. However, the other side will have to provide the same type of documents to your attorney.

Typically documents have to be copied and given to the opposing party in a fashion similar to how you keep them. Therefore, if you have each contract in a separate file, you would allow the other side to pay to have them copied in that form. Sending the other side a big trash can full of poorly copied, crumpled documents would not be playing by the discovery rules. Give all requested documents to your attorney to review and send. Don't hide the documents that are not in your favor. Chances are the attorney for the other side has a copy of the things you don't want seen and is waiting to see if each document is produced.

What about depositions? You have probably seen quite a few courtroom scenes where the witness is called to the stand to testify. Actually, parties and witnesses may be required to testify long before the trial occurs if they are *deposed,* which means they have their *depositions* (statements) taken. Just as in a trial, you swear to tell the truth and then the opposing attorney starts asking you very detailed questions. Generally, you are asked to remember past events in great detail.

A deposition can be a painstakingly slow process. While a deposition may be videotaped, your answers are usually recorded by a court reporter typing everything you say, exactly as you say it. The worst part is later reading your deposition and thinking, "Where did that answer come from?" If you have not had your deposition taken in the past, ask someone who has. Chances are they have not forgotten the experience.

There are things you can do to improve your deposition experience. Your attorney can explain these in detail. Typical suggestions for improving your depositions are identified in Exhibit 16.2.

> **Exhibit 16.2. Tips to Improve Your Deposition.**
>
> - Get a good night's sleep.
> - Review the information you have already provided the other side.
> - Look through the documents to be discussed.
> - Take breaks when needed.
> - Ask questions when questions to you are not clear.
> - Don't answer anything you don't understand.
> - Answer only the question asked.
> - Don't volunteer anything that is not asked.
> - Be polite.
> - Don't ramble.
> - Don't worry about what the other attorney's strategy is.
> - Don't guess. "I don't know" is a perfectly good answer if it is true.
> - Speak clearly, loudly, and don't try to speak when someone else is talking.
> - Most important, tell the truth.

Do not think that your attorney will just go to court on your appointed trial date. Before a typical trial, attorneys have had at least a few meetings or *hearings* with the court. Sometimes hearings are used to make the trial process run smoother and more efficiently. At other times, hearings are used by disagreeing attorneys who want the court to break up the argument.

A NOTE ABOUT ATTORNEYS

It is tempting to place the blame for the costs and time-consuming process on attorneys. The benefits of having a trusting relationship with your attorney have been referred to repeatedly. Most attorneys are very committed to their clients and are faced with a tough job. If trial attorneys don't follow all the rules, observe the deadlines, and file all the motions they should, they can be accused of malpractice or not actively representing their clients. Most of the blame for lawsuits should fall on people who mishandle complaints, miscommunicate, do not read or understand agreements entered, or are not proactive in finding resolutions.

MEDIATION

With all the procedures and steps of litigation, the surprising reality is that most cases don't reach an actual trial. Somewhere along the way, the parties settle or one party realizes it doesn't have a case or a judge determines that the case is not worthy of a trial because the rules weren't followed properly or a party doesn't have a case under the law.

Because judges have so many cases to determine, many states require that the parties try to settle their differences with someone who is impartial, a mediator, in a process called mediation. What are the chances of a settlement agreement in cases where the parties have been fighting each other for many months or even many years?

It may be surprising that the chances of settlement are very good. If a great number of cases settle at mediation when people are in the throes of battle, it makes sense that most of these cases could have been resolved when the problem first arose and while the parties had an opportunity to salvage the relationship.

SCENARIO

Terik started his consulting firm six years ago. He has eight employees: six consultants and two administrative assistants. Because of his firm's continued growth, he decided to expand his office space to almost three times the size. He and the landlord drew up the plans, which included bathrooms within the space. Shortly thereafter Terik took off for Europe, where he combined a ten-day consulting assignment and a two-week vacation.

When Terik returned to his remodeled office space he found many changes to the plan and no bathroom! When Terik called the landlord, the landlord said he had faxed Terik the changes before Terik left for Europe, including the fact that local code did not allow the bathroom addition as originally planned. He also said that Terik had agreed to the changes before he left for Europe. In addition to having verbal approval from Terik, the landlord states that in lieu of the bathroom he built bookcases to make up for the difference.

Terik insisted that he knew nothing about the changes and will not pay the monthly rent the landlord quoted him. He insists that had he known of the changes, he would not have agreed and would have moved his office to other space. Terik brought a lawsuit against the landlord and has not paid rent for the last five months.

Terik is used to being in control and making decisions. He has not enjoyed this five-month battle. He didn't like having his deposition taken. Being interrogated by the opposing counsel was the most irritating thing he'd been through in a long time. Now Terik is being told that if he doesn't settle in mediation, the case will cost him almost as much in attorney's fees as he has spent to date. In addition, Terik just found out that his case isn't as good as he first thought because the landlord found out about a note Terik thought no one knew about. It seems that three months into the lawsuit Terik's secretary found the dated fax the landlord claimed to have sent. On it were Terik's handwritten notes: "same rent," "bookcases," "no bathroom," and "code." When she showed him the fax, he started to recall the phone call that came the same day he left for Europe. He had completely forgotten the conversation. To save face Terik pretended he had not seen the fax. Now the landlord is threatening to bring a counterclaim against Terik. Terik's attorney has told him that hiding the document really makes him look bad and could be a violation of court rules regarding full disclosure.

If things weren't bad enough, his attorney has told Terik that he estimates the trial will take more than three days and that Terik must be there the entire time sitting beside him. The court clerk has set the trial for the week before Terik's quarterly financials are due. His attorney also says that if he asks for a continuance it could be another three months before the case is called for trial again.

Commentary

Welcome to litigation—where the courts make the rules, the attorneys use the rules to compete with one another, and the clients feel out of control most of the time. Terik has just learned a hard lesson. Bringing lawsuits can cost big bucks as well as time commitments. Not being honest with your attorney can cost you even more.

TRIALS

The last part of the litigation process is the actual trial. Most trials don't conform to the exciting moments of questioning and the rapid-fire attorney banter as portrayed in the movies. Instead, much of the trial process is slow moving. Questions are asked and objections are made. Attorneys approach the judge and argue outside of everyone else's hearing about which document can be used as evidence. Rules are followed in introducing that evidence. Witness testimony is disjointed. Jurors watch in silence, relying on attorneys and witnesses to fill them in on the important details. Attorneys and judges use words that no one understands outside the legal profession. Courtrooms are not comfortable. As a party to the lawsuit, you have little to do but watch, listen, and write little notes to your attorney about who is not telling the truth and why.

Trials are always a gamble because the outcomes are decided by juries and judges. A juror's chief qualifications are a voter's registration card or a driver's license and a lack of knowledge about the parties. While the U.S. jury system is a good one, it still has flaws. Despite the best intentions and the judge's instructions otherwise, a juror's personal bias does come out. A juror may not like the personality of a witness or an attorney, which can subconsciously affect a decision.

At the end of the trial, there will be a verdict. That verdict can award nothing to either party or something to you and nothing to the other side or vice versa. What is important is the cost associated with arriving at that verdict. Look at all the stages during a lawsuit where you will spend time and money.

THE FUTURE FOR OPPOSING PARTIES

After you survive your brush with the legal system, will you ever repair your relationship with the other party? Do you want to? It is rare after battling it out that parties will ever want to see each other again. Sometimes you can't avoid an individual due to the close professional or personal community you share. Sometimes the other party may still remain the only way to obtain a service, for instance the phone company or a provider of training materials.

However, in other instances, opposing parties have decided to take a lawsuit out of their attorneys' hands and out of the legal system entirely. Some pick up the phone and arrange a compromise. These conversations are best when your attorney has been notified of your intention and asked for advice. Some people resolve issues at a settlement meeting or have a frank talk with each other at a mediation. Some litigating parties maintain or even create a positive relationship after the fighting ceases.

SOME BATTLES MUST BE FOUGHT

Like it or not, some lawsuits are necessary. If there truly are competing interests and no compromise is possible, a lawsuit may be your only option. And some people have to see that you are willing to fight before they will concede or compromise.

Having acknowledged this fact, the authors still stress that if there is a theme to this book it is this . . . *if at all possible, avoid the courthouse.* Intentionally avoid litigation through planning, negotiating, and resolving disputes wherever possible when they arise.

LEGAL TERMS GLOSSARY

Abate means to suspend actions or obligations for a period; a tenant's right under a certain lease agreement to suspend rental payments in whole or part until a problem is corrected.

Acceleration is to increase obligations; clause in a contract to make all the future payments due when one payment is missed.

Acceptance is the agreement to an offer or proposal by words or actions; one of the elements of a contract.

Agent is one acting for another by permission or apparent authority.

Agent of service is the designated representative for a company who receives the notice of a lawsuit.

Apparent authority means the appearance of permission to act for someone.

Application is requesting court action; see also petition.

Articles of organization are the documents filed with a state to create a Limited Liability Company.

Assign means to transfer the right the owner or contracting party has to another.

Assume is to pretend or do business under another name; also to agree to take on another's obligations.

At-will employment means that an employee or employer can terminate the employment relationship for any reason without any prior notice to each other. Found in some states.

Bad faith means dealing unfairly with the intention to mislead, commit fraud, or infringe on another's rights.

Blended rate is one billing method of attorneys in which the higher-level attorney's rate is reduced and the lower-level associate's rate is raised to find a medium rate.

Bona fide means genuine, sincere, open, and dealing in good faith.

Breach is violating an agreement, law, or right; breaking a contract or failure to live up to the terms.

Cause of action means the facts that support the legal action one wants to pursue.

Citation informs a party of a lawsuit and contains information regarding parties, court, and reference number; usually served with a petition.

Common law means those laws created from tradition, practice, and by court rulings as opposed to those laws created by various legislatures.

Consideration means the value that will be exchanged; one of the essential elements of a contract.

Contingency fees are arrangements where some or all of the attorney's fees are postponed until the client recovers money; most commonly seen in personal injury or collection suits.

Contract is an agreement between parties; minimum requirements are an offer, acceptance, and consideration.

Counterclaim is when a defendant brings a claim against the plaintiff which defeats or weakens the plaintiff's claim.

Counteroffer is to respond to a proposal with another proposal instead of accepting the offer.

Deep pockets are those individuals and businesses who are considered good sources of money to pay a judgment if the court rules against them.

Defendants are the parties who are contesting or defending against the lawsuit brought against them.

Depositions are where parties and witnesses testify or have their statements taken under oath.

Disclaimer is a statement that denies or rejects responsibility for something.

Discovery is the process used to gather information and documents to prepare for a trial; usually interrogatories, requests for production, requests for admissions, and depositions.

Disclosure means to reveal or make something known.

Doing business as ("d/b/a") is a term for people or companies conducting businesses under an assumed name.

Equitable describes those actions or standards that are considered fair for the situation.

Fair use is an exception to the copyright holder's rights in ownership; usually used for research, teaching, library use, and in parody of material.

Finish out is the remodeling or interior construction to be completed in leased space.

Flat fee is a set amount for an attorney's fee based on the project or work to be completed, instead of billable hours.

Flexi-place arrangements is the term used to describe the various nontraditional working environments.

Fraud is misleading, misrepresenting, or omitting information so that someone will act upon the information and suffer a legal injury.

Goodwill is an intangible asset that refers to the positive image or favorable impression people have about a business, service, object, or person.

Hearings are proceedings or meetings before the court.

Indemnity and hold harmless clauses are agreements to shift the responsibility of one's actions to another; agreeing to pay for another's costs of legal work, fees, and any judgment taken.

Infringement means violating a law, contract, or right; used with patents, trademarks, and copyrights.

Intellectual property means an ownership in something intangible such as processes, inventions, formulas, or writings.

Interrogatories are written questions posed to parties during the discovery process of the trial.

Judgment proof is a term used for people or businesses who would be unable to pay a judgment if a court found against them.

Jurisdiction refers to the proper place to file a lawsuit; usually depends on residence of parties, subject matter of the lawsuit, or amount in controversy.

Licenses give legal permission to take a certain action such as driving a car or using another's property.

Limited liability refers to certain business owners' ability to restrict the collection efforts of creditors to the amount invested in a business.

Liquidated damages are contractual provisions that predetermine a sum that both parties have agreed would be fair compensation if the contract was unfulfilled.

Litigation refers to all of the actions involved in a lawsuit.

Mediation is an alternative way to settle a dispute by use of a neutral person.

Nondisclosure agreements identify what information is considered private or a "trade secret" and what property belongs to the company or person.

Noncompetition agreements are contracts to limit one's ability in attempts to secure the business of another.

Offer is a proposal; essential element of a contract.

Opt out means choosing not to participate in a contractual agreement or legal right; used to describe the ability to choose not to have workers' compensation insurance; allowed in limited instances and in certain states.

Pain and suffering describe damages for physical discomfort as well as mental and emotional distress related to an injury.

Petitions are written applications filed with the court to request relief; they identify the parties involved in a lawsuit, the right to bring the suit, the reasons the suit has been filed, and what action is requested from the court.

Piercing the corporate veil refers to selected instances where courts allow creditors to disregard limited liability and reach into a business owner's personal assets; used to avoid fraud or wrongdoing.

Plaintiff is a person who brings a lawsuit; also known in various jurisdictions as a complainant or petitioner.

Pleadings are written documents filed with the court to present a party's position on a particular matter.

Prayer is the formal demand or request for relief from the court.

Proprietary means belonging to an owner.

Quantum meruit, a Latin expression meaning "as much as one deserves," is a way to pay someone for the value of the goods or services provided even if the agreement or contract is not completed; equitable relief to avoid someone's being unjustly enriched to the detriment of another.

Quid pro quo is a Latin term meaning "this for that" and is used to describe the exchange of consideration; a type of sexual harassment. The term is often used to describe instances of sexual harassment where the victim is urged to put up with unwelcome behavior in order to receive some reward on the job or receives penalty if behavior is not tolerated.

Quiet enjoyment refers to a tenant's right to possess the premises peacefully without being disturbed.

Requests for production ask for documents and materials related to the lawsuit; used during the discovery portion of litigation.

Retainers are considered down payments or engagement fees for attorneys' services.

Service of process or *service* relates to the manner and rules in which notice of a lawsuit is delivered.

Service marks identify the source of services (as opposed to trademarks, which identify products); once registered the "ˢᴹ" symbol changes to "®."

Sovereign immunity is the doctrine that limits people in the types of lawsuits they may bring against the government.

Statute of frauds prevents suits on certain matters unless placed in writing and signed by the party held responsible or the party's agent.

Statute of limitations is the time period allowed by law for bringing a certain type of lawsuit; also refers to the time limit in which an individual faces exposure to prosecution for a crime.

Statutory protection refers to those rights given under laws enacted by a legislative body.

Terms of art are words or phrases with a particular legal significance.

Torts are civil claims, other than claims for a violating a contract, in which a party can recover for the damages caused by another; before recovering for a tort, one must show a duty was owed by another, the duty was breached, and damages resulted from the breach.

Tortious interference refers to someone's wrong actions that have disturbed or hindered the rights of another.

Trademarks identify a word, symbol, phrase, or design associated with a product such as a soft drink's name or logo; once registered the "ᵀᴹ" symbol changes to "®."

Trade secrets are private information or property that belongs to a company or individual and gives a competitive advantage over others who do not know the information; proprietary business information includes such things as manufacturing processes, blueprints, formulas, customer lists, and the patterns for machines.

Unjustly enriched means receive wrongfully something of benefit at another's expense; see quantum meruit.

Verdicts are the decisions by the jury or judge in a lawsuit.

Waive means surrender the right to do something; the resulting statement is a *waiver*.

ABOUT THE AUTHORS

Elaine Biech is president and managing principal of ebb associates with offices in Portage, Wisconsin, and Norfolk, Virginia. The management development firm specializes in the custom design of training programs and consulting services. She has been in the consulting field for twenty-one years and has developed training packages for both profit and nonprofit organizations.

She is the coauthor of two dozen books and articles, including *The Business of Consulting,* Jossey-Bass/Pfeiffer, 1999; *Interpersonal Skills: Understanding Your Impact on Others,* Kendall/Hunt Publishing Company, 1996; *The ASTD Sourcebook: Creativity and Innovation—Widen Your Spectrum,* McGraw-Hill Business and Professional Division and ASTD, 1996; *The HR Handbook,* Elaine Biech and John E. Jones, Eds., HRD Press, 1996; "Ten Mistakes CEOs Make About Training," *William & Mary Business Review,* Summer, 1995; *TQM for Training,* McGraw-Hill, Inc., 1994; *Diagnostic Tools for Total Quality, INFO-LINE,* American Society for Training and Development, 1991; *Managing Teamwork,* 1994; *Process Improvement: Achieving Quality Together,* 1994; *Business Communications,* 1992; *Delegating for Results,* 1992, Kendall/Hunt Publishing Company; "So You Want To Be a Consultant," *Careers and the MBA,* Winter, 1994; "Increased Productivity Through Effective Meetings," *STC Technical Communication,* 1987; "Stress Management," *Building Healthy Families,* 1984, Cooperative Educational Service Agency, No. 12; and others.

She has developed media presentations and training manuals and has presented at dozens of national and international conferences. Known as a trainers' trainer, she custom designs training programs for managers, leaders, trainers, and consultants.

As a management and executive consultant, trainer, and designer she has provided services to Land O' Lakes, McDonald's, Lands' End, General Casualty Insurance, PriceWaterhouseCoopers, American Family Insurance, Marathon Oil, Hershey Chocolate, Johnson Wax, Federal Reserve Bank, U.S. Navy, NASA, Newport News Shipbuilding, Coopers & Lybrand, the Naval Supply Center Pearl Harbor, Kohler Company, ASTD, American Red Cross, Association of Independent Certified Public Accountants, the University of Wisconsin, the College of William and Mary, ODU, and numerous other public and private sector organizations to help them prepare for the challenges of the new millennium.

Elaine specializes in helping people work together as teams to maximize their effectiveness. She implements corporate-wide systems such as quality improvement, reengineering of business processes, and mentoring programs, and facilitates topics such as organizational communication, conflict resolution, effective listening, customer service, time management, stress management, speaking skills, training competence, and how to coach today's employee, foster creativity, conduct productive meetings, manage change, and handle the difficult employee.

Elaine has her B.S. from the University of Wisconsin-Superior in business and education consulting, and her M.S. in human resource development. She served as the 1986 president of the South Central Wisconsin ASTD Chapter. At the national level she has been a member of the Chapter Services Committee, the HRD Consulting Network Board, and the 1990 National Conference Design Committee. Elaine was a member of the national ASTD board of directors and the society's secretary from 1991 to 1994.

In addition to her work with ASTD, she is also a member of the American Society for Quality (ASQ), Madison Area Quality Improvement Network (MAQIN), Organizational Development Network (ODN), and the National Professional Speakers Association (NSA).

Biech is the recipient of the 1992 National ASTD Torch Award. She was also selected for the 1995 Wisconsin Women Entrepreneur's Mentor Award. She is the consulting editor for the prestigious *Annuals* published by Jossey-Bass/ Pfeiffer.

Linda Byars Swindling is an attorney-mediator with the Law Offices of Withrow, Fiscus & Swindling. She practices in the areas of employment law and negotiations and develops training programs for both profit and nonprofit organizations. A consultant and professional speaker, she has helped other consultants and business owners build their practices while avoiding legal disputes. She is appointed by judges to resolve cases on their dockets and is regularly consulted for negotiation strategy.

Linda has created four video training programs: *Managing Without Legal Hassle, Hiring and Firing the Legal Way, Workplace Violence,* and *Employee Retainment: Keeping Your Key People.* She has appeared as a subject expert on numerous news programs, and she has hosted the television program Legal*Ease.* Linda has written numerous articles on employment law, business legal issues, and meeting industry concerns.

An award-winning speaker, Linda gives presentations at national and international conferences that are well attended and consistently ranked among the highest by participants. She has provided consulting, training, or presentation services to a number of leading organizations, including the American Heart Association, ProStaff, Bank United, GTE Supply, Comdata, Inc., Meeting Professionals International, Texas Employment Commission, Legend Print and Design, Texas Association of Personnel Services, American Society of Training and Development, the Dallas Bar Association, Richland College, North Lake College, Brookhaven College, Clemson University, Dallas Baptist University, Society of Human Resource Management, Primedia Workplace Learning, Integrated Concepts, Inc., the Dallas Convention and Visitors Bureau, Hotel/Motel Association of Greater Dallas, Mothers Against Drunk Drivers, and the National Society of Hispanic MBAs.

Linda is a member of the State Bar of Texas, the Carrollton/Farmers Branch Bar Association, and the College of the State Bar. She is admitted to practice in the state of Texas and in the U.S. District Courts for the Northern and Eastern Districts of Texas.

Linda graduated *cum laude* with her B.A. in journalism from Texas Tech University. She received her Doctor of Jurisprudence from Texas Tech School of Law, where she was a Board of Regents Scholarship recipient and held an academic clerkship with the U.S. Attorney's Office. She has received advanced mediation and negotiation training from the Attorney-Mediators Institute, the University of Houston's A. A. White Dispute Institute, and the Program on Negotiations at Harvard Law School. She has been recognized by *Who's Who in American Law* and was the Hospitality Sales and Marketing Association International Dallas Chapter's Outstanding Speaker of the Year.

She is president-elect of the Metrocrest Social Services Center and founder of Women Speak Business. She is a member of the Society of Professionals in Dispute Resolution, the Texas Association of Mediators, the Society of Human Resource Management, the National Speakers Association, American Society of Training and Development, and Meeting Professionals International.

Linda has been recognized by Carrollton/Farmer's Branch School District for her support of education and was one of two representatives from Dallas to Leadership Texas's prestigious Power Pipeline. She received the President's Award from the North Texas Speakers Association and serves on NSA's National Meetings Industry Council.

Ethics: and client's agenda, 21–22; consultant's adherence to, 16–20; professional standards of, 9, 16; in subcontracting relationship, 117, 120, 123

Executive suites, office in, 54

Expense report, 20

F

Fair Labor Standards Act (FLSA), 102

Fair use doctrine, 207–208

Fairness, and legality, 251

Family Medical Leave Act, 103

Federal Acquisition Regulations (FAR), 157

Federal employer-identification number (FEIN), 39

Federal and state laws, posting of, 99–100

Fee(s): alternate forms of, 160 (Ex.9.2), 161; arrangements, in contracts, 143, 145; attorney, 3–5, 11; and late payments, 156; negotiations, ethics in, 145; schedule, 143; structure, 20. *See also* Debt collection

Financial plan worksheet, 27–28 (Ex.3.2)

Foreign laws and procedures, 167–168

G

General partnerships, 39–40

Good business principles, 251–252

Government agencies, and employment issues, 99–100, 101

Government contracts: cancellation of, 158–159; and payment problems, 156, 158–159; proposal process, 156–157

H

Health insurance, 226

Home office, 56–57

I

Immigration Reform and Control Act, 102

Incorporation considerations, 30–31, 41

Independent contractor(s): consultant viewed as, 87; former employees as, 84–87; insuring against, 230–231; status, determination of, 81–84

Institute of Management Consultants, 16

Insurance coverage: and choice of carrier, 232; of contract workers, 230–231; lawsuits and, 223–224; need for, 223–225; and "reservation of right" letter, 232; types of, 225–228

Intellectual property: foreign laws and, 167; ownership rights, 180, 188, 191–192, 193–195; and trade secret protection, 180–186. *See also* Work product

Internal Revenue Service: and home office deductions, 57; and independent contractor status, 81; and limited liability companies/partnerships, 43. *See also* Taxes

Internet, and copyright law, 212

J

Joint ventures: confidentiality and legal concerns in, 113–114; nondisclosure agreement in, 182, 185. *See also* Subcontractors

L

Lawsuits: alternatives to, 264–265, 270–271; in business sale, 245; against consultant, 266–270; costs of, 261, 271; and decision to file, 260–264, 266; default judgment in, 267; depositions in, 268, 267 (Ex.16.2); discovery requests in, 268; and insurance coverage, 223–224; and hearings, 269; interrogatories in, 268; necessity of, 273; petition in, 266; pleadings in, 267–268; requests for production in, 268; service of processor in, 266; time demands of, 266; trial process in, 272

Lease arrangements: and executive suites, 54; landlord duties in, 52; practical and legal issues in, 49–50, 51–52 (Ex.4.2); rental rate in, 48–49; and shared office space, 53–54; sub-tenant agreement in, 53; tenant duties in, 53

Legal advice: and business plan, 30; and business start-up, 31–32; on contracts and agreements, 253; by consultant, 168–169, 252

Letters of agreement, 127, 136

Liability exposure: and choice of business structure, 31, 33; of corporations, 41–42; in employee termination, 109; in employment issues, 88–89, 100–102; in general partnerships, 39–40; and insurance protection, 223–233; in joint ventures, 113–114; in lease agreements, 50; and libel and slander, 106–107; in limited and limited liability partnerships, 40–41; prevention and reduction of, 12–13, 16–20, 220–222; and religious beliefs, 175–177; and risk assessment, 220–222; and sexual harassment, 96–97; in sole proprietorship, 38; in unique consulting situations, 165–177

Liability insurance, 226

Licensing agreements, 183

Limited liability company (LLC), 42–43

Limited liability partnership (LLP), 40–41, 42–43

Limited partnership, 40

Logo, 198

M

Marketing plan worksheet, 29–30 (Ex.3.3)

Mediation, 270–271

Minimum wage law, 102

Moonlighting, 92–93

Music and sound recordings, use of, 214–215

N

National Labor Relations Act (NLRA), 104

Non-compete agreement: in business sale, 246–247; with employees, 92, 186; with subcontractors, 117–118

Nondisclosure agreements: with employees, 92, 186; enforcement of, 92; in joint venture, 182, 185; with previous employer, 149; required by client, 147–148; with subcontractors, 118

Nonprofit clients, 159–161

No-solicitation agreements, 117–118

O

Occupational Safety and Health Administration (OSHA), 57, 102

Office: in executive suite, 54; home-based, 56–57; lease negotiations, 48–53; shared, 53–54; start-up cost worksheet, 58–59 (Ex.4.4); subleased, 53

Older Workers Protection Act, 103

Outsourcing, 75

Ownership transfer, publicizing of, 248

P

Partnership: agreement, 39; d/b/a (doing business as) designation, 43; general, 39–40; inadvertent appearance of, 39–40, 53; limited, 40; limited liability, 40–41, 42

Patent(s): application process, 201–202, 203 (Ex.11.3); foreign protection for, 202; infringement penalties, 217; needs evaluation, 202–204; types of, 200–201

Photographs, copyright protection of, 212

Plant patent, 201

Polygraph Protection Act, 91, 102

Practice start-up: assumed name in, 38, 43; business plan in, 24–30; business structure selection in, 31–43; checklist, 46 (Ex.3.6); legal advice in, 30. *See also* Office

Practice valuation, 241–242

Pregnancy Discrimination Act (PDA), 103–104

Print materials, and copyright issues, 209–214

Problem clients, warning signs of, 21–22

Professional associations, 43; ethical standards of, 16

Professional corporations, 43

Professional liability insurance, 226

Professional limited liability company (PLLC), 43

Prompt Payment Act, 156

Property and casualty insurance, 226

"Practical, compassionate, and a good alternative to an MBA."

Peter Block, author, *Flawless Consulting*

Elaine Biech

The Business of Consulting

The Basics and Beyond

Lacking a basic primer, many consultants have had to learn their jobs by trial and error. Now you can put an end to the guesswork. This how-to book gives you the actual tools and techniques you need in order to pursue a successful and profitable career in the world of consulting.

This book is sure to become a consulting classic!

"Here are the nuts and bolts for a successful career in consulting. A few hours with Elaine's book will save you years of trial and error."
Jerry C. Noack, vice president/group publisher, *TRAINING Magazine*

"If I were just starting into the consulting field today, this is the one book I would choose to advise me, caution me, support me in my business, and 'professionalize' me!"
Marjorie Blanchard, chief financial officer, Blanchard International

"Every consultant should apply her principled practices to guarantee satisfied customers."
John E. Gherty, president and chief executive officer, Land O'Lakes

"This book is filled with real-world, practical and proven tactics that can be used to grow and build a successful consulting practice. It is a must-have resource for people who are thinking of becoming a consultant — and for those who already are one!"
Dana Gaines Robinson, author; president, Partners in Change

"Read her book. She shares all her secrets!"
Gail Hammack, regional vice president, McDonald's

"*The Business of Consulting* will serve as my consulting practice workbook. The comprehensive coverage of the subject — along with the practical tips — make it the best tool I have."
Pam Schmidt, vice president, American Society for Training and Development (ASTD)

There's more to consulting than just being a good consultant. You've got to manage your business.

When Elaine Biech asked Peter Block, the legendary author of *Flawless Consulting*, for a book or article that might answer some of her questions about running a consulting business, he could suggest no resource. There wasn't a source that illuminated the day-to-day life of a consultant. You learned by trial and error. Or you begged your peers for advice.

That was then; this is now. Here's the book that all consultants, new and old, have desperately needed.

FREE diskette includes sample invoices, correspondence, planning templates, and more!

Biech shows you how to:

- *Develop* a business plan
- *Market* your business
- *Charge* for your services
- *Build* a client relationship
- *Grow* your consulting business
- *Ensure* your continued professional growth
- *Make* money in the profession . . . and much more!

The enclosed disk contains the worksheets and forms presented in *The Business of Consulting*. Personalize these tools as needed and print them out in order to project cash flow, track your time, tabulate your expenses, hire a subcontractor, plan your marketing campaigns, and much more!

Whether you're embarking on a new career as a consultant or whether you've been a consultant for years, you'll be able to employ this resource right away. And if you're deciding whether consulting is the right profession for you, *The Business of Consulting* will show you just what you can expect to encounter. For years, consultants have depended on Peter Block's *Flawless Consulting* for advice on being an effective consultant. Now there's a source for advice on running an effective consulting business—*The Business of Consulting* is indispensable.

For a free catalog of more than 300 consulting, training and HRD products, call 800-274-4434 or visit www.pfeiffer.com.

hardcover / 272 pages / includes a Microsoft Word diskette

• • • • • • • • • • • • • • • •
The Business of Consulting
ISBN 0–7879–4021–6
Item #F510

EXHIBITS ON DISK

The minimum configuration needed to utilize the files included on this disk is a computer system with one 3.5" floppy disk drive capable of reading double-sided low-density IBM formatted floppy disks and wordprocessing or desktop publishing software able to read Microsoft WORD 6.0/95 files. Document memory needs will vary, but your system should be capable of opening file sizes of 75+K. No monitor requirements other than the ones established by your document software need be met.

Each of the exhibits in your textbook that are marked with a disk icon have been saved onto the enclosed disk as a Microsoft WORD 6.0/95 file. These files can be opened with many Windows- and Macintosh-based wordprocessors or desktop publishers for viewing or editing as you see fit. The files were originally created and saved as WORD 6.0/95 DOC file by Microsoft Word 97. Not all software will read the files exactly the same, but the DOC format is an honest attempt by Jossey-Bass/ Pfeiffer Publishers to preserve the composition of the exhibits such as borders, fonts, character attributes, bullets, etc., as accurately as possible.

Copy all DOC files to a directory/folder in your computer system. To read the files using your Windows-based document software, select File from the main menu followed by Open to display the Open dialog box. Set the correct drive letter and subdirectory shown in the Open dialog box by using the Look in control. In the Files of type text box enter *.doc to display the list of DOC files available in the subdirectory.

Each file name is coded to the text Exhibit number to make it easy for you to find the one you want. For example, Exhibit 5.2 has a filename of EXH05-02.DOC. You can open the file by either double-clicking your mouse on the file name that you want to open or by clicking once on the file name to select it and then once on the Open command button.